the Unofficial Guide™ to Starting a Small Business

Marcia Layton Turner

Hungry Minds, Inc.

Hungry Minds, Inc.
909 Third Avenue
New York, NY 10022

ISBN: 0-02-862525-0

Manufactured in the United States of America

10 9 8 7 6 5

First edition

*This book is dedicated to the people who've made
me a better business owner:*

*My father, Richard Layton, who convinced me as a child
that "can't" is a word that does not exist,
My mother, Deborah Layton, who demonstrated that anything you want badly enough is possible, and
My brother, Jonathan Layton, whose determination and
networking skills constantly inspire me.*

Acknowledgments

Many people helped to develop and polish this book, adding valuable content and advice that will certainly benefit the reader. In addition to the panel of experts, the following people helped make this book a reality.

Thanks go to researcher, reviewer, and entrepreneur, Audrey Seybold, who helped tremendously throughout the process of writing this book.

Thanks also go to Matthew X. Kiernan, Development Editor, who kept the project on track and frequently added his two-cents, which was always worth much more.

Randy Ladenheim-Gil was responsible for starting the whole process and Jennifer Perillo did a great job as managing editor.

Contents

The *Unofficial Guide* Reader's Bill of Rights

We Give You More Than the Official Line

Welcome to the *Unofficial Guide* series of Lifestyles titles—books that deliver critical, unbiased information that other books can't or won't reveal—*the inside scoop*. Our goal is to provide you with the *most accessible, useful* information and advice possible. The recommendations we offer in these pages are not influenced by the corporate line of any organization or industry; we give you the hard facts, whether those institutions like them or not. If something is ill-advised or will cause a loss of time and/or money, we'll give you ample warning. And if it is a worthwhile option, we'll let you know that, too.

Armed and Ready

Our hand-picked authors confidently and critically report on a wide range of topics that matter to smart readers like you. Our authors are passionate about their subjects, but have distanced themselves enough from them to help you be armed and protected, and help you make educated decisions as you go through your process. It is our intent that, from having read this book, you will avoid the pitfalls everyone else falls into and get it right the first time.

Don't be fooled by cheap imitations; this is the *genuine article Unofficial Guide* series from Macmillan Publishing. You may be familiar with our proven track record of the travel *Unofficial Guides*, which have more than two million copies in print. Each year thousands of travelers—new and old—are armed with a brand new, fully updated edition of the flagship *Unofficial Guide to Walt Disney World*, by Bob Sehlinger. It is our intention here to provide you with the same level of objective authority that Mr. Sehlinger does in his brainchild.

The Unofficial Panel of Experts

Every word in the Lifestyle *Unofficial Guides* is intensively inspected by a team of three top professionals in their fields. These experts review the manuscript for factual accuracy, comprehensiveness, and an insider's determination as to whether the manuscript fulfills the credo in this Reader's Bill of Rights. In other words, our Panel ensures that you are, in fact, getting "the inside scoop."

Our Pledge

The authors, the editorial staff, and the Unofficial Panel of Experts assembled for *Unofficial Guides* are determined to lay out the most valuable alternatives available for our readers. This dictum means that our writers must be explicit, prescriptive, and above all, direct. We strive to be thorough and complete, but our goal is not necessarily to have the "most" or "all" of the information on a topic; this is not, after all, an encyclopedia. Our objective is to help you narrow down your options to the best of what is available, unbiased by affiliation with any industry or organization.

In each *Unofficial Guide* we give you:

- Comprehensive coverage of necessary and vital information
- Authoritative, rigidly fact-checked data
- The most up-to-date insights into trends
- Savvy, sophisticated writing that's also readable
- Sensible, applicable facts and secrets that only an insider knows

Special Features

Every book in our series offers the following six special sidebars in the margins that were devised to help you get things done cheaply, efficiently, and smartly.

1. "Timesaver"—tips and shortcuts that save you time.
2. "Moneysaver"—tips and shortcuts that save you money.
3. "Watch Out!"—more serious cautions and warnings.
4. "Bright Idea"—general tips and shortcuts to help you find an easier or smarter way to do something.
5. "Quote"—statements from real people that are intended to be prescriptive and valuable to you.
6. "Unofficially . . ."—an insider's fact or anecdote.

We also recognize your need to have quick information at your fingertips, and have thus provided the following comprehensive sections at the back of the book:

1. **Glossary:** Definitions of complicated terminology and jargon.

2. **Resource Guide:** Lists of relevant agencies, associations, institutions, Web sites, etc.

3. **Recommended Reading List:** Suggested titles that can help you get more in-depth information on related topics.

4. **Important Documents:** "Official" pieces of information you need to refer to, such as government forms.

5. **Important Statistics:** Facts and numbers presented at-a-glance for easy reference.

6. **Index**

Letters, Comments, and Questions from Readers

We strive to continually improve the Unofficial series, and input from our readers is a valuable way for us to do that. Many of those who have used the *Unofficial Guide* travel books write to the authors to ask questions, make comments, or share their own discoveries and lessons. For lifestyle *Unofficial Guides*, we would also appreciate all such correspondence, both positive and critical, and we will make best efforts to incorporate appropriate readers' feedback and comments in revised editions of this work.

How to write to us:

Unofficial Guides
Hungry Minds, Inc.
909 Third Avenue
New York, NY 10022

Attention: Reader's Comments

The *Unofficial Guide* Panel of Experts

The *Unofficial* editorial team recognizes that you've purchased this book with the expectation of getting the most authoritative, carefully inspected information currently available. Toward that end, on each and every title in this series, we have selected a minimum of three "official" experts comprising the "Unofficial Panel" who painstakingly review the manuscripts to ensure: factual accuracy of all data; inclusion of the most up-to-date and relevant information; and that, from an insider's perspective, the authors have armed you with all the necessary facts you need—but the institutions don't want you to know.

For *The Unofficial Guide to Starting a Small Business,* we are proud to introduce the following panel of experts:

> **Richard Enger**   Richard Enger and his partner started Strata Systems, Inc., a technical marketing and manufacturing firm in the geosynthetic industry, in 1994. Mr. Enger's experience includes direct sales and sales management,

strategic planning and merger/acquisition positions in a Fortune 500 company, and consulting assignments involving the set up of inventory control and production scheduling systems. He has assisted in the planning and start-up of a number of businesses in industries as diverse as animal genetics, the Internet, and contract agricultural production. Mr. Enger has a B.A. in Economics from the University of Chicago and an M.B.A. from the University of Minnesota.

John Flores With the hope of utilizing technology to compensate for his lack of size, John Flores started jf interactive inc. in 1995. After cutting his teeth for several years with small, fast paced marketing and multimedia companies, John Flores had decided that he would rather put his nose to his own grindstone and burn his own candles and midnight oil. Now cellphoned, Palm Piloted, cable modemed, digital cameraed, and Think Padded, John creates CD-ROMs and Web sites for corporate clients by utilizing a network of freelancers, including one in faraway Manila, the Philippines.

Daniel C. Marotta Dan Marotta is a partner in the Manhattan-based law firm of Dowd & Marotta, PC, representing various New York-based companies and start-up businesses. Mr. Marotta oversees the corporate and real estate practice areas of the firm, and provides copyright and trademark counseling for the new media, music, film, fashion, restaurant and computer industries. He serves on the Board of Directors of the Richmond County Bar Association and the Board of Directors for the

Neighborhood Preservation Coalition, a state-
wide consortium of 180 nonprofit organizations
dedicated to urban renewal and revitalization.
Mr. Marotta earned a B.A. in Economics from
Manhattan College and his law degree from
Fordham University School of Law.

Introduction

If you're currently considering starting your own business, you're almost in the majority, says a study by the Entrepreneurial Research Consortium (ERC). According to a first-of-its-kind study compiled in 1996, one of every three U.S. households includes someone who has had a primary role in a new or small business. That's 35 million households, or 37 percent of the country.

This shift towards entrepreneurship is no fad, argues Jeffry Timmons in his book, *The Entrepreneurial Mind*. In fact, it is part of a larger cultural movement, he says. Signs that he may be right include the fact that most new employment growth during the 1990s stemmed from entrepreneurs or start-ups in hiring mode. Even the financial community has recognized the potential of entrepreneurial enterprises; available capital is increasingly finding its way into more high risk, high growth start-ups and emerging ventures.

Entrepreneur Versus Business Owner

Some people differentiate between entrepreneurs and business owners, suggesting that to be an entrepreneur, one must create a new product, service, or process. A business owner, on the other hand, simply manages an enterprise.

In my mind, however, business owners demonstrate innovations on a daily basis in how they serve customers, manage employees, and strive to improve their operations. For that reason, the terms entrepreneur and business owner will be used interchangeably in this book.

Why More People Are Choosing to Become Their Own Bosses

Although owning a business has been the great American dream for more than two centuries, more and more people worldwide are making that dream a reality. Increasing numbers of workers are deciding that their role as "employee" is overrated and undervalued. Some of the most common reasons people choose to become their own boss are:

- **Flexibility** (read Control). The escalating numbers of women entrepreneurs should be a sign that we're growing weary of trying to juggle work and family lives within the strict confines of an 8-to-5 day. Although the hours may be long initially, many business owners value the ability to work when it is most convenient and choose to be available for family at other times. For some, this reason alone is reason enough to strike out on their own.

- **Independence.** Just as control over one's time is important to some individuals, control over the type of work to be done and the type of customer to be served are other issues near and dear to business owners. The need to decide for oneself when, how, and where a project will be completed is what separates many business owners from lifelong employees.

- **Financial potential.** When you work for someone else, the potential amount of money you can earn in a day, or in a year, is set by your employer. However, many business owners prefer to decide for themselves what their earning ceiling is. The more an entrepreneur works, the more he or she can potentially earn.

- **Less bureaucracy.** If there is one thing entrepreneurs universally hate, it is bureaucracy. Office politics, corporate games, and internal bickering are all unproductive and destructive. In your own business, you can make it your mission to keep politicking to a minimum.

- **Ability to reach one's full potential.** This is the most important reason for many entrepreneurs.

Part of the impetus for this cultural shift may have, in fact, started at the corporate level. As multinational employers determined that their policy of lifelong employment was no longer financially viable, long-term employees suddenly found themselves without a job. For many, the experience of being unemployed made them reluctant to put their professional lives in the hands of anyone other than themselves. These corporate refugees have become some of the most experienced and better-funded entrepreneurs in history. Their knowledge and administrative skills have frequently made them more successful than entrepreneurs of the past.

While some entrepreneurs were pushed into business ownership, new technology has created more opportunities for individuals looking for a reason to leave. Computer and telecommunications technology have made it possible for a single individual to accomplish the workload of many. As the cost of technology has steadily dropped, so has the cost of self-employment. The availability of Internet access and the acceptance of e-mail as a new standard communications media have totally changed how some types of business operate; often putting small businesses on equal footing with established firms.

Another trend that has shaped the ranks of the self-employed has been the increasing acceptance of the home as workplace. As computers have come down in price and size, it has become possible for businesses to be located within the home. For some, that may be a one-room apartment, for others, a rural farmhouse; the size and location makes no difference, as long as there is space available for completing work. Without the cost of a commercial location, one of the major barriers to starting a business has been eliminated. Hence, the emergence of the small office/home office (SOHO) market as a recognized growth category for many consumer and business-to-business companies.

Technology has also made it possible to do business internationally, without racking up the frequent flier miles. For many businesses, the quality of product or service has become much more important than the location of the supplier. Greater access to information makes starting a business easier and improves its chances of success.

Growth Trends

One of the trends that has spawned new ventures and hastened the entrepreneurial endeavors of many former employees is that of outsourcing. Initiated in the early 1990s by major corporations looking for a way to concentrate on what they were best at, outsourcing gave them a means of "farming out" administrative and technical activities the corporations no longer wanted in-house. To fill this need for outside consultants and specialists, many new companies were born. New companies also have access to these experienced consultants, who can advise them on starting off on the right foot.

Since that time, outsourcing has grown and expanded beyond the largest companies into the small business marketplace. In response, the ranks of the small business owner continue to swell.

Another trend impacting business ownership is the changing nature of the employer/employee relationship. Corporate downsizing has demonstrated to employees the importance of watching out for their interests. And it seems that those interests are generally not to be working for someone else.

Choice is frequently the name of the game as a business owner.

Many entrepreneurs start businesses they hope will become multimillion dollar enterprises that span the globe. But as it becomes more acceptable to merge personal and business goals, more business owners are setting limits to the amount of growth they will pursue. Why expand the company beyond the house if the result is simply more work and more stress? Why add dozens of employees if the result is less time spent in front of clients? Why assume the burden of a hefty commercial loan if the business can continue to grow at its current pace without it? These are just some of the questions entrepreneurs face every day.

A decade ago, few would have chosen the slow-growth path. But today, aggressive growth is increasingly the road not taken. "Balance" and "quality of life" are taking increasing priority over revenue growth, longer hours, and more frequent travel.

The Business Owner Personality

There is no one profile of what a successful business owner looks like, nor is there one test to be shared

Bright Idea
If you're inter-
ested in a quick
assessment of
your entrepre-
neurial potential,
take the
Entrepreneurial
Test at
www.onlinewbc.
Although it's on
a site oriented
for women in
business, the
evaluation
applies to men
as well. As with
all assessments,
take it with a
grain of salt.

that can help you determine whether you're meant
to be a business owner. But there are some com-
monalities among entrepreneurs. Generally they are

- Hard-working.

- Ambitious.

- Administrative.

- Optimistic.

- Prudent.

Until now, I've stressed the advantages of being a
business owner, but there are certainly disadvantages. Among them, long hours (the average entrepreneur works 50+ hours a week, says Dun &
Bradstreet), potentially lower pay than your current
job (especially at the outset), and the stress of trying
to meet the needs of your many customers (where
you had one employer before, now you have many).

It may take several months before you're even
able to pay yourself a salary. Setting aside a year's
worth of savings to cover your living costs is a realistic and smart move.

These issues, and many more, will face you as you
begin the entrepreneurial journey. During the next
few months, you'll learn more than you probably
ever have in the same amount of time—more about
business, about your products and services, and
about yourself. Fortunately, as a business owner,
you'll never stop learning.

There are some experiences and pieces of information, however, that are purely a waste of your
time. Recognizing this, we've tried to create a start-
up manual that will save you time, money, and frustration. By the end of the book, my hope is that you
will already be a business owner.

Do Your Homework First

PART I

GET THE SCOOP ON...
Start-up strategies that work ▪ Must-do to-dos ▪
The entrepreneurial personality ▪ Free help from
the government

Starting from Scratch

Chapter 1

Anyone who tells you that there is a standard, tried-and-true method of starting a new business has obviously never done it. If there is one thing for you to remember as you start this exciting process, it is that there is no one right way to go about starting a business. Scholars have studied entrepreneurship for years, trying to discover the formula for success. And what they've learned so far for sure is that there is no *one* formula.

This is good news for you. Since most successful entrepreneurs are nonconformists who hate to be told that "it can't be done that way," you undoubtedly want to do it your way—which is fine. There are, however, some helpful guidelines to follow that should help keep you out of trouble.

Some steps toward business ownership need to be taken in a certain order. For example, until you file incorporation or DBA paperwork to establish your business, no bank will grant you a business account. And until you've decided on your business's location, there's no point in calling the phone company to have a phone number assigned. Some of these steps are common sense, but use the handy

3

checklist that follows to be sure you haven't missed anything.

As you move ahead with your plans to become a business owner, this chapter should help you finalize some of the details.

Startup checklist—a to-do list for budding business owners

Before you quit your day job, take a look at the following list of activities you need to complete before becoming an official business owner. Do as many as you can while still employed.

☐ Decide on the products and/or services you will sell.

☐ Determine how many product or service lines you will offer.

☐ Settle on a company name.

☐ Determine whether you will need to hire employees at the outset and set a schedule for new hires.

☐ Decide on where your business will be located.

☐ Consult an accountant about the appropriate corporate structure.

☐ Meet with an attorney to file the necessary paperwork; discuss any trademark and copyright issues.

☐ Estimate your monthly expenses and projected sales on a cash flow statement.

☐ Complete a break-even analysis to confirm you can actually make money at this.

☐ Establish a business bank account.

☐ Have a business phone line installed.

☐ Buy any needed equipment (e.g., computer or manufacturing).

☐ Draft a list of potential customers.

☐ Hire a graphic designer to lay out corporate letterhead, business cards, and envelopes.

☐ Determine what minimum percentage of ownership you need to retain over time to stay involved in the business.

Time lines

Every new company has its own schedule or time line to follow, based totally on the owner's personality, resources, and plan. Some entrepreneurs will have the ambition and financial wherewithal to be fully functional in a matter of days; others may need six months to make the same progress. One pace is no better than the other as long as you're comfortable with it.

Of course, there is something to be said for moving quickly to take advantage of an opportunity. In some industries and markets, moving slowly to make decisions may not work, so you'll need to decide whether to give up on business ownership or simply switch industries.

One tool that is useful, no matter what your start-up pace, is a time line. Quite simply, it is a sheet of paper that plots graphically all the things you need to do and what the due dates are. Without identifying all the action items you're responsible for and applying a deadline for each, you'll never get them done. I can't remember who said "A goal is a dream with a deadline," but it's so true.

Figuring out the finances

In Chapter 3, "Your Business Plan," you'll hear all about the process of preparing your business plan. However, before you go to the trouble of drafting

Bright Idea
A great site for budding entrepreneurs is the Kauffman Center for Entrepreneurial Leadership, at www.entreworld. org. Visit it for an amazing array of information and resources for people considering starting their own business.

such a document, take a few minutes to roughly estimate your future financial situation.

You want to do this for a couple of reasons: 1) to
make sure you have enough money to actually start
the business, and 2) to make sure that, long-term,
the company will be profitable. What's the point of
starting a business that has no possibility of being a
moneymaker?

To estimate what you'll need to start your business, make a list of all the things you should have on
the day that you open for business. Do you need a
computer? How about a phone system? Advice from
your accountant on incorporating? Office furniture? A printed brochure? A car? Make a complete
list and then attach an estimated cost with each
item. This will help you see the total amount of
money you'll need to invest up front. Here's a sample list:

Item Estimated Cost

Computer	$3,000
Laser printer	$500
Phone	$75
Phone service hookup with voice mail	$150
Office furniture	$500
Chair	$300
Fax machine	$300
Copier	$700
Brochure	$1,500
Stationery, business cards	$1,000
Yellow Page advertising	$500
Office supplies	$500

As you complete this analysis, be sure that you're
estimating your needed resources based on the true

requirements of the business and not the current balance of your bank account. Put aside thoughts of how much money you may have available to invest in a new business and focus on realistically assessing what it will take to get up-and-running with everything you need.

Now estimate what your first-year revenues will be—that is, what you can realistically sell in your first year in business. How many customers do you expect to be able to win in your first month? How about your second? And so on. Make a grid and count how many sales per month you anticipate.

Now estimate what your average sale will be worth. If you're opening a restaurant, for example, will the typical bill be $20 or $40?

For professionals who charge by the hour, it may be easier for you to estimate the number of hours you'll bill per month. Then multiply that by your hourly rate to get your projected monthly revenue. Now calculate the total for the year. How are you doing?

For Product Estimates

Average number of products sold per week:

_____

Average sale amount:

× _____

Number of weeks per year:

× 52

Total Revenue Projection

= _____

For Service Estimates

Average number of hours billed per week:

_____

Hourly rate:

× _____

Number of weeks per year:

× 52

Total Revenue Projection

= _____

These figures are certainly not cast in stone, but they do give you a down-and-dirty idea of how far you are from covering your expenses, and how long it will be before your business is profitable.

Doing Your Homework

Most businesses fail because the owner simply didn't do enough research—that is, he or she didn't gather enough information about the realities of running a company. In the end, that results in one or more of the following scenarios:

Bright Idea
It's much easier to qualify for credit when you're employed by someone else. So accept a few of those offers for credit cards with no annual fee that arrive on your doorstep. Although you may never use them, at least you'll have them in hand. After the start-up phase, you'll want to cut back on the cards you carry to reduce the risk of a negative credit rating.

■ **Not enough working capital.** Some businesses require a large amount of capital to get started. Even after the equipment is purchased, the location renovated, and the staff hired, you need money left over to stay afloat until your sales more than cover your expenses. Some business owners fail to account for the time it will take to build up sales to their break-even point. Few businesses break even immediately, much less make a profit.

To avoid this trap, arrange for financing before you need it. Start by setting aside some of your personal savings to tide you over for up to a year while you're not drawing a salary from the business. Set up lines of credit with your bank, too.

■ **Not enough sales.** Lack of sales, or sales well below projections, can frequently be attributed to a lack of market research up-front. Too few business owners bother to ask potential customers whether they would actually buy a particular product or service before sinking thousands of dollars into trying to sell it.

The best way to avoid this problem is to talk to as many potential customers as possible, inquiring about what products or services they currently buy that are similar to yours. What do they typically spend on them? Where do they buy them? Is there anything they would like to be different about that particular product or service? Then use this information as you move forward to ensure that there are enough customers to make your venture profitable.

Another potential solution to this problem is ongoing marketing efforts to keep your business in the public eye. People can't buy from you unless they know that you're out there. Too many businesses invest too little time in marketing to attract customers.

■ **Overspending on nonessentials.** For some businesses, this means paying too much for office space, or going overboard on fancy furniture. For others, it may mean overusing your attorney or accountant, or hiring employees before you can afford to. In the end, your start-up costs skyrocket.

During the first year, your challenge will be to spend as little as possible—period. Yes, you'll need computer equipment. Yes, you'll need letterhead. But you don't need every bell and whistle on your computer system, nor do you need 20,000 sheets of four-color stationery.

Moneysaver
Yes, there is such a thing as too much research—it's referred to as "analysis paralysis." But too little research is an even scarier proposition. If you don't know how to begin to research your market, call your local SBDC (Small Business Development Center) for some free assistance.

First steps for starting a business

If you know that you're destined to be a business owner but you haven't discovered your true calling, don't give up. By taking a look at your strengths and marrying them with a current market need, you'll be on your way in no time. The first step is in evaluating what you're good at.

Assess your strengths

The most successful business owners are those individuals who absolutely love what they do. They're enthused about their services, believe in their products, and are constantly looking for ways to improve how they serve customers. To a large extent, they are successful because they have found a business that matches their interests.

To brainstorm businesses that may be appropriate for you, evaluate these six aspects of your life:

1. Strengths

2. Preferences

3. Hobbies

4. Skills

5. Previous experience

6. Network of potential customers and "helpers"

Take a look at those activities you most enjoy, as well as those where you excel. They may or may not be one and the same. Consider your hobbies and interests beyond work, as well as past business experience. Where have you felt most fulfilled? These questions can lead you towards types of businesses that fit your personality and interests.

Evaluating what the market needs

While your individual interests are essential in selecting a business to start, the other half of the equation is what the market needs or wants. You could be the best dogsled guide in the world, for instance, but your market for such services is going to be severely limited outside the Arctic.

Take a look at trends in the market and products or services that both businesses and individuals are buying. Consider the types of companies that seem to be doing well in other parts of the world but that haven't yet taken off in your immediate area.

For example, the coffee craze started just a few years ago as the "hot" Seattle coffee shop decided to expand nationwide, seemingly increasing the per capita consumption of coffee exponentially. Interest in alternative medicines is also skyrocketing, as the world's aging population searches for answers beyond traditional medicine. What other shifts are you witnessing that are changing what, how, or where we buy goods?

Up-and-coming businesses to look into

Some of the fastest growth ventures right now are Internet-related; e-commerce firms are raking in venture capital left and right as companies race to set up shop on the Web.

Other types of businesses with great potential are:

- Products or services that save people time.
- Information products, especially self-help.
- Health-related products and services, especially preventive measures that keep us feeling young.
- Computer-related services.

Identifying underserved markets is easier than you think—look at Starbucks, for example. But be careful of trying to ride the coattails of a new trend; by the time you jump on it, the trend may be hitting

Unofficially . . .
In 1999, every second the World Wide Web expands by 17 pages, according to the NEC Research Institute. That means that every day the job of managing information becomes that much more difficult for the average business.

its peak. If the national media has already covered a fast-growing company in a particular market, you may have missed your chance.

Of course, finding an untapped market can be a goldmine. But you have a better chance of developing a new approach to an age-old problem, or finding an alternative product or service to what's been available forever. Successful companies are more often built on evolutionary improvements, rather than revolutionary changes.

Look for product and service needs with stable demand, such as auto repair service or supermarkets, and come up with a radical new way to do business in that market. Some companies offer added benefits, such as a free car wash with every oil change, or free delivery of groceries, as a way to set themselves apart.

Location, location, location

Your first decision regarding the location of your new business is "home or away." Do you want to try to establish your company in a home office, or should you shop for space outside the home? For many service businesses, the answer is to keep expenses to a minimum and work from home. But for others, such as manufacturing enterprises, a home office just isn't a good fit—literally as well as figuratively.

Once you've made the decision to locate the company in a separate building, you'll need to consider exactly how much space you'll need.

During the start-up phase, it's generally smart to stick with a lease arrangement rather than to buy a building (or virtually any capital-intensive asset). Buying property requires a significant cash investment, which could be diverted to more essential

Timesaver
Don't waste your time trying to scout out potential locations on your own. Turn to a seasoned real estate professional who knows your local market and can advise you on available properties throughout your area, reasonable lease rates, and unusual opportunities. To find such a pro, note the names of Realtors on local commercial properties and ask colleagues for recommendations.

expenditures right now, and commits you to a location and facility that may not fit your needs in five—or even three—years. So many aspects of your business will change in the coming months that you'll want to remain as flexible as possible in all your financial commitments.

When to quit your day job

The short answer to this question is "only when it starts to interfere with the operation of your company." Hold onto that steady paycheck for as long as possible because you're going to need all the money you can get once the company is operating full steam ahead.

Partner or perish

At this point, you may be planning to start your venture alone, without support from other partners. While this approach will certainly avoid any potential conflicts that inevitably arise among partners, it ignores some of the major benefits of having one or more business partners:

- Enhanced aggregate skill set and optimal use of skill sets
- Reduced individual risk
- Improved chance of investor interest
- Time demands reduced to a manageable level

Fast-growth companies have been shown to benefit significantly from the involvement of more than one person in the start-up phase. MIT Professor Edward Roberts reported in his book, *Entrepreneurs in High Technology*, that a study of fast-growth high tech companies bears this out. He found that only 6 percent of the companies surveyed had one founder; 94 percent had two or more partners.

> **"**
> Starting a business as a team greatly enhances your chances for success. The main reason is that by bringing together individuals with complementary skills, you're improving the quality of your business operations.
> —William J. Stolze, cofounder of RF Communications, a division of Harris Corporation, and author of *Start Up: An Entrepreneur's Guide to Launching and Managing a New Business* (Career Press, 1996)
> **"**

Starting a company solo may be the simplest and fastest way to get going on your new business, but is it the smartest? You'll have to decide for yourself.

Pooling your resources

A secondary reason for bringing on partners, besides their skills and abilities, is for the emotional and financial support that they can provide.

Anyone who has owned a solo business will tell you how lonely it can get. Home-based business owners frequently find that they miss the camaraderie of teammates and colleagues. Working together towards a goal is more satisfying and fulfilling for many owners than doing everything alone.

But there is a financial benefit as well. Partners should be expected to make some type of financial contribution to the business. This investment can take the form of equipment, professional services, space, cold hard cash, or some other combination of needed goods and services in return for a stake in the company. Obviously, the more partners, the more resources the company has to draw from.

Turn to available resources for help and feedback

Watch Out! Although SCORE can be a valuable organization to turn to for problem-solving advice, in reality, it is not equipped to help start-up ventures. Don't waste your time contacting them while you're starting your company.

There are a number of organizations you can turn to for start-up advice, problem solving, and brainstorming. Many of the executive directors of organizations in your area are well-connected in your community and could be excellent referral sources for you. Keep that in mind as you arrange your first contact with them.

Small Business Administration (SBA)

The Small Business Administration offers financing guarantees, low-cost publications, training, and advocacy services nationwide. Call (800) UASKSBA for a listing of their services in your area.

Small Business Development Centers (SBDC)

When you need some work done on·your behalf, such as help in writing a business plan or research on your local market, start with the SBDC in your area. SBDCs provide free information about starting and running a small business. Such counseling centers are generally cooperative arrangements between a local college and the SBA.

Minority Business Development Centers (MBDCs)

Only available in some cities, MBDCs were established specifically to aid minority and women business owners through training and consulting. Most MBDCs charge a nominal fee ($10–$25 per hour) for their services, however, so you may want to start at the SBDC and turn to an MBDC if you can't get the services you need.

Women Business Development Centers (WBDC)

Like their MBDC cousins, WBDCs were established to help women business owners start and run successful companies. In addition to training programs, many WBDCs provide certification assistance, helping to qualify women-owned businesses for corporate and government contracts.

Local economic development departments

Cities and counties nationwide have established local offices dedicated to increasing the number of businesses in the area. With the help of your local economic development department, you may qualify for loan programs, earn tax credits for job creation, or learn about other incentives to locate your business in a particular location.

Timesaver
Find the SBDC closest to you by going to www6. americanexpress.com/ smallbusiness/ resources/ expanding/ sdbc.

Just the facts

- There is no standard formula for entrepreneurial success—your approach has just as much potential as anything that has been done before.

- Arrange financing now, before you need it, by establishing lines of credit or applying for credit cards.

- Evaluating what the market needs now and how that will change in the coming decade will improve your odds of long-term success.

- Partnering improves your odds of success by bringing in complementary skills to the business, rather than you trying to do everything yourself.

- There are a number of national and locally based organizations available to help you start your business at little or no cost.

GET THE SCOOP ON...
Choosing your perfect business ▪ Deciding
what's most important to you ▪
Making sure you can make money ▪ The best
business research sources

What Kind of Business Makes Sense for You?

Chapter 2

Once you've made the decision to become a business owner, the next logical step is to begin evaluating your options. The secret to establishing a successful venture is choosing a product or service you love and believe in.

When you're excited about what you do, you'll have boundless energy and excitement. In itself, that's priceless. But what it does for your business is ensure that you'll give it your all.

Of course, the key to finding that perfect business is first assessing your personal strengths and weaknesses, as well as your interests and abilities. Don't think of this as limiting your options; it's really just helping to organize the thousands of possibilities that are out there.

After you determine what industry you should be in, you'll need to design the optimum business structure and format. That means blending your business with your personal life in a way that makes you most productive, and your business most profitable.

Selecting a business

Beginning the process of choosing your new business may seem daunting. But there are a number of criteria you can work through to help weed out businesses that don't fit your personality, your financial resources, or your skills.

The options

In general terms, the basic types of businesses include those that are:

■ Manufacturing/production.

■ Service.

■ Home-based.

■ Web-based.

■ Direct mail.

■ Multilevel marketing.

Manufacturing/production

Unless you have significant financial resources, this type of business is going to be difficult to own. Whether you establish it from scratch or buy an existing operation, manufacturing companies have sizeable assets and workforces, which means that the cash needed to invest will be considerable. The upside, however, is that this type of business can yield huge profits without the owner being on the job 24 hours a day.

Although manufacturing operations require more financial resources to get started, that fact is also a barrier to entry for potential competitors; individuals who can't afford to invest significant funds in a manufacturing operation face a barrier to entering that business. For business owners who have made such an investment, the barrier to entry becomes a protective measure that prevents competitor overload.

Service

Service businesses, such as consulting, hair salons, or daycare centers, are less expensive to start because there are typically fewer equipment requirements. Except for licenses and permits, there are few barriers to entry. However, the owner's earnings are frequently tied to how much time he or she invests in the company. For instance, an accountant only makes money when she is performing billable work for a client.

Home-based

The past decade has witnessed a tremendous jump in the type and number of businesses being operated from the owner's home. Government restrictions on such activities have been reduced and the public acceptance of such businesses has risen.

Parents frequently like the flexibility that a home-based setup provides, while others can't imagine getting work done with children in the house. Depending on the age of your children, your tolerance for distractions, and your ability to creatively juggle, this may or may not be an ideal situation for you. Only you can judge for yourself. The advantage is reduced cost; the disadvantage is distractions.

Keep in mind, however, that once children hit school age, you may have more free time to potentially invest in a business.

Children aren't the only potential distraction, however. Friends and neighbors may perceive your home-based status to mean that you have plenty of free time. Some may ask that you baby-sit their kids during the day "since you're home," or feel free to call and chat at length while you're trying to work. Be clear when communicating that you are *working* from home. Ask to return calls to friends after work hours and refer needy neighbors to a local daycare.

Web-based

Companies that consist of a Web site and a product
or service are becoming increasingly common as the
Internet becomes a central source for information,
communication, and shopping.

Up-front costs for equipment or Web-site design
can run at least several thousand dollars, but do-it-
yourselfers have established sites on their own for
far less. Like a manufacturing operation, the
owner's income is not tied to how much time he or
she invests in the company, but this type of business
is far from proven.

Direct mail

Much like Web-based businesses that provide a
means of ordering products and services from a central source, direct mail businesses enable shoppers
to order from a catalog or flyer. Armed with a
product or service, a targeted mailing list, a flyer or
information piece, and money for postage, you can
establish a direct mail venture from your garage in
your spare time. The quality of your list and your
mailer are critical components of this profit
equation.

Multilevel marketing (MLM)

Multilevel or network marketing has made million-
aires out of housewives and part-time workers by
inviting them to act as agents for the company. In
this capacity, individuals sell products and services
to their friends and colleagues and recruit new
agents for the company. As their recruits sell products and attract new recruits, a portion of their earnings is paid to the originator.

Granted, those housewives and part-time participants are few and far between, but there are some
success stories.

To protect yourself, stay away from organizations that require a large cash investment to become an agent, or expect you to buy a large quantity of their products. Spend time carefully evaluating each MLM opportunity before deciding to invest.

What best fits your financial resources

Your current financial resources—that is, your personal checking and savings accounts and any investments you can draw on to start your company—should play a major role in settling on your dream business. If you don't have tens of thousands of dollars to invest, you'll need to limit your options or scale down to fit your budget. That may mean starting your company from home, bartering services in return for professional services, buying furniture at auction, and hiring independent contractors or college interns instead of employees.

What meets your lifestyle needs

Although your finances will create a framework within which you need to work, deciding the type of lifestyle you want to have is an even bigger issue. Some people are intent on throwing themselves into a venture 110 percent. Others need time for family and personal obligations. You should evaluate your answers to these questions:

- Can I make this work part-time, or do I need to be full-time at the start?

- Can I operate this company solo or do I need employees right off the bat?

- Will a home-based office suffice or do I need to rent space in a commercial area?

Unofficially . . .
Data collected in 1998 by ActivMedia Research shows "Web site annual business revenues now regularly exceed $100,000, and in many cases, $1 million . . . . Web-generated revenues are predicted to exceed $1.2 trillion by 2002."

Researching your market

In addition to defining the type of company you'll be operating, you need to confirm that you can actually support yourself in your new venture. The only way to answer this question is to conduct market research.

Can you make money in your own business?

No matter what you want to sell, your market will determine whether you can make money at it. Carefully study what your target market—the type of people or businesses most likely to buy from you— wants and needs, and what they're having difficulty getting.

What does the market need?

One sign of what the market needs is what it is currently buying. What types of products and services are experiencing an upswing? Which are on the decline?

And what is happening to your target market itself? As the group ages, how are its needs changing? Do its members have children now? Are they retiring? Are they starting school? What do these changes mean in terms of the products and services they are willing to pay for?

For companies selling to other businesses, what are the changes that those organizations are experiencing? Are customers taking longer to pay? Is employee turnover becoming a bigger issue? How is telecommuting affecting worker expectations? Is the marketplace becoming more competitive in certain industries? Are costs rising? How are these changes affecting how the company does business?

What are people willing to pay for your product or service?

One way to find out what your product or service is worth is to conduct a survey. Although there is no guarantee that what you learn in your survey will play itself out exactly the same way in real life, asking people about their buying habits should help you price your product or service in line with your potential customers' expectations.

You can also evaluate the prices for "substitute products"—those products that people are using now *instead* of yours. For example, tap water is a substitute for bottled water, just as frozen burritos at the convenience store are a substitute for a drive-thru fast-food meal.

Determine what substitute products already exist and turn to the multivolume set of Mediamark Research (MRI) reports for pricing information. This will help you assess the financial potential of your new product and company.

Who is the competition?

Which companies are currently selling something similar to what you want to offer? These are your competitors. Although you may argue that no one is selling exactly what you have, there are certainly companies selling substitute products. Identify them and research everything you can about them.

What can you learn from them?

Although competitors are notoriously tight-lipped about their business, you can learn a lot about them from their customers, their suppliers, and the way they conduct business. One way to get information is to become one of their customers and study how you are treated.

Bright Idea
Simmons Market Research Reports provide annual data on a long list of consumer products. Demographic profiles of everyone who bought luggage, toothpaste, a refrigerator, and virtually everything in between can be found in this multivolume set. Visit a business library at a local university to find this very useful report.

The process of selecting your business should entail a combination of personal assessment matched with solid research. You may find yourself going back and forth between evaluating your needs and those of the market, as you discover them through your information gathering. Use the following tools to help you understand where the greatest market potential may lie.

Tools and references

Combining information culled from both print and online resources will yield the most complete picture of an industry or business, suggests Kim Fukui, business information specialist with Infokui.

Start with an industry overview and then move to investigate specific companies to be most efficient in your research. The following sources will be of most help to you:

- **Internet sites**—Search engines, company Web sites, news sources, and association sites
- **Associations**—Print and online organizational information
- **Publications**—Trade journals, local newspapers and magazines, newsletters, reports, and national publications
- **Industry experts**—Government experts on the payroll of the Department of Commerce and frequently referenced industry leaders
- **Market analysts**—Stock market seers who monitor every aspect of an industry or market's growth
- **College and university professors**—Academicians involved in research and consulting can often be at the leading edge of a market or profession. Don't be shy about contacting them

Timesaver
Check out the SBA Web site at www.onlinewbc. org for detailed instruction on analyzing and researching your competitors, all in one place.

for reference material or referrals. University management libraries will also have valuable business reference material no public library will.

- **Competitors**—Companies doing what you aspire to do, but in other parts of the country or world, who may be willing to share sensitive data because you are not a local threat

Using these sources, start compiling a thorough industry overview to better understand the potential for your planned company. Then research companies already in your field.

Industry research

The Internet is a market researcher's dream come true. Countless information sources in one place, many available for free—how can you go wrong?! Although you won't be able to find everything you need, surfing the Internet for information will save you considerable time and money. What you can't find online will most likely be available at a local college library.

Some of the best places for industry information include:

- **Encyclopedia of Associations.** This print directory of more than 88,000 organizations worldwide can also be searched online for a fee at www. gale.com. Associations are some of the few organizations that track industry-specific statistics for their members.

The directory of American Society of Association Executives (ASAE) can also be searched at www.asaenet.org/gateway.

- **U.S. Industry and Trade Outlook.** Published annually by the U.S. Department of Commerce,

Consider going outside of your geographic region to have a frank conversation with someone who owns a business that mirrors what you hope to set up. In my case, I went to Maine and benefited tremendously from hearing specific aspects of running my proposed business.
—Audrey Seybold, founder, Tic Tac Toys

this publication provides helpful overviews of many major industries.

- **Encyclopedia of American Industries.** Available at the library and at the Gale site (www.gale.com), this publication provides background information on industries, especially service.

- **Standard and Poor's Industry Surveys.** This print and online resource offers current overviews of 20+ industries. Their Web site is at www.standardandpoors.com, though the printed reports are only available in hardcopy at this writing.

- **Article indexes.** Indexes for specific publications, such as the *Wall Street Journal* at bis.dowjones.com, are available for a fee, as are more general business indexes, such as CARL UnCover, at uncweb.carl.org. Carl can be searched for free, but ordering specific articles will cost you. Other article indexes can be found in Appendix F.

- **Hoover's Industry Zone.** This Web site at www.hoovers.com provides industry overviews as well as company-specific details.

- **Small Business Sourcebook.** This annual two-volume publication lists sources of information for starting various types of businesses. The hefty reference has a hefty price, too, costing more than $400 to own.

- **MarketFull.** This database of full-text market research from several major publishers can be broken up, so that you can buy only the sections that you need at a cost of $20 per page. Published by Dialog.

Once you've done your background information gathering, you can focus in on specific companies in your industry. Some sources that will help you hunt down information include:

- **Ward's Business Directory.** Available at the library or online at the Gale site (www.gale.com), this seven-volume set is a directory of 130,000 U.S. companies with sales of more than $500,000.

- **Hoover's List of Major U.S. Companies.** The Hoover's Web site (www.hoovers.com) can be searched for information on 9,000 public and private companies, or the published book can be referenced.

- **Big Yellow.** This is Bell Atlantic's interactive yellow pages. Search more than 16 million U.S. and Canadian companies online at www.bigyellow.com.

- **Thomas Register.** This directory of 140,000 manufacturers in the U.S. and Canada can be searched by product category online at www.thomasregister.com or in the print version.

- **SEC filings.** Check corporate SEC filings for free at www.sec.gov.

- **RMA Annual Statement Studies.** Published by Robert Morris Associates, this print manual provides financial ratios by SIC code, allowing you to compare your projections with companies that are already established in your industry.

- **Company site locator.** Check out www.linkonline.net/company/listings.html for a comprehensive directory of company Web sites.

- **Credit reports.** Check private company credit reports at www.dnb.com for $75.

Bright Idea
Call or visit a local graduate business school library or a metropolitan library with a business division to learn which stock market analysts track which companies. The library's microfiche should provide a list of expert contacts who have their fingers on the pulse of companies in virtually every industry.

This list is just the beginning of potential information sources. As you begin to check out the sites we've recommended, they will undoubtedly lead you to others. Together, they should give you a much better picture of what is currently happening in your chosen industry and where the opportunities lie.

Just the facts

- The perfect business for you will be determined by your interests, abilities, lifestyle preferences, and resources.

- Start your market research process by investigating industry data first. With that in hand, move on to study specific companies next.

- Competitors can also be a handy source of information, helping to validate or refute things that you've heard or learned through research.

- Think ahead to what future customers will need as you develop a picture of your business; demographic shifts, technological trends, and economic changes all affect what products and services will be most in demand.

Planning for Success

GET THE SCOOP ON...
Increasing your odds of financial success ▪
Organizations that can help you write your plan
▪ Why business plan software may not be
a good idea ▪ How to use your plan as your
business grows

PART II

Your Business Plan

Chapter 3

You've probably heard the analogy between a business plan and a road map—you wouldn't get in a car and drive cross-country without a road map, yet the majority of business owners today operate without a plan to lead them in the direction they want to go. Unfortunately, this may also explain why there are so many small business failures each year. Too many business owners are operating by the seat of their pants, with too little capital, too little experience, and too little planning.

Successful business plans are always written, always researched up front, and always well thought-out. Unfortunately, too few business owners take the time to go through the process. Many use the excuse of not being a writer to justify the lack of a plan, although being a writer is not a pre-requisite for a good plan.

The key to planning is not in the writing, which is where everyone gets bogged down, but in the thinking that occurs before the writing. The amount of time invested in writing a business plan should be inversely proportional to the amount spent considering the many different paths to be taken.

31

Unofficially . . .
AT&T and the
University of
Pennsylvania's
Wharton School
conducted a
small business
survey back in
1993 that deter-
mined that only
42 percent of
small businesses
in the U.S. actu-
ally had a writ-
ten business
plan. But of
those that had
grown in the
past three years,
59 percent had
a plan.

This chapter will help you turn your goals and ideas into a document you can use to manage your business or to pursue funding, or both.

Setting achievable goals

What are the major reasons that you want to own a business? Is it for the potential financial rewards? The control over your work life or schedule? The opportunity to build something from scratch? There are probably a million different reasons that people start businesses. But what's important right now is why you want to start yours.

Those reasons will guide what you hope to achieve by owning a business. And they will also guide your plan for starting and growing your business.

Setting business and personal goals is so important because it will shape what your business becomes. The adage "Be careful what you wish for" certainly applies here. Think about what a business will help you attain, and what you don't want it to impact.

If you decide that your goal is to run a multimillion dollar international manufacturing operation, your business plan will be designed to help you accomplish that. But in order to do so, you may have to spend a lot of time away from home and your family. For some people, that won't be a problem. But for others who may be looking for more control over their family life, the plan for the business will need to be tempered by a desire for a personal life.

One potential solution is to bring on staff members at the outset who can support the business, relieving you, the business owner, from having to do it all.

"

Most people
don't realize
their objectives
because they
don't take
planned steps to
achieve them.
—Hyrum W.
Smith, chairman
of Franklin Covey
Co., in *Black
Enterprise*
magazine.

"

As another example, a part-time, home-based sewing cooperative may provide the means to be available for young children while generating an income. One potential challenge could be in growing the business beyond the confines of the home, or in limiting the amount of growth the company aspires to.

Think about your business and personal aspirations, what you want to achieve and why you want to achieve it. Imagine how you want your life to be as a business owner. Take into account all aspects of your life as you ponder your future.

Now write down a series of one-year and five-year goals for yourself that are *SMART*—specific, measurable, action-oriented, realistic, and timely.

- **Specific**—Be as detailed as possible about your goals. For example, don't just say that you want to own a business; say that you want to own a drycleaning operation consisting of three locations by the end of the first year in business.

- **Measurable**—Quantify your goals. For example, state them in terms of when you will reach certain milestones, or in monetary terms.

- **Action-oriented**—Instead of dwelling on feelings or characteristics, such as being more assertive, state which actions you will take.

- **Realistic**—Be reasonable about what you expect of yourself. Stating that you will generate $250,000 in business the first month of operation, for instance, is not likely if you're just starting out.

- **Timely**—Set deadlines for completion. Some goals will take much longer than others, obviously, depending on how big a step each is for you.

Once your goals have been established, the next step is to break them down into manageable chunks. Review each goal and identify all of the steps necessary to attain it. Some may take three steps, others 10. That's okay. Some are much more difficult to achieve than others.

Then break down each of those steps into smaller steps. Working month by month, continue this until each step is just 15 to 20 minutes long. Work on this year's goals first, breaking each down into smaller steps month-by-month. Not only will it help you see your way to achieving them, but you'll also get past being overwhelmed by the enormity of some of the tasks.

Many of the large-scale steps are common to all businesses; the more detailed you get, the more different the steps become for different businesses. For example, most businesses will need to

- Prepare a projected cash flow to determine how much money you need to get started, and how much you'll spend just to get up and running.

- Develop an organizational chart to identify which functions are critical to success.

- Select a location from which to operate, or identify which markets you'll enter during the first year.

- Research potential suppliers, vendors, or manufacturers. Have preliminary conversations with them about a potential relationship.

- Consider which marketing methods will be used at the outset.

It's a given that service businesses will have different steps than product-driven companies, but the basic action items will be the same.

The process you've just gone through is the beginning of the creation of your business plan. Some of the steps for achieving your goals will become part of the plan for your business.

The business plan myth

Many people erroneously believe that you only need a business plan if you are trying to secure business financing. Most small businesses are financed from personal savings or investments by family and friends, so contact with outside financial sources doesn't occur initially. However, colleagues, family, and friends frequently still want to know how their money will be used to build your company. A business plan is not just used for financing. Long-term a plan can have a much greater impact—far beyond funding.

Interestingly, larger companies may prepare a plan to land start-up funding but don't necessarily follow them once the company is up and running.

In fact, anyone planning to start—and stay—in business needs a plan. Studies repeatedly demonstrate that companies that plan for growth achieve growth.

The only outline you'll ever need

There is no magic business plan outline that can guarantee success in your venture—each plan is as unique as the business being described. However, the following framework has been developed and used by companies around the world to get started. Many ventures have secured funding using this approach, which emphasizes industry research up-front to educate the reader.

Cover Page

Table of Contents

Unofficially . . .
At a 1994 Canadian Bankers Association conference, it was reported that companies with a written business plan made, on average, 10 times more than companies without a written plan.

Executive Summary

Industry/Market Analysis

Business Overview

Product or Service Description

Management and Staffing

Marketing Plan

Operations Plan

Financial Plan

Appendix

Bright Idea
To jump-start your writing, tape-record yourself. Pretend that you are describing your plans for your new business to your best friend. Walk him or her through each section of your plan, explaining why you think there is an opportunity and how you'll run the company. When you're done, have your audio tape transcribed, and there you have a rough draft of your business plan.

The secret to writing your plan

People who think that they can't write or who feel that it takes them too long to write anything, take heart. Your business plan is not a novel. It won't be as difficult to write because you don't have to use flowery prose or formal sentence structure. Concentrate on getting your thoughts down on paper on the first go-round. Don't even worry about complete sentences at this point. Start by focusing on your ideas for starting and running your business and jotting down a few words here and there, in the appropriate section. You can edit and proofread later.

Your first draft

So that you understand what information should and should not be a part of each section of your plan, let's run through each one.

Cover page

Your cover page, the first page of your plan, should reflect the image of your new company. For some, this means simple elegance, for others, high tech graphics. Whatever your image, there are some key pieces of information that must appear somewhere on the cover. These are

- The name of your company.
- A brief description of the type of company it is, if the name doesn't clarify it.
- The words "Business Plan," to identify what the document is.
- The date on which the plan is completed, to help you track your progress.
- A key contact person. This is essential if you will be distributing your plan to outside funders.
- An address and phone number for your contact person.

Although you may decide to add an attractive graphic or logo here, be sure to leave plenty of white space. Your cover page should be clean, not cluttered, and welcome the reader to turn the page. Don't overdo it with information here.

Table of contents

The whole purpose of a table of contents is to aid the reader in quickly locating a particular section of a plan. It also gives a hint as to what kind of information will be covered—a mini-preview. Most importantly, it should be easy to read.

Using any table of contents capability on your word processor is the easiest way to prepare a table of contents section for your plan. The key items that need to appear here are:

- The words "Table of Contents" at the top of the page.
- The name of each section, which should match exactly the title of each header within the plan.
- The page number on which the section can be found, so that the reader can quickly flip to a particular page of interest.

Avoid adding too much detail to the table of contents, such as subheads and more subheads. One level of subheads is more than enough, if you must. Subheads help the reader quickly locate main topics they want to investigate. Keep in mind that a table of contents should be no more than two pages.

Executive summary

Your executive summary should be a one- to two-page synopsis of your entire business plan. Note that I said synopsis, not introduction. An executive summary section that is longer than three pages can no longer be considered a summary.

The executive summary should also be able to stand on its own, giving a complete, albeit brief, overview of your plan.

Headers that lead the reader through the section are useful, as are bullet points. However, the executive summary should tell a story—a laundry list of bullet points won't give the reader a complete picture, only snippets.

If you are planning to send your plan out to potential financiers, consider sending only the executive summary out first, to gauge their interest. Once the recipient has determined that they may be able to fund it, send the complete plan. Using the summary as a qualification tool saves you money because you're not sending out boxes of bound plans, and it protects your concept.

Industry/market analysis

Assume at the outset that the person reading your plan—your employee, banker, or investor—knows nothing about your industry or your target market. Since they don't understand what opportunities exist for your new business, you need to educate them in this section.

Timesaver
Write your executive summary after all the other sections have been written. Only after the rest of the plan is complete can you really summarize the entire document. You'll waste hours if you try to write this first.

The most important pieces of information you'll want to cover include:

- What is the size of the industry?
- What is the industry growth rate?
- -What are standard profit margins?
- Who are the major players?
- What are the standard channels of distribution?
- What percent of the market do they account for—that is, do the little guys have any chance of winning business?
- What are some of the trends and forecasts for the future?
- What changes are occurring that are creating new opportunities for businesses such as yours (e.g., technological or cost shifts)?

After giving a macro view of your industry, talk specifically about what's happening in your geographic market. Besides market size and growth rate, also describe how you can differentiate yourself and how you will succeed, given market demands and trends.

For companies that will do business nationally or internationally, don't spend time now analyzing each individual market in the nation. However, if you intend to focus on specific cities or regions initially, an evaluation of each would be smart.

Business overview

This section is typically short and sweet. In one to two pages, you should be able to describe

- The products and/or services you'll be selling.
- How long the company has been in operation.

- What the legal structure is (i.e., corporation, sole proprietorship, LLC, or some new form of doing business).

- Who the owners are.

- What your short-term and long-term goals are for the business.

If you're pursuing financing, you'll also want to explain why you need money now (for expansion, marketing, working capital, equipment purchase, debt reduction, etc.).

Product or service description

To be sure that the reader has a firm handle on what your business will be selling, take the time to fully educate him or her on your products and/or services. For some businesses, this will be a simple task, such as if you're starting a restaurant. But especially in technology-focused businesses, it may take several pages to clearly explain how the product works and why customers will buy it. Don't overdo it, however; too much detail can drag the plan down. Use product literature as an Appendix if it will help to keep the section short.

Focusing on describing the benefits of your product or service is key, so that the reader fully grasps why someone would want it. Where charts and graphs help to explain your product or service, feel free to use them. But be sure that such illustrations help to clarify and aren't there just to break up the page.

The worst plans are those that are heavy on jargon and technical data about how a product is operated. Not only can the reader not understand a word of what's being said, but he or she is really not interested in its functioning as much as what the *benefits* are. The fact that a car can drive up to 100 miles an hour through the use of fuel is of less interest here than the fact that the use of a car makes cross-country travel possible. Speak to the lay person and explain why we all will want your product or service; what pain does it eliminate.

Management and staffing

After describing how your business is structured, describe who is responsible for making it work.

First, you'll want to write a brief paragraph about each of your top managers, detailing their expertise and background. Convince the investors that these are the people most capable of making your business a success. Also describe what their roles and responsibilities will be in the new venture, which hopefully dovetails with their previous experience. Include an organizational chart and describe your plans for adding new staff members over time.

Sometimes a plan's success at getting financing hinges on this particular section. For many investors, the issue is not so much whether a business concept will work, but whether the current management team is strong enough to make it happen. Make sure you've fully explained why your group has the best chance for success.

Marketing plan

This section is one of the most important in the plan, because businesses often fail due to poor marketing. In this section, detail the four *P*'s of marketing: product, price, place of distribution, and promotion. We'll discuss these concepts in more detail in Chapter 9, "Getting Business."

After restating your product or service, describe how you will be pricing your product/service versus those already on the market. Do you have a competitive advantage? If so, explain how it will make a difference in gaining market share over the competition.

Also explain how people will be able to do business with you—will you sell via mail order, the Internet, personal appointment, or in retail outlets? And then explain the various marketing methods you plan to use to promote your business and its wares.

Operations plan

This section is most important in manufacturing operations, which have many different pieces of equipment and operational processes that need to be described.

For service businesses, describe how your business is being run, what the departments are within the business, and how you will be able to expand (by hiring, buying equipment, moving location, outsourcing production, etc.). If you will rely on certain pieces of equipment to produce your work, list them and describe what they do.

Financial plan

Start this section with a "Funding Needed" header, which tells the reader the total amount of money you need to start your business. After providing that number, explain how it will be used—such as for marketing materials, working capital, hiring, equipment purchases—as well as the reasoning for spending it.

The next pieces of information to be provided here are any historical financial statements. If your company has been in operation for more than a year, include the past three years' balance sheets and income statements.

Finally, you'll need to develop and include three years of projections, balance sheets, income statements, and a three-year cash flow with monthly projections. We'll discuss how to put those together later in this section.

Appendix

This section should be used for important reference information that need not appear in the body of the plan. For instance, a summary of a recent contract you won, an article that supports your belief that your company has discovered an untapped niche, a map of planned locations, résumés of key managers, or proposed marketing literature.

Your final draft

With your first draft in hand, ask for feedback from trusted advisers. These may include business colleagues, a mentor, business professor, or trusted friend. Now is the time to refine any strategies that are weak, or to identify potential pitfalls you hadn't noticed. An outside perspective can help bring these weaknesses to the forefront.

The most important reason to develop a business plan is to confirm that the company is viable—that is, that you can make money running it. If you've written a plan for a business that isn't potentially profitable, think long and hard about moving ahead. If you're destined for failure from the outset, think about doing something else.

Finally, before taking your plan to be bound, be sure to proofread, proofread, proofread. Ask a friend who is a writer or hire a copyeditor to read your work and find all the misspellings and grammatical goofs. No matter how much money you invest in printing and binding it, your plan will look foolish if there are spelling and typographical errors.

Should you buy the software?

Bright Idea
Small Business Development Centers across the country will help you write your business plan for FREE! Find the Small Business Development Center nearest you by visiting the American Express Web site at www6.ameri-canexpress.com/smallbusiness.

People who hate to write, or think that they can't, often turn to business plan software for help. Unfortunately, what they discover is that a software package can't do the strategic thinking that is at the heart of your business concept.

Don't rely on a $100 business plan software package as the answer to your prayers. Unless you've thought through your goals and strategies for managing your business, you'll find a software template very difficult to use. You're also taking a big risk that the package you've selected is asking all the important questions relevant to your particular industry.

The real advantage is in the formatting—software packages provide some nice financial templates for you to follow. Instead of having to set up your own spreadsheet on Microsoft Excel or Lotus, you can use the preformatted versions provided. It is a potential timesaver, to be sure.

Some of the most popular packages are:

- Business Plan Master
- Business Plan Toolkit
- Business Plan Builder
- Guerrilla Business-Automated Business Plan

Financial projections

The outline you just worked through is primarily focused on the narrative portion of the business plan. The narrative portion is the material in the front of the plan that describes what the business is and how you will run it.

The second portion is the section called the "Financial Plan," which we quickly reviewed. In this section, you'll provide detailed financial information to prove to yourself and anyone else that you can make money running this business. After all, if you can't make money at it, why do it?

Three critical financial statements

As you begin the process of estimating your sales and your expenses for your business, you need to come to grips with one fact—the numbers you are developing are *guesses*. There are no right or wrong answers here. Of course, the guesses are based on a significant amount of research that you've already conducted, but they are still your best estimate.

Cash flow statement

The first financial statement you need to prepare is the cash flow statement. This is an estimate of how much money you'll collect and how much you'll spend in the next three years, broken down month by month.

Start by estimating your annual sales for the coming year, then break that down into monthly income. If you're aware of any seasonality or cyclicality in your industry, try to take that into account as you plot your monthly sales. If you simply divide your annual figure by 12, you'll find it more difficult to manage your cash flow later.

Keep in mind that you should record your sales in your cash flow statement when you expect to receive payment. So if you sell a widget one month and don't expect to receive a check until the next month, you don't record the sale until the second month, when you receive the cash in hand.

Watch Out!
Be aware that most lenders and venture capitalists can spot a "plan-in-a-can" document a mile away. If you use business plan software, the finished plan will look very similar to any other plan created with that package. Funders may not be impressed that you took the easy way out.

Next, estimate your monthly expenses. These may include:

- Rent or mortgage payments for your offices
- Salaries for you and your employees
- Utility payments
- Tax payments
- Insurance payments
- Equipment leases or loan payments
- Professional service fees, such as for attorneys or accountants
- Supplies
- Raw materials
- Phone service
- Travel costs

Use the examples above as a starting point to help you identify all the potential expenses your business will have. It's much better to overestimate your expenses up front than to discover that you forgot to include some.

After you've calculated your monthly income and expense projections, subtract your expenses from your income each month. Be sure to carry forward any leftover cash from the month before. Those months where you have a negative number indicate that you'll need to find a cash infusion to stay afloat; typically, that means a line of credit or a prearranged loan. Another alternative is to investigate means of reducing your expenses, so that your income can cover all of the costs of doing business.

This tool is the most important one you'll develop. Once you're up and running, you'll want to review this regularly to make sure you're never short of cash.

Income statement

An income statement is very similar to a cash flow statement. It reflects all the revenue and expenses the business has had for a particular period of time, which is usually a year. One simple way to construct a projected income statement is to develop a cash flow statement, listing a total column at the end. Take that total column as the starting point for your income statement. Then add in any equipment or building depreciation the company expects. That's an income statement. You'll read more about income statements in Chapter 4, "Financing Techniques."

The reason you can't run a business solely by an income statement is that it's not detailed enough. You may end up with positive figures at the end of the year, but unless you took the time to develop a cash flow statement, you wouldn't recognize that you're short of cash in March and September.

Balance sheet

The balance sheet is the most difficult to put together because the numbers don't relate to any sales or expense figures. The balance sheet is divided into two sections, which equal each other— your assets (what you own) and your liabilities (what you owe).

To begin developing your balance sheet, make a list of everything you believe your company will own by the end of its first year. Do the same for the second and third years in business. Now go back and estimate the value of each of those items.

For example, based on your cash flow statement, how much cash do you think you'll have in the bank by the end of the first year? How much in accounts receivable, equipment, property, and real estate?

Those are your assets. Total them when you've finished making your list.

Next, make a list of your debts and place a value on each. If you have parents or friends who have offered to lend you money, those would be debts to place in your liabilities section. Any balances on equipment purchases or building mortgages would also appear here. Total your liabilities.

If your assets do not currently equal your liabilities, don't despair. You can even them out using two categories in the liabilities section of your balance sheet: paid-in capital and owners equity. The paid-in capital line item is for any investment that the owner (you) has made at the outset. So if you invested $2,000 of your own money in return for 200 shares of stock, you would put $2,000 on that line.

Add that figure to the total liabilities number and subtract that from your assets. That's what goes on the owner's equity line. Most companies have a negative owner's equity at the start because their long-term liabilities exceed their current assets. If this is the case with your balance sheet, you're in the majority.

Tried-and-true templates

Sometimes taking a look at sample business plans can be helpful as you try to envision the finished product. You can find some here:

- **www.bplans.com**—Several business plans for personal services, restaurants, and a distributor can be found here.

- **www.morebusiness.com/templates_worksheets/bplans**—Two samples plans are available here, for a consulting firm and computer dealer.

■ *Business Plan Handbook* (4th edition), by Kahrs and Shupe—The editor has compiled a slew of sample business plans from many industries and types of companies, providing many examples of plans for you to follow.

■ *The Complete Book of Business Plans*, by Covello and Hazelgren—Includes 11 fictional business plans, along with instructions on how to prepare your own.

■ *Start-Up: An Entrepreneur's Guide to Launching and Managing a New Business*, by William Stolze, has several business plans for ongoing businesses, both product- and service-oriented.

Your book will be judged by its cover

Many successful business owners will argue that a business plan's appearance is much less important than the business concept being described within—and they would be right. However, these same success stories probably have personal contacts and connections that will ensure that their business plans get read no matter what. So, unless you can pull some strings to guarantee that your plan will be read (or you have the financial resources to personally fund your new venture), you need to be concerned with the initial impression your plan makes.

Of course, if you're developing a business plan for a venture that doesn't need outside funding, you'll have to decide whether you'll be sharing it with anyone else. If not, the appearance is much less important. It needs to be legible so that you can track your progress, but it doesn't have to impress.

However, if, like many entrepreneurs and business owners, you'll be submitting your business plan to potential lenders or funding sources, you'll want

Watch Out!
Remember to write your plan for the reader who knows nothing about your industry and isn't at all familiar with the technical jargon that may be second nature for you. Technical words and phrases make it more difficult for the reader to focus on your innovative business concept. To be sure, have a friend outside your industry read your plan before distributing it.

Unofficially . . .
The number of business plans received by major venture capital firms can be as many as 100 in an average week. That's a lot of competition for funding.

Bright Idea
Channelbind Inc. has patented a hardcover cloth binder that can be foil-embossed with your company name or logo, giving the appearance of an expensive book binding. For under $20, you can have a top-of-the-line look. Call them at (800) 562-7188 or visit their Web site at www. channelbind.com for pricing and ordering information.

to increase your odds of success. And your first challenge is getting it opened.

To increase your odds of that happening, you'll want to use some or all of the tactics mentioned here.

First impressions count

The first question to ask yourself once your plan is complete is "Does this look professional?" Is it obvious that you've invested time and money to create a solid business document? Simply by its outward appearance, does your plan suggest that it is comprehensive and well-developed?

One measure of that is the quality and appearance of the plan's cover. You don't have to invest in leather binding, but a hardcover does make an impact.

If a hardcover binding isn't feasible or desirable for you, some other options include:

- Have an 8.5' × 11" color cover created by a desktop publisher or graphic designer. Insert this sheet of paper on the front of a presentation-style three-ring binder with a clear cover. You get the best of both worlds—eye-catching color on the front within a hardbound package.

- Order solid color covers from a paper supplier, such as PaperDirect!, with a cutaway on the front for the business name.

- Add an acetate cover and backing to your printed plan and have it spiral or coil bound.

Layout tips

Although there is no standard format for a business plan, there are some guidelines for ensuring that it is easy on the eyes and simple to follow. These include:

- Keep at least a 1' margin around the edges of the page. Leave at least .25' more on the left-hand side of the page, to accommodate the type of binding you select.

- Use short paragraphs, instead of lengthy ones, to make the pages less daunting to read; two to four paragraphs is a good guideline. In doing so, you'll add white space to make reading easier on the eye. Be careful not to go overboard with too much space, however; that could suggest to readers that you're trying to bulk up the page count because there isn't much substance.

- Use headers that indicate the topic to be discussed in the next section. Lead the reader through the plan.

- Insert tables, charts, and graphics whenever they help to illustrate or clarify a point. If they may be confusing, however, it's better to leave them out. Be sure that the graphic clearly supports a point you've made within the text and isn't a stand-alone chart or illustration.

- Use a serif font, such as Times Roman or Garamond, rather than a sans serif, such as Futura or Arial.

- Select one or two fonts to be used throughout the plan—no more. One font for the body copy and a complementary one for the headers provides a nice variety.

- Don't go any smaller than a font size of 11 points for your body copy—12 is preferred.

- Avoid excessive underlining and italics.

- Use color to liven up charts, graphs, images, and photos that appear within the text, but

Watch Out!
Keep in mind that one of the advantages of a three-ring bound plan is that it can be easily photocopied by the recipient for distribution. Coil bound and ChannelBind-type plans are much more difficult to lay flat on a copier, and are sometimes more frustrating for the recipient.

Unofficially . . .
Studies have shown that serif fonts, with their extra tendrils, are easier for our eyes to process and read. Most books are printed using serif fonts for that reason.

never use colored text. Not only is it difficult to read, it looks childish.

■ Once again, be sure to carefully proofread your finished plan before showing it to anyone outside of your circle of friends. An obvious typo or grammatical error can result in your plan being immediately jettisoned.

Measure your progress with your plan

Many business owners pat themselves on the backs at this point, reveling in the fact that they have actually written a business plan for their company. Unfortunately, the next thing they often do is to place the plan on their bookshelf, filing it away. Don't let this be you!

A business plan is not a document, it is an ongoing process. You've taken the first step by putting your goals and your strategies down on paper. But the next step is to take action, using your plan as your guide. It's your to-do list and performance measure all rolled into one.

The only way you'll ever be able to know how you're doing as a business owner is to refer back to your initial plan. Some business owners do this weekly, for example, checking their cash flow religiously. Other review it monthly, making sure that they've taken care of everything they intended. And others do it quarterly, sometimes involving their management team or advisory board in the review.

At start-up, you'll want to refer to your plan almost daily to keep yourself on track. After the first year, you can go to weekly, and monthly after that. Use it as your central repository for any new information related to the growth and success of your business.

Just the facts

- Anyone intending to run a business needs a business plan to make it happen.

- Setting goals and objectives for your business establishes the framework for your plan.

- There are organizations nationwide that provide free help in writing a business plan.

- Completing an industry or market analysis up front helps the reader better understand your business plan.

- The presentation and appearance of your plan can make a difference in getting funding.

"

I've maintained my business plan on a regular basis for nine years; doing so has helped us consistently grow the company. In 1997 we purchased a new building to store our growing inventory. Many of our products are from exclusive lines—lines that we would never have been able to obtain without being able to present credible evidence that we knew what we were doing.
—Brian Cockfield, president, Sports Equipment and Flooring, Monroe, N.C., in *Self-Employed Professional*

"

GET THE SCOOP ON...
When to pursue financing ▪ Money mistakes
that can be avoided ▪
Beefing up your business plan ▪ Evaluating
equity versus debt

Financing Techniques

Chapter 4

M ost businesses fail because they are under-capitalized—that is, they run out of cash. There can be many different reasons that this situation occurs—higher than expected start-up costs, lower than expected sales, sudden loss of a long-time customer. In the end, all of these situations could have been avoided simply by planning ahead.

Financing is not for companies that desperately need money. In fact, if your company is up and running and you already need money, it's too late to ask for it. The trick is to arrange for financing to be available when and if you ever need it.

The best time to apply for funding, whether you're pursuing a loan or an investment, is during the start-up phase. As soon as you have a solid business plan written, it's time to locate potential sources of capital. Although you may not need the money now, you'll probably need it down the road, when you decide to expand, buy a building, invest in new equipment, or hire several new employees.

There are basically two kinds of financing to consider: debt and equity. Debt financing involves agreeing to repay a certain amount of money borrowed, plus a fee. Equity financing, on the other hand, need not be repaid. The major difference is that with equity funding, the owner sells a portion of the company to an investment group in return for an investment in the company. With a loan the owner retains ownership, along with full responsibility for repayment of the debt.

Of course, the element of risk plays a big role here as well. How risk-oriented or risk-averse are you? Do you feel more comfortable making a solid commitment to repaying a large sum of money, or are you happier to potentially give up a chunk of your company for the possibility of great rewards?

The types of investors you may consider approaching are also evaluating their risk tolerance; how likely is it that they'll get their money back? What are the chances of sales going through the roof? How much money can they afford to lose? These are all questions floating around the investors' mind as they weigh making a financial commitment to your business.

One of your first challenges will be to decide which type of financing makes the most sense for your situation.

What financiers and bankers want to see

First and foremost, potential investors or lenders want to see that an entrepreneur understands his or her business. Whether you are seeking debt or equity financing does not matter—you must know your business inside and out in order to convince someone else to hand his or her money over to you.

A concise, well-written business plan is the best way to demonstrate your business savvy. It's useless to try and get around this basic requirement (go back to Chapter 3, "Your Business Plan," if you aren't sure of how to begin).

In addition to a business plan, a one-page summary is key. This summary document highlights the important strengths of the business, provides a financial snapshot, and lists the contact person's name, address, phone, fax, and e-mail. This short summary is a boon to venture capitalists and loan brokers who are trying to wade through piles of business plans each week; you'll impress them if you make their decision-making process easier and faster. But it's also a great way to protect yourself as well, by not laying all your cards on the table up front.

By offering a one-page summary, you should give enough information to pique the financier's interest but not too much that you worry about intellectual property issues.

According to Lawrence Mohr, founding partner of Mohr Davidow Ventures in Silicon Valley, a winning deal consists of the "three *M*s": management, market, and money.

In your business plan, you must demonstrate why this management team is the one most likely to make this venture a success. Communicating who your target market is now and five years from now is a start at documenting how your product or service will change their lives. And, finally, detailing how much money it will take to bring your product or service to market over the next few years is critical. If you can address all three well, you have a shot at getting the attention of someone like Mr. Mohr.

Watch Out!
Don't even think about asking a venture capitalist (VC) or banker to sign a non-disclosure agreement. First, there shouldn't be anything proprietary in this document not already protected by copyright or patent, and no VC can guarantee that they haven't already seen a concept similar to yours, or that they won't tomorrow.

Financing options

Once you determine whether your company is best served by debt or equity funding, your next challenge is to identify potential sources of those funds.

Starting with those individuals you know best and working your way out from there is how people typically compile a list of potential contacts. The following is a list of potential sources you may or may not have thought of:

- Family and friends
- Factoring
- Suppliers
- Private investors
- Loans
- Lines of credit
- Venture capitalists
- Government funds

Family and friends

One of the first sources entrepreneurs turn to are family and friends, the people who may be more willing to invest based on character than any of the other four *C*s of lending (collateral, creditworthiness, capacity, and condition). But don't expect that these investors won't want to see the same types of information that everyone else will ask for—namely, a business plan.

Some people would never ask their family or friends to take a risk with their money because of the strain it can add to the relationship. If you *do* decide to approach the people near and dear to you, make sure you keep the discussion as business-focused as possible and that you fully explain the risks. For everyone's sake, you'll also want to formalize any agreements reached by putting it in writing. Taking this step helps avoid misunderstanding by clarifying the terms of the loan up front. This may help ease the tension later on if things don't go as expected with your enterprise.

Factoring

Companies with contracts, purchase orders, or invoices in hand are in a position to consider factoring to raise cash quickly. Although expensive, factoring provides a means for companies to generate cash in a hurry.

Essentially, factoring companies buy promises from other companies to pay—in the form of purchase orders, invoices, etc.—at a discount. When the company pays, the money goes directly to the factoring company. Although quick cash can be a lifesaver, factoring is expensive; remember that you only get a portion of that original invoice amount, not the total. Although factoring can reduce the need to go into debt to pay obligations, it does add paperwork and new restrictions on how you handle incoming cash.

Suppliers

Companies that have a short-term cash shortfall should consider turning to their suppliers for assistance before going to a bank. In many instances, you may be able to negotiate extended payment plans for a set amount of time, such as six or nine months. This will ease your cash crunch and ensure that your supply of materials won't be cut off.

Some suppliers may consider making an investment in your business if they have seen a steady increase in the amount of work the two companies have been doing together. If you're looking for an investor, a supplier who understands your industry

Timesaver
Save yourself time and aggravation by learning what the criteria are before approaching a funding source. Ask what their minimum and maximum loan amounts are, the types of businesses they invest in, what the funds can be used for, and the stage of development the company should be in.

and your business could be an excellent fit. Not only will you receive the cash you need to keep operating, but you might also gain a valuable adviser and confidant.

Private investors

Private investors (a.k.a. angels) can be lifesavers, coming through to fund a company when no one else would. But as Andy Sack, chief executive of Abuzz, points out in an article on "Angel Financing" on the entreworld Web site (www.entreworld.org), "Angels are idiosyncratic. Rather than dealing with institutions, you're dealing with individuals—and the whims of individuals."

Angel investors are individual investors willing to fund companies in the very early stages. Since they rarely identify themselves as such, you are more likely to find them at a local venture capital meeting or through other business contacts, such as accountants and attorneys.

Loans

One of the first places you should turn for a loan is the bank you currently deal with. If you have a long-term relationship with a certain institution, they have a history of your money management abilities and may be more willing to lend you funds. You may also be able to negotiate a lower interest rate, given your existing relationship.

The Small Business Administration has a number of loan programs for business owners that range from $500 to several million. Visit their Web site at www.sba.gov for information on the microloan, LowDoc, and guaranteed loan programs.

Lines of credit

Lines of credit are very similar to a credit card; the money is available for use, but you need only take

Moneysaver
If you intend to use money raised to purchase equipment for the business, consider an equipment lease through the equipment manufacturer. Less expensive than a term loan and less risky, an equipment lease can get you the equipment you need without the lengthy process of identifying and securing investors for that purpose.

what you need. Repayment amounts vary according to how much of the total you have borrowed, rather than being a set monthly figure, as with a term loan.

Companies that are cyclical or seasonal often rely on a line of credit to help ease the cash swings during their slow months. The extra cash generated during the peak season then pays the line of credit off.

If you don't have a current need for financing, a line of credit will be easier to arrange than a term loan, which is typically approved based on a specific project.

Venture capitalists

Despite the fact that venture capitalists got a bad rap during the 1990s for their aggressive approach to investing (remember the term "vulture capitalists"?), venture funding continues to grow. Especially in the high tech arena, venture-capital firms are eager to make investments.

Be aware that no matter what the source, lump sum funding is rare. That is, most financing is phased, providing a company with several cash infusions over a period of time as long as they meet their stated projections. Phased funding limits an investor's risk and keeps the company focused on meeting its goals. However, it also increases the risk to the entrepreneur, who may encounter difficulties regaining or retaining equity if targets aren't met.

Check out a number of venture capital resources in Appendix E of this book.

Government funds

The truth about government grants is that they are few and far between, and there are no programs out there that will simply hand you cash to start a company. There are certainly programs that can reduce

Timesaver
The SBA has created an online networking site for angel investors and entrepreneurs, called ACE-Net, at www.sba.gov.

Timesaver
Wells Fargo Bank
has established
a loan fund
specifically for
women-owned
businesses. Visit
their Web site at
wellsfargo.com/
biz to learn more
about it and to
apply for a line
of credit.

your tax liabilities and give free incentives to run your business a certain way, such as locating in a particular part of the city, hiring workers on welfare, or buying an abandoned building. But there is no free money.

The one program that provides grants for research and development activities is the Small Business Innovation Research program (SBIR). SBIR grants are awarded competitively to companies in the hopes that information gathered will benefit the sponsoring government agency, as well as the awardee. Information on such grants is available at www.sba.gov.

Through the U.S. Small Business Administration, the government will guarantee repayment of loans to other banks, making it easier for you to qualify for a bank loan, but the government doesn't make loans directly to its citizens.

What they require

All financiers require a written business plan that contains at least three years of projected financial statements. Beyond that, a willingness on your part to answer all of their questions is the only common requirement. Of course, each source will have its own criteria on which you will be evaluated, such as amount of collateral available, your personal net worth, and previous entrepreneurial experience.

Pros and cons

Entrepreneurs so focused on securing financing for their companies may fail to see that the type of financing they are about to get is not in the best interests of the business. There are definite advantages and disadvantages to each funding source that should be considered.

When pursuing debt financing by way of a loan or line of credit, be aware that this money must be repaid in full by the borrower—you. Although the money is being invested in the company, you will also be asked to personally guarantee it; if the company fails, you will still be required to pay up.

Companies already saddled with debt may want to rethink adding an even heavier debt burden to the business. The other option is attracting investors to help share the risk.

The advantage of equity investors is that they will give you money to invest in the company in return for a percentage of future profits. Although the money provided need not be repaid, the investors certainly expect to get their money back, and then some. As the company grows and profits increase, investors take a portion of the profits as a return on their investment.

Keep in mind that investors will take a share of the company in return for their money. And there is the very real possibility that if the company does not perform according to your business plan, they may decide to hire new management to run the company. If they hold a majority of the shares, they are well within their rights to do so. Bringing in new management has happened in a number of high profile companies—remember Apple Computer? Or Mrs. Fields Cookies? The owners had no control over the future direction of the company once they failed to meet their promised sales or profit targets.

One tactic that is frequently used to prevent such a situation from occurring is that the owners place restrictions on the sale of company stock. That is, investors are prevented from reselling corporate stock to unknown third parties as part of the initial agreement. Retaining as much original corporate

Unofficially . . .
The MIT Enterprise Forum was one of the first groups established to link entrepreneurs with investors. Local chapters can be found by visiting the following Web address: www.onlinewbc. org.

stock is always a good idea to reduce the chance of third-party investors gaining a controlling interest.

While it doesn't happen all the time, you, the owner, need to be mindful of this possibility going in.

Just the facts

- Debt financing enables the business owner to retain full ownership but saddles the company with financial obligations up front. Equity financing, on the other hand, requires that the owner give up some control.

- Without a written business plan, financing will be almost impossible to obtain.

- Networking is the best way to get a business plan read by a venture capitalist or investor, rather than just mailing it in to someone you've never met.

- SBIR grants are the only money the government gives away. Funds must be used to finance research and development efforts that may benefit the government.

Taking the Plunge

PART III

GET THE SCOOP ON...
Protecting your product ▪ Getting on the IRS'
good side ▪ Incorporating pros and cons ▪
License and permit prerequisites

Getting Up and Running

or many people, the paperwork involved with starting a business will be fairly minimal. Considering how to best safeguard your business's intellectual property and what form of business structure to adopt are critical aspects of starting a new business. If patents, copyrights, or trademarks are involved, you can count on lots of paperwork being part of your start-up activities. Ensuring that your business has the right to use the name you have carefully selected, to market any products or services you have developed, and to operate using sound financial management practices is critical for longevity.

Not following proper procedures at the outset can cost you thousands of dollars in penalties and fines, not to mention potential lawsuits, if you're careless. Consider your start-up legal fees as an investment in protecting the intellectual property of your business. We've identified the most important procedures and government requirements you'll need to be aware of and have summarized them here.

Mission statement

Although the government doesn't require a mission statement, developing one is a smart first step for new business owners. While you're immersed in paperwork, forms, and legal documents, a mission statement can remind you of why you're doing this; it keeps you focused on the big picture. It will also help when you seek out advice on what form of business structure you should adopt.

Some of the elements of your mission statement might include:

- The ultimate purpose of the business—what you want customers to gain from their association with you

- What are the benefits of the products and services you'll be selling

- What clients should expect from you in terms of service, responsiveness, and professionalism

- How you expect to be treated by customers, suppliers, and partners

- How prominent you intend the company to become in your industry. (Some owners want their companies to stay well-kept secrets in order to keep competitors in the dark, while others strive to be vocal industry leaders.)

- What you want the company to become known for, also known as its Unique Selling Proposition (USP)

- Operating principles you will follow in your efforts to achieve client objectives, including ethical issues or response times, for example.

Developing and establishing your organization's guiding principles will help you in many ways as you grow—in your marketing to clients, in attracting and retaining the right employees, and in determining which growth opportunities should be pursued. Your mission will help to establish the corporate culture for your company by setting standards and expectations for employees, as well as defining priorities.

Once your organization's mission has been set, your focus should be on protecting corporate assets.

Patents, copyrights, and trademarks

A company's intellectual property is often its most valuable asset. As the world economy shifts from industrial- to information-based, ownership of ideas is at the core. Patent, copyright, and trademark documentation helps to determine who is the rightful owner of inventions, concepts, brands, and artistic creations. Copyright or trademarks can also dramatically increase the marketability of a business. So protecting intellectual property rights can significantly increase the potential value of a business. And whoever files first has a clear advantage.

Patents

Patents are the worldwide standard for assigning ownership of an invention or process. Before filing a patent application, an inventor should first confirm that a patent is not currently held by someone else for the same product or process. To qualify for patenting, an invention must be new, proven to work, and tangible; intangible ideas are not patentable.

Moneysaver
The U.S. Patent and Trademark Office assists businesses in protecting their investments and in promoting their goods and services. They can be reached at (703) 305-8600, or visit their Web site at www.doc.gov.

Bright Idea
As soon as you have confirmed that your idea can be patented, proceed to file the paperwork. Even if you have no immediate plans to manufacture or market your product, you will retain the right to do so within the next 17 years without competition. You can also license or sell the idea, once you've patented it. The only downside is that your exclusive rights begin to run out as soon as you file.

Patent searches can be done for free through a local library with direct computer access to the U.S. Patent and Trademark database. Another more costly yet less time-consuming option is to work with an attorney who specializes in patent filings. Costs range anywhere from $2,000 to $6,000 for a typical search and filing process.

Keep in mind, however, that having a patented product does not guarantee business success. At the same time, a patented product or process is not necessary to establish a thriving company. Legal documents such as patents and trademarks merely help to protect your ownership rights.

Copyrights

Where patents protect tangible ideas or products, copyrights protect the ownership of creative ideas and products, such as fine artwork, music, and books. The creator of such works has the right to prevent others from using, copying, or distributing his or her works without permission.

Copyrights are easier to secure than patents but much harder to enforce, unfortunately. The U.S. Copyright Office of the Library of Congress issues and administers copyrights that are registered with their office.

To apply for a copyright, complete an application and send it along with a check for $20 and a complete copy of whatever work you are seeking to copyright. You can download an application at the Library of Congress Web site at www.lcweb.loc.gov/copyright/forms.

Be sure to complete and file the appropriate application for the copyright, whether it's for music, art, or written work.

Trademarks

In some cases, a company's identity or brand name is its most valuable asset. A well-known brand name connotes a certain level of quality or prestige that many consumers have come to trust and associate with a particular company. To allow someone to tamper with that brand image could be extremely damaging and costly to a company—which is where trademarks come in.

Trademarks protect both product and service names and their associated symbols for an initial period of 20 years. During that time, no one else may use that symbol or name without the company's approval. By definition, trademarks identify the source or owner of the mark.

Name search

Selecting a company's name is one of the most important decisions you will make as you start your business. A business's name will help identify what the company does, as well as establish its image. Discount Duds, for example, presents a very different image than Van Wert Clothiers.

Begin the process of generating potential names by brainstorming with managers, consultants, and/or friends. Consider the ambiance you plan for the company, the level of service and pricing strategy you have defined, as well as synonyms or phrases frequently associated with your product or service.

The strongest and most protectable trademarks are those that consist of words or phrases that have been newly created or coined, rather than a collection of several common words. Made-up words are considered the most distinctive trademarks and are more easily protected than generic or common terms.

Bright Idea
One cheap and popular way to establish yourself as the true creator of a work of art, written work, or concept is to document it, place those pieces of paper in an envelope, and mail it to yourself. If your authority is ever challenged, you can present the unopened, date-stamped envelope as proof of when you came up with the idea.

Once you have settled on a name, the next step is confirming that no one else in your service area is already using it. "Service area" is a key issue; if you intend to operate only in your local area, you may need only check local records. However, if you will be operating nationally or internationally, it is best to conduct a national or international name search to ensure that you won't encounter problems down the road. If another company has already registered a business name as its own, by trademarking it or incorporating, you cannot use it without their permission.

The process of running a name search through your attorney's office can cost anywhere from $500 on up, depending on the geographic area being searched. An international search will cost several thousand dollars. Weigh that against the potential loss of business if you are prevented from exporting your company's name to other countries.

Although you'll want to complete the search before expanding into a new area, it's not necessary to make the investment now, when cash may be tight. Reevaluate the need to register your company name in other areas every six months, as your business grows and matures.

Corporate structure

Selection of your business's corporate structure affects how you track revenue, pay employees, and complete government paperwork. Your options currently range from operating as a sole proprietorship, a partnership, a corporation, a limited liability company, or a limited partnership. Most importantly, it shifts liability for financial obligations or lawsuits from the business owner to the business itself. This is the major reason many business owners

Unofficially . . .
According to *FinancialWorld Magazine,* the value of Coca-Cola's brand was an estimated $39 billion in 1995. The Marlboro name was worth $38.7 billion, while Microsoft was worth a mere $11.7 billion and IBM $7.1 billion.

incorporate, choosing to shield themselves from corporate liabilities.

Be aware, however, that individuals and businesses can choose to sue whomever they please, so despite the fact that you've incorporated, you can still be named personally in any lawsuit. Incorporating generally helps protect personal assets, such as a house or car, in such instances.

Timesaver
To learn whether a company name has already been trademarked, visit www. tmcenter.com.

Sole proprietorship

Many companies start out as one-person operations. These solo businesses are often run as sole proprietorships, which are taxed at individual rates rather than corporate tax rates. As the IRS sees it, any income generated for the business is passed through directly to the business owner.

To establish a sole proprietorship, you need only complete a Doing Business As (DBA) certificate, available at a legal stationery shop, search courthouse records to confirm that no other business has already registered the same name, and pay the requisite fee, typically under $50.

If you have a partner in the business, you can also file a DBA for a partnership. The main difference with a partnership, however, is that each partner is equally responsible for the acts and ommissions of the other. So if your partner chooses to buy a building for your new business, you are both responsible for the mortgage payments.

Corporation

Incorporating enables you to separate your business obligations from your personal obligations. Once your business is incorporated, you become an employee. Any revenue earned is paid to the company, not to you personally. Taxes are also paid monthly, not quarterly or annually, on salaries and wages paid to employees—like you, the owner—as they are with sole proprietorships.

The major advantage is that if the company is ever sued, you may be able to shield some of your personal property.

Although the actual process of incorporating can be handled in minutes, consulting your attorney and accountant before initiating anything will also save you time and money. Doing so will ensure that you've selected the appropriate form of incorporation, that you've elected appropriate officers, and that the paperwork is all in order.

Keep in mind that incorporating in a state different from your home state, such as Delaware, frequently does not eliminate the annual franchise fee which home states charge of all corporations operating in their borders. This franchise fee is also payable regardless of the size of your sales; if you incorporate before you actually plan to start operating, you will still be expected to cough up the annual fee (which is generally somewhere between $250 and $400).

Depending on the number of shareholders involved in the company, you may elect to file as a Subchapter S corporation or as a Subchapter C. Most smaller companies are Subchapter S corporations. Operating as a Subchapter S corporation allows you to avoid being "double taxed." Instead of reporting profits on the corporate return, shareholders (including the business owner) are taxed on amounts received from the company. Allowing profits to be distributed to shareholders without taxation at the corporate level is called "pass through" tax treatment.

Limited liability companies

Both limited liability companies (LLC) and limited liability partnerships (LLP) have a general partner, who is personally liable for the actions of the organization, and limited partners, who are not liable. LLPs are frequently used in real estate transactions, where there are several silent partners not involved in the day-to-day decision-making. LLCs are becoming very popular among law and consulting firms, where the partners are active in daily operations; they are less expensive and less complex to set up and manage than corporations.

Reporting and paying taxes

The Internal Revenue Service requires that Americans pay taxes on a wide variety of items, including:

- Salary and wages
- Owned property
- Sales
- Luxury items
- Capital gains on investments

As a business owner, you are responsible for paying a number of taxes, based on your annual sales and employees' wages, to both federal and state governments.

Earnings of sole proprietorships are taxed as part of the owner's personal income, rather than as a separate business. IRS Schedule C allows the sole proprietor to itemize all income and expenses for the year.

Partnerships, corporations, and limited liability companies (LLC) file separate business and personal tax returns, on the other hand. Partnerships and LLCs file a tax return, with each partner also

Unofficially . . .
Companies frequently incorporate in Delaware rather than their own home state because of its business-friendly courts. When lawsuits are filed, Delaware will rule in favor of the corporation more often than not. However, any licenses or permits required by your home state still need to be obtained.

Watch Out!
Employers are
required to com-
plete an I-9 form
when an
employee is
hired, document-
ing that the
individual is a
U.S. citizen or
resident alien
with two forms
of ID. Employees
must also com-
plete a W-4
form, authorizing
their employer to
withhold their
taxes.

responsible for paying personal taxes on his or her
share of the business's earnings. Corporations file a
tax return for the organization while the owner pays
taxes on any salary or dividends received from the
company during the year.

Income

Employers are responsible for withholding a portion
of each employee's salary or wages, according to his
or her individual tax bracket. The company then
pays that withholding figure to the government, by
making a payment to its own bank, each month.

Failure to withhold and pay the required tax
amounts on time each month will cost your company big bucks in fines and penalties.

Unemployment Taxes

In addition to income taxes, employees must pay a
portion of their earnings to the state unemployment
fund. Under the Federal Unemployment Tax Act
(FUTA), employees pay 8 percent of their wages up
to the first $7,000 earned. This means that employ-
ers must withhold this amount and pay the state
accordingly.

Social Security

Employee and employer also split the social security
tax, which is 12.4 percent of the first $68,400
earned. An additional 1.45 percent of the
employee's salary is paid to Medicare.

Insurance

Although some business owners decide to risk not
having insurance to cover their business against loss,
most entrepreneurs would agree that having no
insurance is the most risky situation of all. Especially
at the start of a business, when your financial risk is
the greatest, insurance is crucial.

If you are leasing, be sure to read your lease closely as it may specify the type and minimum amount of insurance you are required to carry. The building owner or leasing agent may require written proof from your insurance carrier annually that you have coverage in place.

The whole purpose of insurance is to reduce the risk of loss and keep a company up and running following a disaster. Of course, a disaster could be anything from an earthquake, to a fire, to an owner's serious illness, to one of your employees cleaning out your bank account and skipping town.

Worker's compensation, which provides for any employee who is injured on the job, is the only type of insurance required by law in every state. However, some states may also require additional insurance beyond worker's compensation. In New York, for example, you are required to have disability insurance to provide for any employee who is injured off the job. Be sure you know your state's particular requirements.

Business owners can often be exempted, however, from certain types of insurance. Although not necessarily smart to restrict yourself from insurance protection, you can often save money by exempting yourself from coverage.

Other valuable types of insurance include:

■ **General liability**—protects against a lawsuit that may result if someone is injured at your place of business

■ **Errors and omissions (E&O)**—protects against a lawsuit that alleges that your advice was either damaging or incomplete. Lawyers and consultants typically buy this type of protection. E&O may also provide coverage for discrimination claims or negligent acts of corporate officers.

Watch Out!
Failing to pay monthly corporate withholding amounts is extremely costly. Making the deposit even one day late can result in fines of several hundred dollars. Avoid these penalties by paying your monthly tax withholding figures by the 15th of each month.

- **Business interruption**—provides funds to compensate the company for some event that caused business to be lost.

- **Key man**—enables the company to continue to operate even if one of the owners or senior managers becomes ill or dies.

- **Auto**—ensures that the company isn't penalized if an accident occurs by an employee while on the job.

Licenses and permits

Some service businesses require licenses of those individuals providing services, such as hairstylists and cosmetologists, while companies are often required to have a business permit in order to operate. The list of businesses and professions that must be licensed varies by state, as does the list of businesses needing a permit in order to operate.

Each state has an office that handles the processing of licenses and permits. To learn whether you are required to be licensed or have a permit, call your local SBA office or Chamber of Commerce.

Just the Facts

- Writing a mission statement for your company helps your employees understand the purpose and top priorities for your business, making it easier for you to reach your goals.

- To protect your company's intellectual property, such as written work, product brand name, or innovative manufacturing processes, consult an attorney and complete all the necessary forms to register a patent, copyright, or trademark.

- Consult a tax accountant to be sure that you are withholding all the necessary taxes from your

> **"**
> Talk to both a reputable property and casualty insurance agency and an agency whose specialty is life and health insurance. Together they can evaluate your business premises and operations and advise you of potential risks and appropriate types and levels of insurance coverage.
> —William Seybold, John Hancock Insurance
> **"**

employees' paychecks and that you are paying the least amount required under the law.

■ Business insurance is essential to ensure that your company continues to operate after disaster strikes.

GET THE SCOOP ON...
Selecting the best business location ▪ When to
lease, when to buy ▪
Must-have business tools ▪ Negotiating an
even better deal

Setting Up Shop

Chapter 6

The success of some businesses can be determined solely by their location. Even with the best products, the most appealing signage and displays, reasonable pricing, and helpful employees, companies have failed simply due to a poor location.

Of course, location is of greatest importance to businesses that rely on foot or drive-by traffic; these customers are looking for convenience when they shop. Retail businesses are those that are most affected by their selection of a location.

On the other hand, manufacturing companies, distributors, and consulting firms that typically travel to meet with clients are less concerned with visibility and more with image, accessibility from major roadways, and parking availability. Location is less of a factor in the success of these types of companies because their customers don't choose to do business with them solely due to their location, as with retailers. And physical location of the corporate offices is of least importance to Internet-based ventures, which operate in cyberspace.

Moneysaver
Many cities have small business incubators, which are low-cost facilities established to foster start-ups. New businesses located within an incubator pay a nominal rent and share space and resources, such as office equipment and secretarial support, with fellow start-ups. For information on the incubator closest to you, call your local SBA office.

Since your lease or mortgage payment will likely be a relatively sizeable expense at the outset, invest carefully in a location that will serve you well at the outset and for several years. Moving to a new location is also costly, so try to avoid moving again until you absolutely have to.

Finding a location

As you begin your search, first make a list of your top priorities. Finding your perfect location is only possible when you've defined what "perfect" is for you. Consider:

- What is it that your location must have?
- Are there geographic areas that are particularly desirable/undesirable?
- What would be nice to have?
- What is your budget?
- Where are your competitors located?
- What market trends are affecting where companies are locating?
- What other businesses that may relate to yours are nearby?
- Where are potential suppliers or distributors located?

Next, you'll find that a commercial real estate broker or Realtor can be of great assistance in advising you of available sites and reasonable rents. Take a look at the names on many of the buildings you've seen. A well-connected Realtor can be a big time-saver and may be able to alert you to space that is coming on the market soon.

Confirm that the landlord will pay the Realtor's fee before engaging someone, but in most cases, you will incur no additional fees.

Tools to evaluate sites

In addition to a location's cost, business owners need to evaluate a laundry list of factors before selecting the best site for their company. The right location will match the business's needs in many, if not all, of the following areas:

- Amount of traffic—foot or car
- Visibility of location
- Appearance of building exterior
- Neighboring businesses that complement your own
- Amount of space available for operations
- Space available for expansion, if necessary
- Parking availability and accessibility
- Shipping and loading dock availability
- Accessibility from main roads
- Proximity to employees' homes
- Proximity to customer locations
- Renovation costs
- Utility costs
- Length of lease
- Local taxes, fees, and licensing requirements

In addition to these factors, keep in mind population shifts in your area. Are families or businesses moving into new areas? New office park and residential developments on the outskirts of existing towns or neighborhoods create opportunities for forward-thinking companies.

Negotiating a buy or lease deal

When you know that you'll be in a location for several years, perhaps because of equipment that can't easily be moved or a technology infrastructure you

66
Restaurants and retail businesses need visibility, so the location must be clearly seen from either direction of the road; signage is also key. On the other hand, if you rarely see customers at your place of business, low overhead is important. Only pay for a first-class location if it is required.
—Matthew Korona, Olver, Korts, Korona, and Russell
99

don't want to risk compromising, buying a building can make a lot of sense. And if your other options include leased space that require you to pay utilities, a portion of the taxes, and maintenance and repairs (also called a triple net lease), purchasing a facility won't cost much more.

Although purchasing a building can be more costly up front, over the long run the benefits of building ownership can be substantial. In addition to tax advantages, being able to modify the facility layout, the ability to hand select other tenants, and the prestige and credibility that go hand-in-hand with owning a property are bonuses that may be even more important than the financial aspects.

Whether you're buying or leasing, double-check that you are permitted to operate your type of business in that particular space. Depending on how the building is zoned, you may or may not be able to legally operate there. Just because a space is zoned commercial doesn't necessarily mean that you can locate a heavy industrial plant there, for example. If you're unsure of whether it's permitted, consult your attorney or a local architect.

When leasing, you may be asked to sign a personal guarantee by the landlord. Obviously, this is to protect them from deadbeat tenants who move out before the end of the lease term. If you can't get out of signing a personal guarantee, try to have an early termination clause added which could enable you to leave before the end of the lease under certain circumstances. The last thing you want is to be personally responsible for lease payments for several years if you find that there are problems with the building, you outgrow it, or you go out of business.

Starting out at home

Another popular start-up strategy is to start out at home. Instead of investing money up front in commercial space, many business owners decide to operate from a home office. In addition to saving money on rent, the business owner can also take a tax write-off for the portion of the house or apartment set aside for business activities. But be careful, the home office deduction is one of those red flags that generate IRS audits. To play it safe, check the IRS criteria before taking the home office deduction.

While home-based businesses may have had a shady or unprofessional image years ago, they are certainly accepted nowadays. One sign of how prevalent home-based businesses are is the number of publications devoted to serving this huge market; *Home Office Computing* is one of the largest. Fortune 500 companies have also established whole divisions to serve the growing "small office, home office" (SOHO) market.

If you plan to operate a product-oriented company from your home, be aware that neighbors may not like having huge delivery trucks pulling into your driveway each week. Have a conversation with your neighbors to ensure that there will be no problem if you decide to operate from home. Neighbors are generally the people who will report you to the zoning board if an incident occurs, so try to stay on their good side. Steering clear of any parking problems on your street is also a good idea.

Equipping your enterprise

Your location is just one component of the image you'll project to customers and prospects. The

Timesaver
To quickly identify buildings that may be available for sale at reduced prices or that are located in target Economic Development Zones (EDZ), call your local economic development department or city real estate department. Such properties typically need renovating, but there are often additional grants, low-interest loans, and tax abatements available to the buyer.

Watch Out!
The primary
threat to operat-
ing from home
are zoning laws
designed to dis-
courage home-
based concerns.
Although few
towns still have
laws on the
books that pre-
vent home-based
businesses,
investigate your
town's or city's
laws to be sure
you aren't in vio-
lation. Call your
local zoning
board to ask
about restrictions
on home-based
businesses.

professionalism of your operations is another—and probably more important—component. The primary way to control the image of your operations is to ensure you have quality office equipment.

The quality of the output from your office will demonstrate your professionalism. That output ranges from the sound quality on your phone system, including your voice messaging system, the quality of your printed documents, the clarity of your outgoing faxes, and the crispness of your photocopies. Each item doesn't have to be perfect, but overall, you'll want their appearance to be above average.

Since many companies assume that home-based businesses are somewhat less professional than commercially based companies, you need to go above and beyond the expectations for most businesses to overcome some misconceptions. Don't scrimp when it comes to designing and printing your marketing materials; they represent the quality and level of professionalism you'll be providing. Cutting corners here suggests that you'll cut corners in your work with clients.

Some individuals expect that they can get a bargain price from a home-based business, since there is much less overhead. But cutting your prices below competitive levels only suggests that the quality is lower; don't do it.

Despite your residential address, your clients and prospects should not be able to tell that you're working from a home office. And the only way to ensure that is to invest in all the extras that commercially based businesses do.

Basic tools you won't want to be without

These days, one of the biggest operating issues is communication—how can customers reach you.

Providing more ways for customers and potential customers to contact you has been the trend, causing business owners to invest in a myriad of tools to stay in touch. From cellular phones to pagers, to Web sites, immediate access has been the goal.

Once you're connected, you'll want to appear well organized and on the ball. With the help of your speedy computing system and a contact management program or database, you can reference your customer's particulars on the spot.

Checklist

There are some pieces of office equipment you just can't operate without. These "must-haves" include:

- **Computer** (Estimated cost: $1,000)—Today the standard processing speed is 350 MHz, but you'll want to buy yours to stay a little ahead of the curve. Expect to have to completely upgrade your computer every five years, with minor upgrades along the way, in order to stay current.

- **Computer software** ($800)—Word processing is critical, as is a customer database or contact management program. Accounting software also makes a lot of sense and will save you considerable headaches down the road. Many packages are included as part of the purchase of a new computer, fortunately. But for those of us who have to purchase separately, look into buying a suit of applications bundled together. Microsoft Office and Corel's WordPerfect Office Suite are two very popular packages that combine several types of software for one lower price.

- **Printer** ($400)—Depending on your frequency of usage, you can consider either an inkjet or

Bright Idea
Operating from home doesn't mean that you have lower standards of professionalism. Invest in a second business line, which will provide you with both white and yellow page telephone listings, and will ensure that callers know they have reached a quality company. Keep that impression alive by preventing children from ever answering your business line.

Unofficially . . .
According to research and consulting firm Find/SVP, there are approximately 18.3 million self-employed people who work at home. However, only about 8.7 million Americans who do any type of work at home said they operated a home-based business.
Source: *Entrepreneur's Home Office Magazine*

laser printer. Inkjets are fine for infrequent use, for invoicing, for example. However, print-intensive businesses, such as consulting firms, will want to step up to laser quality printing for just a little more.

■ **Office telephone with answering machine or voice mail** ($100)—When someone calls, give them the opportunity to leave a message for you if you're not available. A busy signal is one of the worst sounds a potential customer can hear.

■ **Facsimile machine** ($300)—Although your computer may have direct fax capability, meaning that you can fax documents directly from your PC, you'll still need a way to transmit documents you've received in hard-copy form. Buy a plain-paper version and avoid having to photocopy incoming documents.

■ **Copier** ($400)—You can often find multiple-use printer/scanner/fax/copier machines ($600–$700) that will function well and negate the need for separate pieces of equipment. But you'll need some way to photocopy documents for distribution to colleagues, prospects, and customers.

■ **Merchant status** (percentage of sales)—For manufacturing and service companies, credit card transactions will be the exception rather than the rule. But for retail businesses, being a merchant able to accept credit cards is essential for survival, as is a cash register.

■ **Filing cabinet** ($100)—Don't even think about trying to operate without a means to keep your documents well-organized.

There are also other items that are "nice to have" and will potentially make your life a lot easier. These productivity-enhancing tools include:

- **Postage meter** ($50/month)—If you anticipate doing a lot of mailing, the fee for the rental of a postage meter may far outweigh the time lost driving to the post office each day with packages.

- **Color printer** ($250)—Increasing use of the Internet has driven the sale of color printers, which can showcase color featured on Web pages. Color printers can also be helpful in putting together overhead cells for presentations.

- **Telephone headset** ($150)—People who are constantly on the phone swear by telephone headsets, which allow them to move about the office during a call.

If you're unsure how useful a particular piece of office equipment will be for your operations, hold off buying it until you're sure you need it. Monitor how many times in the first month you could have used the item. In the meantime, rent it or turn to other service providers to meet your needs. For example, rely on a quick copy business until you know that you need a copier in your office.

Low-cost ways to furnish your space

Once you've settled on a location, you'll want to be sure not to break the bank furnishing it. Some of the best ways to get the furniture and equipment you need for less than you'd expect include:

- **Auctions**—watch your local paper for listings of upcoming auctions. Companies being sold or

Watch Out!
Be aware that providing multiple ways for customers to reach you means that you'll never be out of touch. For those of us who like to have a life beyond business, that becomes virtually impossible once you've given out your home phone number, cell phone, and pager number. Think about the downsides of 24-hour accessibility to everyone before you print your home number on your business card.

Bright Idea
Voice mail has a
major advantage
over an answer-
ing machine—
callers can leave
a message if
you're on another
call or logged
onto the
Internet, instead
of hearing a busy
signal and hav-
ing to call back.
Essentially, you
have the capac-
ity to take two
calls at once
with voice mail.
Answering
machines are less
expensive long-
term, with the
only cost being
the up-front pur-
chase, but the
recording quality
is generally poor.

going out of business will frequently auction off office furnishings, filing cabinets, and other accessories at pennies on the dollar. You'll find some of your best deals here. But be ready to pay cash on the spot and arrange for delivery yourself.

- **Used furniture stores**—When companies upgrade their furniture, they frequently sell the lot of older items. Check your yellow pages for used office furniture businesses. The prices are good and any upholstered items can be recovered to meet your color scheme.

- **Classified ads**—Skim your local classified ads to find companies selling off their old furniture themselves.

- **Internet suppliers**—Increasingly, Internet Web sites are providing very competitive pricing. In a few cases, you set the price you want to pay for certain items and the company tries to acquire it for you. Priceline.com is just one example of a company that works this way; you set your lowest price and see if they can locate a seller willing to accept your bid. Although Priceline isn't yet offering bidding on office furniture, they probably will in the future. Other auction sites that do have furniture include eBay.com and Amazon.com Auctions. There are also Internet auction sites that have access to office equipment and furnishings.

- **Sharing space**—Instead of going out on your own, check with other businesses to learn whether they have extra space they would rent you. Freelance consultants often locate their firms within larger companies that are, or later become, their clients. In renting space, you'll often avoid having to buy any furniture and office equipment. Make a list of suppliers and customers you'd like to be associated with and start contacting them.

Setting up a multiperson office

Designing an office for yourself is very different from setting up space to meet the needs of several workers. In addition to buying multiples of each type of furniture—desk, chair, telephone, computer, filing cabinet—you'll also want to lay the space out to provide privacy for each individual.

Allowing each worker to control their own work area has been shown to boost productivity. Whether you use cubicles, moveable partitions, or build offices with ceilings and walls, take into account the number of employees you have, the type of work they will be doing, and how much space they'll need to function properly. Nothing gets in the way of productivity more than an uncomfortable workspace.

After the desks are in, the computers are on, and the phones are ringing, don't forget to encourage employees to decorate their offices with personal mementos, such as photos, plaques, and plants. Having employees make an investment in their space may also increase their commitment to the company.

Getting the best deals on equipment and technology

In almost every case, buying equipment outright will yield you the best long-term cost. However, in some cases, the lower monthly cost of leasing will be the only option during the start-up phase.

Whether you're buying or leasing, you'll want to calculate the greatest amount of money you can

Watch Out!
Before purchasing a multifunction machine, determine what the primary use will be and shop for a model strongest in that function. Be aware, however, that multifunction units tend to break down more than stand-alone units, and when one function goes, you lose access to the others while the whole unit is in the shop.

Bright Idea
Renting space in an executive suite can be a great way to get started. Sharing space with other small businesses, frequently in a Class A building, can enhance your image without requiring that you rent more space than you need. Generally, you also gain access to a receptionist, furniture, phones, copier, and conference rooms. A list of national executive suite companies is in Appendix D.

afford to invest up front and use this as the basis for negotiating the best possible deal.

Ask the equipment dealer about any special financing packages that may be available. In many cases, 90-day free or "same-as-cash" financing is the rule.

If you're leaning towards leasing, you'll also want to ask about buyouts during the lease period. In some cases, after the lease is in place, you can buy the equipment from the lessor for less than the total cost of the lease payments. This happens more with national dealers, such as Xerox or Canon, than with smaller businesses.

Get price quotes from at least three suppliers before making a decision. And ask if this is their best price. In most cases it is, but it never hurts to ask. When you have the lowest price, see if another vendor will beat it.

Just the facts

- Take into consideration your type of business and its particular requirements in selecting your business location.

- Don't pay full price for office furnishings. Unless customers frequently come to your place of business, the appearance of the furniture is less important than how well it functions.

- If you scrimp on office equipment, you can potentially undermine your professional image. A dot matrix printer or telephone answering machine spell low budget.

- Leasing office equipment may enable you to have equipment you couldn't afford to buy up front. But you can usually buy it during the lease term at favorable rates.

GET THE SCOOP ON...
Accounting action items ▪ Empowering
employees ▪ Preventing paper overload ▪
Managing yourself

Internal Management

Chapter 7

Managing your business involves creating systems to better track your finances, your employees, and your workload. These elements are your company's most valued resources. Keeping better track of your money, your staff, and your paperwork will mean higher profitability for your business.

To start, you'll need to set up a bookkeeping system to manage your finances. Monitoring your cash flow, profitability, assets, and liabilities will keep you in business. It will also help you to grow and expand your company, making the best use of your financial resources.

Helping your employees to understand how they can best serve the company is your second challenge. The answer is to develop reference manuals for them. Keeping employees in the loop regarding your goals and objectives will make it possible for them to help you reach those goals. In the absence of information, employees will make their best guess of how to do something. To reduce the chance of employees taking action you'd prefer they didn't, give them plenty of guidance.

93

Finally, in addition to helping your employees be their best, you need to take steps to manage yourself better. Controlling how you use your time will improve your productivity, your effectiveness as a manager, and your business's profitability.

Accounting

Since your first year in business is the most important, seek out professional help if necessary to make sure you correctly address these critical first-year decisions:

- Selecting an accounting method—cash or accrual. Do you know whether an expenditure should be expensed or capitalized? Decide now to reduce the chance of having to convert all of your records later.

- Determining which expenditures constitute start-up expenses, handling the election, amortizing organizational expenditures, etc.

- Choosing a depreciation method.

- Choosing an inventory valuation method.

- Setting up systems for tracking accounts receivable, accounts payable, fixed assets, etc.

- Establishing the optimum ratio of debt to equity.

- Applying IRS rules to setting officers' salaries.

- Knowing which tax deductions you are entitled to, and which are disallowed and will result in penalties.

- Arranging/itemizing expenses correctly for IRS forms.

- Filing all the necessary employment taxes, special business taxes, etc., and the right forms for reporting income and other taxes.

Bright Idea
Check out the Web version of the Small Business Tax Review at www.smbiz.com. The site is focused on providing tax and management assistance to small and mid-size business owners. The goal is to help you do as much of your accounting, tax, and analysis work as you feel inclined to do.

To keep your expenses down, hire an accountant to set up a bookkeeping system for you to follow. Setting up an efficient and cost-effective system may involve computerization. Even niche businesses like specialty toy stores have access to software specifically written for the needs of their particular business. Computerization of your operations is the only practical way to manage your accounting functions if your business has a large volume of cash transactions on a daily basis or if you maintain a large inventory.

At a minimum, you want to streamline daily transactions, payroll functions, and tax reporting. Research vendors who produce software written specifically for use in your industry. The up-front cost could prove to be the very difference between your business succeeding or failing. Even if your business doesn't merit specialized software, small business software, such as Intuit's QuickBooks and Peachtree Accounting, have modules for invoicing, accounts receivables, and accounts payables that can help tremendously in tracking and managing your cash flow. Such programs, as well as specialized packages, are great for quickly creating sales, profitability, inventory, and expense reports.

Software vendors can be a good source of start-up help, providing tips on how other companies in your same industry set up their books and manage their business.

Even if you have no intentions of managing your own books, you'll want to be knowledgeable enough to recognize whether your bookkeeper or accountant is doing an adequate job.

Watch Out
Be as careful about selecting an accountant as you would about selecting a business partner. Check references, interview current clients, call the Better Business Bureau, and talk to anyone who may know your candidates. Since you'll be trusting this person with sensitive information about your business as well as potential access to your funds, be extra careful to find someone reputable and trustworthy.

Personnel management

Just as your money can help you achieve success or block your path, so can your staff. And whether that staff consists of you alone or several workers, you'll want to take some steps to make your workforce as organized and productive as possible.

We'll discuss the pros and cons of having hired help in Chapter 12, "Adding Staff," once you're fully established in business. But for right now, here are some tips to manage your work habits—and the habits of those already on board.

Information you should have on-hand

Whenever a new employee is hired, you'll want to create a personnel file, which contains the following:

- **A copy of the I-9 form** the employee completed, documenting U.S. citizenship. You're required by law to have this documentation on file for easy access by the Department of Labor.

- **A copy of the W-4 form** on which the employee specified his or her tax bracket and withholding amounts. The IRS requires this document.

- **A copy of the employee's job description.** Although this information will undoubtedly change as the employee's role changes or grows, having documentation to illustrate what duties the employee understood he or she was to fulfill can be useful in unemployment hearings if the employee is ever fired for poor performance.

- **Employee's signed confidentiality agreement.** Should the employee ever reveal sensitive information that is damaging to the company, you may want to pursue legal action. Be sure you have something to back you up.

Bright Idea
To help you select an accountant or bookkeeper and conquer potentially intimidating accounting terminology, browse through Jan Zobel's *Minding Her Own Business: The Self-Employed Woman's Guide to Taxes and Recordkeeping.*

- **Employee's signed noncompete agreement.** Since job hopping among competitors is common, try to have a non-compete in force that prevents former employees from sharing proprietary information that would be harmful to your business.

- **Employee's resumé and references.** Should any question ever arise about the employee's qualifications or background, such as if your firm were applying for a government clearance, you'd need such information available.

- **Background check details.** Although background check information is not routinely reviewed after hiring an employee, it can provide useful information like current address, former employers' names and contact information, as well as a credit report. During litigation, you may find it necessary to go back to those references.

- **Drug test results.** Many corporations require their suppliers to drug test employees working on their premises. You'll need to document that your employees have passed such tests.

Company policies

Employees make it possible for you, the business owner, to be concerned less with the day-to-day details of getting the work done and more with the strategic issues affecting your company. Instead of having to take orders, fill the orders, bill customers, and manage your business, you can focus solely on improving the functioning of your company.

However, to take this step back from the daily activities, you'll need to establish procedures and systems to guide your employees' actions. You

Timesaver
Nothing saves more time than learning from someone with experience. Look for opportunities to gain a mentor who can lead you around potential trouble spots in your business. The SBA has a free mentoring program for women called WNET that has helped numerous new business owners achieve success faster.

Watch Out!
"Getting it right
the first year can
make all the dif-
ference. If you
make a mistake in
the first year, you
may not be able
to rectify the
error, or may only
be able to do so
at a substantial
cost . . . . And it
could take time
away from your
regular business.
In some cases you
may not be able
to undo a first-
year error." So
says *Small
Business Taxes and
Management*.

should have written policies and procedures in place right from the beginning. Since your employees are a direct reflection on your business, cover all your bases by specifying procedures for every task, even how the phone should be answered. Keep instructions and policies simple in order to avoid misunderstanding and misinterpretation.

Your goal should be to develop clear procedures for employees to follow so that over time you can delegate more and more as your employees demonstrate their ability to take on more responsibilities.

- Analyze frequent tasks and write down the steps and/or questions that need to be addressed to obtain the outcome you want. For example, if you write a lot of press releases, create a form that features all the questions you need answered. Check for understanding, then let your employee take a crack at it.

- Establish controls and checkpoints for monitoring progress on large projects.

- Create a project-tracking sheet. Break down each step in the process of each major activity and insert next to each step the initials of the person whose responsibility it is to complete the work.

- Increasing your business momentum is going to come from committing yourself to coach, train, and encourage your employees. In general, employees want to do their job well. Most are conscientious and hardworking, but they need guidance in order to know what a "job well done" looks like to you. That's exactly what your policies and procedures manual should contain.

▪ Set up regular feedback procedures. Feedback given only in times of crisis will almost always be taken in a negative fashion.

According to David Elzey in the *Small Business Journal,* "The Small Business Administration estimates that the average small business owner spends 7 to 25 percent of their time handling employee-related paperwork . . . . The increasingly complex tax codes and regulation, pension rules and requirements, workers' compensation laws, anti-discrimination laws, OSHA, etc. . . . have added to the administrative complexity, not to mention the legal ramifications of being an employer." This paper-intensive work associated with running a business has driven the growth of the PEO industry. A PEO can be hired to administer all personnel and payroll functions, handling anything that would be managed by an internal human resources department. The PEO is the employer of record for insurance, tax, and payroll purposes.

An advantage for employees is that PEOs are generally able to provide better benefit options than smaller businesses. Because they are pooling workers from lots of small businesses and purchasing benefit packages on a volume basis, they can negotiate very low rates.

If you want to pursue this option for your business, look for a PEO that is a member of the National Association of Professional Employer Organizations (NAPEO) and the Institute of Accreditation for Professional Employer Organizations. Take the time to really investigate the PEO you are considering; ask for bank and client references, and get your attorney to review the agreement and the provisions for cancellation.

Timesaver
Leasing employees through a Professional Employer Organization (PEO) allows you to select your workers without assuming responsibility for all the necessary—and time-consuming—paperwork. Instead of being employed by your business, they are employed by the leasing firm and assigned to your company for as long as you require them. PEO fees range from 2–6 percent of your gross payroll.

Processes and systems

Productivity is the name of the game in being a successful business owner. Service businesses that bill by the hour can only make more money by increasing the billable hours generated each year. And product-focused businesses can only hope to continue to build a customer base by doing more in less time. Consider increasing productivity by offering your employees more flexibility as to where they accomplish their work. Focus on the results they produce and not how many hours they spend in the office.

The research company Cyberdialogue reported that "in 1997, (telecommuting expert Tom Miller) counted 11 million teleworkers in the U.S, growing to 15 million by the year 2000. (Miller's) most recent study (in October 1998) counts 15.7 million teleworkers (a.k.a. telecommuters). That's about 8 percent of the U.S. population, and is about 41 percent higher than the previous year's figures. He predicts 18 million by the year 2000."

The key to increasing the productivity and momentum of your business lies in setting up systems to manage your workflow, paper flow, and human resources or human capital.

Filing

Divide all of your work based on what needs to be done today, what needs to be done in the future, and what has already been done. Keep the information for your immediate tasks handy on your desk, and put all other files away in your filing cabinet.

Make a pile of paper to be filed, and label it in the top right-hand corner with the name of the appropriate file in which the material should be placed. Doing this eliminates the need for you to

Unofficially . . . According to the Canadian Telework Association, a full 55 percent of AT&T's managers already telework at least one day a week. The key benefits for the company are productivity gains and real property savings. AT&T in New Jersey realized 50 percent savings on real estate.

personally file the information and reminds you quickly of where the papers need to go.

Procedures

While a policies and procedures manual will help employees complete activities to your satisfaction, your staff also needs to be informed of your larger goals. Creating a personnel manual is a smart idea, as it educates employees about the company they work for and informs them of your expectations.

Some of the elements of a personnel manual include:

- A company history
- Company mission statement
- Dress code
- Drug policy
- Holiday schedule and sick day allowance
- Starting compensation
- Benefits provided, such as health care, retirement account, vacation time, and even child care assistance.
- Pay periods and overtime provisions
- Performance reviews and promotion policies
- Provisions for continued employment/termination
- Confidentiality or non-disclosure policy
- Training and education
- Grievance process

The more comprehensive your company's personnel manual, the less the risk of miscommunication and claims of discriminatory or harassing treatment or wrongful termination. Ask an attorney specializing in labor law to review your personnel

Timesaver
Color-code all of your files to make it easy to immediately identify their purposes. Customer and prospects files should be differentiated from your business management files and your reference files.

manual for completeness and any potentially discriminatory language. Then, when questions arise,
you can confidently direct employees to review their
manual for guidance.

Time management techniques

The biggest challenge to managing your time is controlling it. Some of the most effective tips for managing your time include:

- Bunching your calls both in the morning and
  evening

- Grouping any meetings or errands to reduce
  the amount of separate trips out of the office

- Ignoring the ringing phone if you're in the middle of another project

- Delegating activities that can be completed by
  employees whenever possible

- Scheduling phone appointments to avoid
  "phone tag"

- Sending a response or query by fax, which an
  employee can do on your behalf

- Reducing potential distractions in your office by
  cleaning off your desk frequently

- If you're a procrastinator, setting a deadline for
  starting a project, rather than a deadline for
  completing it

- Learning to say "no" in order to avoid being
  overburdened

Whether your business bills by the hour, by the
job, or by the product, knowing how much time has
been spent creating each product or completing
each job can be useful in understanding how your
company is doing financially, as well as learning
more about how well your employees are working

out. Asking employees to track how they spend their time during the day can be amazingly illuminating. Using 15-minute intervals, ask employees to note what they accomplished. The results can be great learning and training tools, as well as helpful financial management devices.

In service businesses, tracking time by the quarter hour is standard procedure, both to ensure that you're billing clients for every minute you spend on their work as much as to confirm you're spending enough time on their behalf. By tracking hours, you'll know which employees are generating the most money for the company, as well as identify people who may need some additional training in productivity.

Just the facts

- In your first year, doing your own accounting and taxes can be a big mistake.

- Have a written personnel manual in place right from the beginning.

- Take time to coach, train, and encourage employees so you can delegate effectively.

- Adopt time-saving strategies to maximize your productivity and consider alternative work arrangements to increase employee job satisfaction and productivity.

> "
> The very notion of time management is a misnomer, for we cannot manage time. We can only manage ourselves in relation to time. We cannot control how much time we have; we can only control how we use it.
> —Alec Mackenzie, *The Time Trap*
> "

A Marketing Mindset

GET THE SCOOP ON...
Calculating your costs ▪ Preferred pricing
methods ▪ Enhancing your image ▪ Collecting
what's owed

PART IV

Pricing Strategies for Profitability

Chapter 8

Pricing your products and services appropriately will yield the highest sales and best profits for your company. The trick is in determining what "appropriate" is for your business. Some of the questions you'll need to ask as you set your prices are:

- How do you want your company positioned/ perceived in the marketplace?

- Where will the business be located?

- Who is your target market?

- Is your target market growing? By how much annually?

- What are your competitors charging?

- What are your fixed and variable costs?

- What is your break-even point?

While your costs are an essential part of setting profitable prices, they are only one component to determining pricing that will bring you the highest sales. You also need to evaluate what your customers are willing to pay.

Bright Idea
Increase the profitability of each customer relationship by increasing the amount sold to each customer. One tactic for doing this is by providing information about a related service or product with each product or service purchased, such as with a printed flyer or coupon. There is no additional cost to provide this information beyond the printing cost, and it increases the likelihood of an additional sale exponentially.

Products with desirable brand names have cachet for which consumers are generally willing to pay more. Ralph Lauren and IBM are two brand names that demand a premium price. Popular service businesses can also charge more because there is enough demand to sustain higher rates. Like brand names, certain service businesses will earn a reputation that increases demand, enabling the owner to raise prices.

On the other hand, targeting price-sensitive shoppers can result in substantial sales as well. Companies such as All for a Dollar and Discount Auto Rentals position themselves as lowest cost to attract customers in search of the lowest price. The most successful companies on this end of the pricing spectrum focus on generating volume; although each sale yields a small dollar amount, the number of transactions is high, resulting in higher sales.

The only way to know which pricing approach will yield the best results for your business is to carefully calculate your costs and to set your end price above that amount. Companies that are losing money on each sale can never hope to "make it up on volume," as the joke goes. Instead, they can only look forward to a speedy bankruptcy.

Know your costs first

Although there are three general approaches to pricing, each requires that you know your total costs. No matter whether you opt to use cost-plus, market-based, or perceived-value pricing, you'll want to confirm that your approach is actually profitable.

A break-even analysis will alert you as to whether your current cost and pricing structure is profitable. However, it will not tell you what the market response may be—that is, you still don't know whether customers will buy your products and services at the prices you've set.

To determine which strategy will work best for your business, consider the three major approaches.

Cost-plus pricing method

In many industries, the standard pricing strategy is to bill for the total cost to produce an order, plus an industry-standard profit percentage. The automotive and commercial printing industries, for example, have printed pricing guides that businesses refer to when quoting jobs. Retail establishments also typically have standard markups, or margins, above their wholesale cost.

If you are in such an industry, the most important component of your pricing strategy is the accuracy of your cost calculations. Since you can't control your profit margin, you'll want to be 100 percent sure that you've accounted for all your costs on each and every job. In many cases, that means adding a margin for error—that is, adding an additional percentage to cover unforeseen problems. This additional amount covers product spoilage, damage, failure, non-paying customers, or additional costs associated with providing a service.

Companies that advertise huge discounts on their products or services can still be making a profit if their margins are high enough. Even after a 40 percent discount, a business with a 100 percent margin is still highly profitable.

Becoming more profitable in such industries is only possible by cutting your costs. With your end price set, you'll need to bring your costs to a minimum. Improving product quality and reducing waste is just one way many manufacturing companies boost their bottom line.

> 66
> Setting prices is an art, not a science. The art is in striking a balance between the money you need to stay in business and the customer's perception of what your product or service is worth.
> —Edith Quick, partner, Quick Tax & Accounting Service
> 99

Note! ➔
Determine
whether your
current pricing
strategy makes
sense, given your
costs, by con-
ducting a break-
even analysis.
This calculation
will tell you how
many units must
be sold before
you start making
a profit. Make
sure that number
is one you
expect to
achieve, or
change your pric-
ing approach.

Moneysaver
Be sure you know
the difference
between discounts
and margins. A dis-
count is calculated
as a percentage off
of the retail price
of a product; cus-
tomers will ask for
a discount to get a
better final price.
Your challenge is
to make sure that
you maintain a
profit margin,
which is the
amount above the
cost to produce
your product or
service when you
make a sale. A dis-
count shouldn't cut
too much into your
profit margin.

Break-Even Analysis
Example

Let's assume that you're a management consultant charging $125 per hour for your services. Your fixed costs are those expenses that don't vary with how many hours you bill each month; your variable costs do. Your profit is the difference between the two numbers. Calculate each figure to determine your break-even point.

Fixed costs

Rent/lease	900
Utilities	100
Salaries	5000
Insurance	200
Telephone	300
Marketing	500

Total **$7,000 per month**

Price per unit OR
Price per project   5000

Total **$5,000 per project**

Variable costs

Raw materials	200
Travel	450

Total   **$650 per month**

Profit	=5000-650	
(Price - Variable Cost)	**$4,350**	
Break-even	=7000/4350	
(Fixed costs/Profit)	**1.61 projects/month**	

To break even each month and make a profit, this consultant needs to secure and bill almost 2 projects each month, at an average cost of $5000. Is this doable? Only the consultant can gauge for him or herself.

Market-based pricing

Market-based pricing involves determining what your competitors are charging as a guide to where you set your prices. Of course, relying on your competitors to set your pricing is reactive; trying to follow every pricing move your competition makes is dangerous and essentially puts your pricing decisions in someone else's hands.

If your company positioning goal is to be market leader, you may decide that setting your prices slightly above your competitors' will best support your image. On the other hand, to pick up sales from price shoppers, you may elect to be consistently below the competition. If you do decide to go this route, however, be sure you communicate that loud and clear to your prospects and customers; being assured of lower prices is an important benefit of doing business with you.

Of course, once you have your competitors' prices, you'll want to double-check your costs. No matter what your competitors' prices are, you still need to confirm that you can be *both* profitable and competitive.

Perceived-value pricing

Although perceived-value pricing is thought to be the highest profit strategy, the opportunity for huge profits is generally short-term. Using a perceived-value strategy, the business owner charges whatever the market will bear—whatever customers are willing to pay.

Typically, the opportunity to charge prices based on value to the customer arises suddenly, perhaps due to a major marketing push or new product announcement. When this occurs, demand for the product or service is so high that competitor pricing is only a minor concern; competitors may not even be able to get products in inventory. Costs, however, should always be evaluated to ensure that each product sold earns a profit.

Although many businesses would absolutely love to price their goods using a perceived-value pricing strategy, the reality is that few products or services can sustain such an approach long-term. Once production capacity increases and product availability ceases to be a challenge, demand no longer exceeds supply and prices must drop in response.

The best perceived-value pricing example I can think of is that used by Mazda dealers in the 1980s, with the release of their extremely popular Miata. At that time, the car's MSRP was approximately $14,000, and yet dealers were asking up to $30,000—and getting it—because consumers wanted the hard-to-get car. Of course, this strategy didn't work forever, but for the period of six months

Timesaver
To compare your costs to your competition quickly and easily, turn to the Robert Morris Associates *Statement Study*. Using your Standard Industrial Code (SIC) code (found in the *SIC Code Index*), you can determine how your financial ratios compare to other businesses in your industry. This will alert you as to how your profit margins stack up against fellow industry participants.

or so during which the cars didn't stay on the lots, the dealers maximized their profitability.

Be sure you're looking for those opportunities, just as the Mazda dealers did. Whenever you encounter a situation where demand for your products or services exceeds your capacity, increase your pricing until demand falls off. Try a 10 percent increase and see if customers balk. If not, try 20 percent. And stop increasing when sales start to decline—at that point, you've exceeded the perceived value of the product or service.

Y2K consulting is another situation where, for a limited period of time, consultants and computer programmers with knowledge in this area could increase their fees to take advantage of demand exceeding supply, especially as 1999 came to a close. Organizations that realized too late their dire need for help in becoming Y2K compliant were forced to pay elevated fees just to get a consultant in to scope the situation out.

Value-added pricing

Related to perceived-value pricing, which brings a higher profit margin, is valued-added pricing. Unlike perceived–value, which has a limited window of opportunity, valued-added pricing allows businesses to introduce an extra product or service in exchange for charging a premium price.

A value-add could include an unlimited warranty for the life of the products you sell, or free follow-up dental checkups after a root canal, for example. Adding something extra to the product or service that increases the value to the customer also strengthens the bond they have to you and increases the number of potential contacts they will have with your business.

How image and positioning play a role in pricing

Your pricing strategy and your image are closely linked, with each affecting the other. Too low a pricing policy and your business will be perceived as average or discount—which could be exactly what you want. The higher your pricing, the more selective and upscale you may be perceived to be.

Neither strategy is right or wrong on its own. However, your image and your pricing need to be in sync or you will have difficulty cultivating relationships with your target customers. And, as always, there are limits beyond which you don't want to go. It's one thing to be slightly higher priced than your competition—you can differentiate yourself on service, response time, or quality—but it's a totally different story to be more than double their prices. You'll knock yourself right out of the market.

When Honda entered the U.S. market, the company priced its cars below comparable models as a way to win market share. They had no image, no brand recognition, so they knew they would have difficulty entering the market at higher than average prices. To win customers and establish the brand name, Honda priced itself below market rates.

This strategy worked extremely well and garnered attention and positive reviews in short order. Over time, the company has used its image of reliability and durability to justify price raises annually. Honda now has a luxury car division and receives well above average fees for its cars.

Keeping its image and pricing in sync was the key to its success, however. Until the brand recognition and positive image were in place, the company

Watch Out!
Consultants and service providers frequently make the mistake of calculating their hourly rate based on the annual salary they desire to earn. Unfortunately, this pricing approach does not take into account the cost of doing business—that is, operating expenses. When setting your hourly rate, add your operating costs to your target salary.

Bright Idea
If you are having difficulty selling your services or products, instead of dropping prices, consider raising them.Interestingly, in many instances, increased prices suggest better quality and may entice customers to buy. Of course, this strategy will backfire if the product or service quality is not equal to the price being charged.

knew it couldn't win above average prices from customers.

Once you've set your prices, you'll want to be sure to reevaluate them on a regular basis, such as semiannually or annually. As the market changes, your prices need to be updated. Here are four ways to assess your current pricing levels:

- **Use proven numbers.** Some prices sell better than others; knowing which will generate more sales. In some cases, lower prices ending in .99 will outperform prices ending in .00. However, higher prices sometimes will outperform lower ones. Test different prices to determine your optimum figure.

- **Use limited-time pricing.** Encourage customers to buy now, rather than "think about it," by putting an expiration date on some prices. You're always better off starting with a higher price and reducing it with a sale, than to start low and have to raise it. Customers believe that the original price quoted reflects the true value of your product or service. Don't overdo it with sales, however. Companies that routinely offer limited time offers have trained customers to wait for the next sale, rather than buying at full price in the meantime.

- **Account for additional services.** Carefully track the additional services or benefits you provide to customers during a project or as part of an order. Estimate the value to your customer and the cost to you to provide those services. Assess whether you should increase your pricing to accommodate such additional services in the future, rather than having to absorb the cost.

■ **Charge what you're worth to customers.** As you gain more experience, your prices should reflect the knowledge and technical expertise you have now. If you haven't raised prices in awhile, you may be due.

Companies that hold the line on pricing but reduce the quantity or quality of the product or service are only doing a disservice to their customers. Most of us would rather pay slightly higher prices in return for the same level of service. Consumer product companies are notorious for slightly reducing the package size on certain products in order to keep prices at the same level and maintain their profit margin. Candy bars seem suspiciously smaller than even a few years ago.

Carefully monitor your sales, noting any increases or decreases as you adjust your pricing strategy. And don't be afraid to make changes if you believe it will improve your business.

Collecting what's due

To reduce or eliminate problems in getting paid, you must first establish your expectations with your customer at the time of sale. Tell your customer immediately what your payment terms are, so that there is no miscommunication or misunderstanding about when you expect to be paid in full.

You may also want to note on any receipts or invoices when payment is expected, to remind your customers of their obligations.

Stating when payments are due makes it much easier to follow up by phone when no payment is received. There's no way your customer can say that he or she was unclear on when the bill had to be paid.

Unofficially . . .
According to the American Collectors Association (ACA), in 1992 there were approximately 533,000,000 checks, totaling $16 billion, returned to U.S. banks for nonsufficient funds, closed accounts, and stop-payment requests.

Bright Idea
When you send out an invoice or bill, be sure to state a due date on it, rather than leaving it open to interpretation. If you expect to be paid immediately on receipt, say so. Or if you allow 30 days for payment, which is standard, note that payment is due on such-and-such a date, 30 days hence.

Of course, you don't need to be the person responsible for making those follow-up calls. In fact, to keep your customer relationships tension-free, you should try and delegate all collections activities to someone else. That person can be an employee, a bookkeeper, or your attorney. It's simplest and least expensive to rely on someone already on your staff, however.

To prevent collections issues before they arise, you may also consider holding back part of a customer's order. Some of us have learned the hard way that giving customers 100 percent of their order without some kind of financial commitment on their part puts your business at greater risk. This means that you may require that a purchase order be issued before you'll ship your product, or that payment be made in full. Once you've given a customer everything he or she needed, there is less of an incentive to make a timely payment.

For example, if you've secured a contract to write a business plan for a new client, you'll want to structure payment so that you receive a deposit of 25–50 percent, perhaps an interim payment on delivery of the first draft, and a final payment of 25–50 percent *prior to* delivery. The key words are "prior to." By requiring full payment before delivery of the completed document, you ensure that there won't be delays after your work is done. You'll want to communicate this up front, as the contract is being signed, so that the customer understands the terms of the deal, but then sticks to them.

Direct mail music clubs like Columbia House and BMG Music have a similar policy. They will continue to send customers mailings encouraging a purchase, but they won't send out a complete shipment of the order until payment for past orders has been received.

Other strategies for being paid on time and in full include

- Enclosing a self-addressed, stamped envelope.

- Providing several payment options, such as credit card and third-party financing.

- Calling the accounts payable department one week after you've mailed an invoice to confirm that it is being processed without problem.

- Offering a sizeable discount for prompt payment, such as 5 percent if paid within 10 days.

- Requiring a rebilling fee or financing charge of customers who are slow to pay.

Just the facts

- Before selecting your pricing strategy, be sure you have accurately calculated your total operating and production costs.

- When demand for your products or services increases beyond your ability to meet it, increase your prices until demand evens out.

- Perceived-value pricing is a short-term strategy to take advantage of a sudden surge in demand and should not be relied on as a long-term approach to pricing.

- Clearly state your payment terms up front and in every invoice or statement you send, so that there can be no miscommunication about when you expect to be paid.

Moneysaver
Eliminate the chance of accepting a bad check by using the services of a check verification and guarantee service, such as Telecheck. Once Telecheck authorizes acceptance of a check, they guarantee payment to the business owner and assume all risks of collecting on it. Fees to use Telecheck range from less than 1 percent to 4 percent of the check value.

GET THE SCOOP ON...
Marketing matters ▪ Promotions on the cheap ▪
Free advertising ▪ Successful sales techniques

Getting Business

The most important word in your marketing vocabulary isn't "promotion" or "advertising" or "sales," it's "consistency." And your marketing efforts will prove much more successful if you develop a standard look and feel that carries through all of your communications with prospects and customers. At its simplest, marketing is how you communicate with your prospects and customers. Deciding up front how you want to be perceived and remembered is important in creating a consistent look.

Part of your look involves a logo design, which you'll feature in any brochures, mailers, newsletters, etc. You'll also need to choose a corporate color scheme that is used repeatedly. A slogan describing the benefits of hiring your company should be used whenever possible.

The absolute worst marketing mistake you can make is to frequently change your look and slogan, because you will confuse your target audience. You also lose any awareness and credibility that you had started to generate and which has already cost you plenty.

Moneysaver
When having
business forms
such as invoices
printed, ask the
printer to "wipe
the plate" after
the quantity of
invoices is
printed so that
only the com-
pany logo, name,
address, etc.,
remain. He or
she can then
continue to print
letterhead for
you at a sub-
stantial discount.

Marketing done well will help prospects under-stand when they should turn to you for help. Your job is to link your product or service with your com-pany's name so that prospects will think of your busi-ness first whenever they have a need for what you provide. Consistency of look and message will help you clear this hurdle. Pick one and stick with it!

At a minimum, you'll need the following mar-keting tools to get started:

- Matching letterhead and envelopes
- Business cards that coordinate with your letter-head
- Return mailing labels featuring your logo
- Company capabilities brochure
- Basic product information sheet with logo

With these printed materials in hand, you'll be taken seriously as a business owner and professional.

Marketing versus sales

Many people incorrectly use the words "marketing" and "sales" interchangeably. Unfortunately, doing so suggests that they are one and the same, when they are definitely not. Skills required by a top notch sales person are quite different from those needed by a successful marketer.

Marketing is everything you do to attract cus-tomers. Your promotional efforts and investments that cause prospects to consider buying from you are part of your marketing program. These would include, for example, any advertising placements you buy, direct mail pieces you send, or press releases you distribute to the media.

Sales are part two of your marketing program, essentially. Everything you do to "close the deal" or complete the transaction of exchanging money for your products or services is sales.

The power of marketing planning

Few small businesses have a written marketing plan, if the truth be known. In most cases, marketing decisions are made as opportunities arise, such as a special advertising deal that is presented or a discount offered on a trade show booth.

Unfortunately, making decisions *ad hoc* like this wastes money and time. A better approach is to set your marketing goals at the beginning of the year and to determine then what kinds of marketing initiatives will be needed to help you reach your sales targets. This document—your marketing plan—will keep your marketing program moving forward even during the busiest times of the year, when you have little time to think about pursuing more business.

To be of greatest assistance to you, your marketing plan should include the following sections:

- **Situation analysis**—Before you can start envisioning your company's future, you need to evaluate where you arc now. What are the company's strengths and weaknesses? How much competition do you have and do you anticipate in the future? What do you believe is the key to success in your industry? Using the market research you conducted in Chapter 3, "Your Business Plan," describe your business today.

- **Market overview**—Since you will be sharing your marketing plan with your employees, who want to help you reach your goals, it's a good idea to document the major developments in your market. It may be second nature to you but totally new to your employees. Tell them how

Unofficially . . .
According to American Express Small Business Services, the amount invested in marketing as a percentage of projected gross sales can be anywhere from 5 percent to 50 percent or more.

Bright Idea
Turn your fac-
simile cover
page into a mar-
keting tool. Add
a list of your
products or ser-
vices to your
contact informa-
tion to alert
recipients to the
range of offer-
ings available.

fast the market is growing and what is causing the growth, and describe your forecasts for the future. Are there any technological trends that will impact how you'll do business three or five years from now?

■ **Market assessment**—After completing these first two sections, you'll want to match them up to identify new opportunities. Based on your analysis of both the market and your company's specific strengths and weaknesses, what does that mean in terms of new marketing opportunities?

■ **Product or service description**—Both to document where you are now and to look ahead, describe your current products or services and the demographics of your current or proposed customer base, as well as the strengths and weaknesses of your offerings. Now think ahead a few years; what new product lines or ancillary services could you envision adding? How will that help build your business?

■ **Annual sales goals**—In a single page, document your sales history (if you have one) and set sales targets for the coming year, in terms of number of customers or unit sales and total sales dollars.

■ **Marketing program**—To reach those sales goals, you'll need to attract inquiries and sell prospects. Which marketing methods make the most sense given your goals, your customer base, and your budget? Describe each tool you intend to use. Now break down those activities month by month. Doing so will keep you on course because you'll know exactly what needs to be tackled every 30 days, as well as the associated expense.

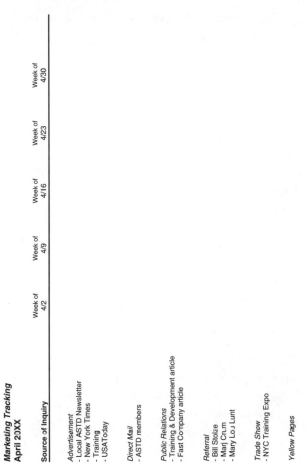

Marketing Tracking
April 20XX

Source of Inquiry	Week of 4/2	Week of 4/9	Week of 4/16	Week of 4/23	Week of 4/30
Advertisement					
- Local ASTD Newsletter					
- New York Times					
- Training					
- USAToday					
Direct Mail					
- ASTD members					
Public Relations					
- Training & Development article					
- Fast Company article					
Referral					
- Bill Stolze					
- Marj Crum					
- Mary Lou Lunt					
Trade Show					
- NYC Training Expo					
Yellow Pages					

← Note!

It's important to know which of your marketing methods are working well and which aren't before you can implement changes to improve results. Use a form like this one to routinely track the sources of your inquiries and sales.

At the end of the next 12 months, review your plan and update it based on your experience during the last year. What will you do differently? What are your new goals? Keep setting higher standards each year.

Low-cost marketing methods

As a start-up, your investment in marketing is critical; unless you put some money into promoting your business, you'll have difficulty attracting customers.

One of the best and least expensive marketing methods—it's free—isn't really a marketing method at all. Word-of-mouth marketing is what business owners crave, yet it can't be bought. This type of marketing is unique in that it uses the spoken word rather than a printed piece, such as a coupon or advertisement. It also carries with it the endorsement of the person doing the speaking.

The best way to generate it is to do good work for your current customers and encourage them to tell others. However, your other marketing methods should also generate discussion among your prospects, which can lead to word-of-mouth referrals and business. For instance, a recent profile of your business in the local paper may get the business community talking about you.

Generally, publicity is the best way to generate word-of-mouth discussions about your business. So in addition to submitting articles related to your company, your area of expertise, or an issue you're passionate about, you could help promote and sponsor a community event.

You can also propose that articles be written that quote you, you could offer to be a radio or television program guest, or you could write letters to the editor of trade publications to demonstrate your professionalism and leadership. Getting noticed a million different ways is the best way to gain notoriety and familiarity, which builds a level of comfort conducive to word-of-mouth referrals.

Since you have no control over word-of-mouth marketing, you'll want to invest some of your budget in methods that have been proven to yield customers.

Advertising tricks

Virtually everyone knows what advertising is—buying space in a publication, or on a direct mail piece, or time on a television or radio station to feature your company's message. The advantage of advertising is that you control what is said about your company and you guarantee when it will appear. The disadvantage is that it is typically the most expensive marketing tool you have to work with.

Don't make advertising your first marketing investment, unless you own a restaurant or retail store. But when you do, commit to at least six placements of your ad. Studies have shown that any less than six ads in a row is a waste of money—it takes that many repetitions for people to notice the ad and process the information.

One small computer retailer began investing in small, business card-size ads in the local daily newspaper, spending a total of about $2,000 a month. Although there wasn't much space for describing the benefits of buying computers from this particular store, the company used the ads to direct people to their Web site. Featuring eye-catching words and the Web site, this company generated tens of thousands of Web hits and hundreds of thousands of dollars worth of business in a matter of months. The key was being in the paper every day, in different sections. The more readers saw the ads, the more visits to the Web site were tracked.

Unfortunately, business owners frequently become bored with their own advertisements well before customers do. This leads companies to change their ads just about the time that customers are beginning to read, remember, and potentially act on the messages.

Moneysaver
If you can wait till the last minute to place your ad, you may be able to take advantage of "remnant space" deals that can save you 50 percent and more on standard ad space. You'll need to alert your ad rep that you're interested in remnant space and have an ad ready to go that fits one of the publication's standard formats.

Also, don't waste money on image ads. Although Fortune 500 corporations may be able to afford to subtly remind you of their products with obscure product references, you need to be more direct. Be sure each ad clearly describes a product or service customer benefit and includes a call to action, such as an invitation to call a phone number or visit a store.

Placing the ad in a particular section of the paper, or during a certain timeslot during the evening newscast, can significantly impact your results. Some companies shoot to have their ads in the sports section of the daily paper when they are targeting male consumers; other companies buy time during the morning radio drive time to get to business professionals.

Direct mail

The three most important elements of a successful direct mail program are

1. An up-to-date targeted mailing list.

2. A solid offer that meets your audience's needs and compels them to take the action you want— place an order or send the reply postcard, for example.

3. Actual follow-up on what each effort produces.

Direct mail works best when you are trying to market to a targeted group of people or businesses, such as doctors' offices in a five-mile radius of your pharmacy, rather than anyone over the age of 21.

On the other hand, if your target market is not so targeted, consisting of everyone in a ten-mile radius of the metro area, advertising may be a better bet. On a cost-per-piece basis, direct mail can be exhorbitant when you're dealing with tens of

Bright Idea
When initiating a direct mail program that you intend to follow up on personally, don't send out 1,000 pieces all at once—you'll never be able to make that many phone calls in a timely manner. Instead, send out 25 or so each week. You'll increase your response rate and spread your investment out over time.

thousands of people; advertising can potentially reach them more economically.

Just as six ads are the minimum needed to generate a response from advertising, a series of direct mail flyers or letters will work better than a single one.

Marketing via e-mail is one of the up-and-coming direct mail tactics. By 2003, International Data estimates 510 million people will be online worldwide. And as the cost of postage rises, e-mail becomes a much more cost-effective tactic. For literally pennies per contact, more customers and prospects can be reached—and reached more often—using inexpensive e-mail distribution software. This is driving retailers and catalog companies to push customers to use their Web sites, which don't have printing and distribution costs associated with them.

The one caution to consider is whether recipients will view your e-mail as junk mail. Internet users rate junk e-mail as one of their biggest pet peeves. You'll need to weigh the effectiveness and cost of e-mail marketing against the potential to irritate your prospects.

Networking

Networking is one of those activities that isn't thought of as marketing, and yet every personal contact or connection you make with someone in your target audience is just that.

One of the worst things you can do is to be too pushy when trying to get to know people at a professional association or civic association meeting. Networking is a long-term activity—referrals and new business relationships will develop as people become comfortable with you. You'll be most

Bright Idea
One of your most valuable business assets is your customer list. Use it to generate more business by establishing ongoing communications via a variety of means. Ask your customers for their e-mail addresses. Encourage repeat purchases through a customer newsletter, coupons, an invitation to a special event at your business, and/or an e-mail with news of particular interest to them.

successful if you aim to be a resource to everyone you come into contact with, rather than seeing them as hot prospects.

Public relations

Public relations activities involve communicating with your target audience, generally using the media to do so. This should be the first marketing method you plan to use.

The reason public relations activities are so popular is that there is little to no cost to provide information to the media about your company. The trick to getting it used is ensuring that it is newsworthy—that is, that it's timely and of interest to the media's audience.

Several public relations tools you'll want to consider using are:

- **Press release**—to make an announcement. Press releases are most appropriate when you are trying to alert the media, and your target audience, to some new information, such as a new product introduction, an award your company has just won, or a seminar you're leading that is scheduled for later this month. Press releases are always used to announce that you've hired a new employee, or promoted an existing one, for example.

- **Press kit**—to give reporters a comprehensive package of information about your product/ service or company. When a press release is just not enough to do justice to your announcement, you use a press kit. Such a package consists of a two-pocket folder, preferably with your company logo on the front, or a label with your company's name on it, and several informative documents.

You'll need a time-sensitive press release that announces your big news, such as the merger of your company with another, the hiring of a new CEO, or the results of a research study you've just completed. In addition to the press release, you can also enclose one or two "backgrounders" which are 2–3 page write-ups providing supporting information to editors and reporters unfamiliar with your business or industry.

When an Upstate New York HMO announced the elimination of the physician referral requirement for specialist visits, a press kit was developed and distributed to regional media. A press release alone wouldn't have done justice to this ground-breaking step and wouldn't have explained why this was such a big deal. A press kit with a press release, two backgrounders on changes in the health care arena, a fact sheet about the organization, and a list of potential interviewees helped secure thousands of dollars of positive publicity via print, radio, and TV coverage.

- **Pitch letter**—to persuade editors to give your company coverage. Pitch letters are one of the under-utilized public relations tools, and yet one of the most successful. Using a one- to two-page letter addressed to the editor at a newspaper, magazine, radio program, or TV show, you propose that an article be written or a show devoted to a certain topic. You state why this topic would be of interest to their audience, why now is the time to cover the story, what role you could play, and why you are qualified to be part of the story.

The attachment of a good photo [to a press release] increases the chances of publication by up to 30 percent.
—Tom Lambert in *High Income Consulting*

After sending the letter, follow up within a week to see whether the editor liked the idea. Numerous times, a pitch letter has led to articles being written or the opportunity for companies to submit articles they've written themselves.

To demonstrate to its customers and prospects that the company was in a different league than its competition, a New York auto repair facility wrote a national auto repair magazine a one-page pitch letter suggesting that they be featured as a "Success Story" in an upcoming issue. Within days of mailing the letter, the feature editor called to set up an interview date. And within a few months, the company's story, complete with color photos, filled nearly four pages of *Underhood Service* magazine. After receiving national attention, the shop then approached the local media with reprints of the article in-hand for added credibility.

▪ **Expertise articles**—to demonstrate your technical knowledge on a particular subject. Expertise articles are the perfect way to show customers and prospects that you know what you're talking about. These write-ups range widely in length, depending on the needs of the particular newspaper, magazine, or newsletter you've approached about accepting one, but always carry a "by-line" naming you as the author, and also feature a photo of you.

To pursue an opportunity for an expertise article, begin scanning magazines and newspapers your target audience is reading. Try to find examples of expertise articles other people have submitted; wherever you find them, there is an existing space set aside for such articles where

yours could be featured. Next send a pitch letter to the editor describing the topic of your
article.

Professionals and business owners who submit
expertise articles to local, regional, national,
and trade publications are seen as experts in
their fields and are frequently contacted for
follow-up opportunities based on the articles
they write.

One advertising agency executive has seen the
size of his projects and his bank account balance increase in a matter of months after submitting marketing and advertising expertise
articles to the local business newspaper.
Presidents and CEOs of area companies began
commenting on his new-found notoriety and
suggesting that they get together to review the
company's current advertising program.

▪ **Case studies**—to describe how other companies
have successfully used your products or services.
Case studies, case histories, success stories, these
are all the same type of article—one that
describes for a reader what your company has
done for another customer. Such articles typically detail what the situation at the organization was before your company got involved,
what you did to improve the situation, and what
the situation is like now. Quotes from executives
at the customer company are always useful,
demonstrating that the company was truly
happy with the results they received with your
help.

Case studies can complement an existing corporate brochure, as well as fit in nicely with a
proposal for new business. But they are most

Bright Idea
To get the most
value from your
publicity success,
request permis-
sion from a
publication's
publisher to
reprint any arti-
cles that appear
about your com-
pany. Then use
those reprints as
direct mail
pieces, newslet-
ter inserts, or
Web site addi-
tions.

valuable when featured in a trade magazine article.

A national commercial printer wanted to find a way to alert its customers that it was now ISO 9000 certified. Given the hype over this process, they decided to let their three best customers describe what it meant to them in a case study. After submitting a one-page pitch letter to the largest trade magazine in one of their vertical markets, seed packaging, the case study was accepted. The printer then had its three customers interviewed and an article written which appeared as the cover story two months later.

Through this case study, not only did the printer communicate that it was ISO certified, but it earned valuable publicity for its biggest customers and significant credibility and prestige by virtue of the cover placement.

Studies have shown that 7 out of 10 people will turn to editorial articles for input on a purchase decision. Because of this added credibility, editorial coverage—publicity—is often valued at seven times the equivalent ad value.

Trade shows

Industry trade shows and conferences can be the most cost-effective way to make contact with numerous prospects and customers at one time. Whether you exhibit your company's wares at a booth or just network with fellow attendees, your presence is frequently worth every penny you had to spend to get to the show. Before making the investment in renting the booth, paying for booth space, shipping, travel, accommodations, and your employees' time, be sure that you are ready and able to follow up promptly on the leads generated at the show. What's the point of going to a major show if you know you can never act on the leads obtained?!

Make the most of your participation at a trade show with the following tactics:

- Use graphics and images in your booth that are eye-catching and legible to people walking by quickly. Make sure the font size is large and that you don't have too much on the back of the booth.

- Send out invitations to encourage customers and prospects to visit your booth. Mention your booth number and consider having a free gift or drawing to encourage visitors to drop by.

- Collect business cards and follow up within 48 hours of the show with literature and a personal note. Although its best to have personal contact at the booth and note specific conversations right on the cards you collect, many companies find that setting out a fish bowl to collect cards works well, too.

- Contact the show guide producer about the opportunity to submit a brief article of interest to industry participants. Handing out reprints of past articles that you've had published is another smart move, demonstrating your expertise and providing a give-away few will throw out immediately.

- Inquire about the opportunity to speak at one of the educational seminars/workshops. Some companies rent a separate suite in a nearby hotel and schedule seminars on their own, for their target customers and prospects. If seminars are key to your marketing, don't give up just because you can't be a featured speaker.

Unofficially . . .
According to the Center for Industry Research (CEIR), the number one reason people decide to attend a trade show is because they've received an invitation from an exhibiting company or sales representative. Source: *Entrepreneurial Woman,* 1991

Watch Out!
Having a Web site designed and hosted isn't enough to encourage people to visit. Be sure to register your site with all the major search engines so that users can easily find you.

Web-based promotions

With increasing use of the Internet for research, purchasing, and communication, a corporate Web site is virtually a requirement. In addition to serving as a sales vehicle, a Web site also provides information about your company.

When designing your site, consider including some of the following elements to increase hits:

- Company background information
- Links to related sites
- Reprints of publicity successes
- A tip or suggestion that changes weekly or monthly
- A contest or survey (to entice users to come back)
- A limited number of graphics and images up front are better than too many. Image overkill will take too long to load, causing some visitors to move on to another site before yours even has time to be seen.

Success at selling

Almost anyone can become a better salesperson simply by listening to what prospects say they need. Instead of trying to force fit your product or service, recommend the best solution, whether it's your product or not. By doing so, you may lose this sale, but you'll gain many more in the future from this prospect and the friends and colleagues he or she tells about your honesty and integrity.

Effective salesmanship

Some of the qualities of a successful salesperson are:

- Friendly
- Empathetic

- Helpful
- Knowledgeable
- Authoritative

When someone approaches you for assistance, they want to be reassured that you're an expert and can help them solve their problem, whether it's as simple as a clogged drain or as complex as lack of capital. They also want someone who seems to truly understand their situation; restating what you perceive to be their challenge is a good way to demonstrate that you've heard them.

Being a good salesperson takes practice, but having a friendly and helpful attitude is 80 percent of the challenge.

Presentations

Whether you're making an oral presentation at a podium or having a seated discussion around a conference table, all eyes are on you as you make your sales pitch. To be at your best, practice, practice, practice. The secret to being a great speaker or presenter is to know your material cold. Only then will you feel at ease and appear confident as you make your presentation.

If you dread having to make any kind of public presentation, seriously consider investing in a public speaking course. The confidence you'll gain will be well worth it, not to mention the additional opportunities to market yourself and your company that will appear once you're open to them.

Of course, unless you're comfortable and fairly polished, public speaking may not be the best idea. Certainly, being seen as a leader is desirable, but not if your presentation is so stilted that the audience is bored.

Tools of the trade

To be most effective at making a sales pitch, you'll want to have:

- **A well-developed speech**—whether on note cards, a note pad, in a Microsoft Powerpoint presentation, or memorized, you'll want to think through the important points you need to mention in your pitch.

- **Visuals of your product or service**—this can be in the form of a portfolio, a series of photographs, a video, or a CD-ROM presentation.

- **Work samples**—if not presented in your visuals, you may want to bring along a product prototype or sample of what you've done for other customers.

- **A leave-behind**—a brochure or information package the prospect can refer to later.

Pay close attention to the body language displayed by your audience and adjust accordingly. For example, crossed arms can suggest defensiveness, that they're protecting their business and their information and aren't yet comfortable with you. Leaning forward, on the other hand, suggests sincere interest and enthusiasm. Smiles and laughs are good and suggest agreement with what you're saying. However, people who display yawning or sneak peaks at their watch are subtly telling you that it's time to end your pitch; they want to move on to other activities.

Follow-up

After your presentation, send each member of the decision-making team a thank you note for their time. This is your first follow-up.

Interestingly, turning a one-time sale into repeat business is as easy as following up on a regular basis. Customers will continue to buy from you if they were satisfied with the last product or service you provided and you stay in contact with them.

The reason people seek out a new supplier is generally because of lack of attention. Jeff Gee, author of *Customer Care, Heart & Soul*, states that "68 percent of people change who they do business with not because of price or product, but because of indifference by one employee." Showing you care about your customers' business will help you keep their business; losing it is very costly. In fact, it is estimated that "it costs five times more to get a new customer than it does to keep one you already have."

This is one area where businesses of all sizes lose opportunities on a regular basis. In many cases, follow-up on a proposal is all that is needed to close a deal; and yet it doesn't happen a good deal of the time. Phone calls, e-mails, faxes, notes, these are all ways of staying in touch. But be sure that you follow-up deliberately after you've made a proposal to someone. Until they tell you that they are no longer interested, they're a solid prospect. Don't lose them as a customer simply because you didn't make a phone call to check in.

Invest in a contact management software program that enables you to track each communication you have with a prospect and to remind yourself of when to check in again. Assigning one individual on your staff the primary responsibility for follow-up is another good way to avoid missed opportunities.

Of course, contact by phone isn't the only way to stay in touch, clipping articles of potential interest and sending them with a personal note can be just as meaningful. Sending birthday and congratulatory cards are other ways to subtly remind your customers and prospects that you're available to meet their needs.

Asking for referrals

Referrals can comprise a large percent of your business if cultivated properly. The advantage of referrals is that the prospect comes to you presold; referred prospects have a much higher close ratio than any other prospect.

The easiest way to encourage referrals is to:

- Make sure everyone knows what you do.
- Ask customers if they know other people who could benefit from your products or services.
- Reward referral sources whenever they send someone your way, whether that person ultimately becomes a customer or not.
- Send a simple thank-you note at every opportunity. It shows that you truly appreciate their efforts on your behalf.

Referrals are often the reward for doing your job well, but you can certainly encourage them. Just asking for them will often yield many new prospects.

Just the facts

- Word-of-mouth marketing can only be generated by satisfied customers willing to tell others about your business; it's a side effect of an effective marketing program rather than a marketing method you can plan on.
- Developing a consistent look and message will significantly improve your marketing results.

Unofficially . . .
Master car salesman Joe Girard estimates that each of us knows an average of 250 people. With this in mind, when Joe was selling, he always took the opportunity to ask current satisfied customers if they might suggest other people in the market for a car.

- Public relations is the least expensive and most effective marketing tool you can use to gain visibility and credibility for little money.

- Selling more to existing customers is much easier than developing new customer relationships.

**Beyond Start-Up:
Managing for Growth**

PART V

GET THE SCOOP ON...
Retention strategies ▪ Calming customer
complaints ▪ Rewarding loyalty ▪
Reaping referrals

Customer Service

Customer service is more than just responding to inquiries or complaints—it's the lengths to which you will go to meet customer needs and wants. Done well, the way you serve your customers can become an important competitive advantage. In recognition of the importance of your relationship with customers, customer service is now frequently referred to as "customer relationship management" (CRM).

When you consistently go above and beyond to make customers happy, you earn a reputation that brings customers back and attracts new ones. Unfortunately, most business owners focus more on securing new customers than on retaining existing customers. To ensure continuous growth for your business, consciously guard against falling into this trap.

One strategy is to provide employee incentives for going above and beyond the call of duty. Employees need to understand how important good customer service is to the success of your company; one way to do that is to provide incentives and

Unofficially . . .
A study con-
ducted by
National Family
Opinion Council
for the Consumer
Research Center
of the
Conference Board
found that "the
vast majority of
consumers
believe that they
receive good
value for their
dollar when they
purchase prod-
ucts. But there is
a rather perva-
sive discontent
with what they
get for the
money they pay
for services."

bonuses when employees demonstrate such customer attention.

Nordstrom department store is the epitome of a company that has used customer service to build enduring relationships with its customers. Tales have been told for years about the customer who returned automotive tires without difficulty (despite the fact that Nordstrom has never sold tires) and the sales associate who personally delivered an order to a customer's home one night. It is those types of stories that enhance a company's image and attract new customers.

Companies with superior service quality can often earn a price premium. Would you rather pay more to a mechanic you trust or take a chance on someone new who's cheaper? Try a new hair stylist or stick with one you know will make you look good? Customers are wary of change, so they will pay higher prices for the peace of mind that comes with being able to rely on their current source for goods or services.

We all know companies whose only hook is a low price. A study by consulting firm Temple, Barker & Sloane found that many companies try to make up for poor quality service with lower pricing.

You see it regularly in the restaurant industry— the fanciest, most expensive eateries typically have the best wait staff, while lower priced locations may not have the cash to pay top dollar for their servers. Computer superstores are also known for the lackluster technical knowledge of their retail help, as well as for their low prices. Wherever you find prices lower than the competition, you need to ask what the company has eliminated from its service in order to keep prices low; then make sure you're not doing the same.

Trying to make a go of it just on the basis of low pricing isn't wise. Companies that are succeeding are obsessed with customer service excellence, say authors Zeithaml, Parasuvaman, and Barry in *Delivering Quality Service*. They use service to:

- Differentiate themselves from the competition
- Improve productivity
- Earn customer loyalty
- Encourage word-of-mouth advertising
- Protect against price wars

Not only can service provide customers with a reason to do business with you initially, it provides an ongoing reason to continue that relationship. Satisfied customers are much less likely to look for new places to spend their money.

Keep existing customers

Anticipate what your customers need and want from your company, beyond what they are buying from you. For example, do they need convenience, do they need comfort, or do they need responsiveness? What is the real benefit of doing business with you? The answer to that question is the key to determining how you can improve service to your customers.

According to Ron Zemke and Dick Schaaf in *The Service Edge*, customers want the following from the companies they do business with:

- **Reliability**—Customers expect a certain unwavering level of quality or service, time after time. The popularity of McDonald's restaurant is in part due to the standardization of food preparation and service. The same can be said of Holiday Inn, which built its initial reputation on reliability through standardization.

Unofficially . . .
Of 100 customers, 1 percent die, 3 percent move away, 5 percent switch suppliers due to a friend or adviser's recommendation, 9 percent switch due to price or a better product, 14 percent switch due to product or service dissatisfaction and 68 percent switch due to perceived indifference on the part of merchant.

- **Assurance**—Customers want companies to do what they say they will do; they hate to be let down. Customers will be much more forgiving if you keep them informed of any anticipated delays.

- **Empathy**—Customers want to feel that you understand exactly what they're looking for. Take a long-term approach and focus on getting to know your customer's business so that you also not only meet their immediate needs, but suggest other ways you can support them. Recognize the risks a buyer faces—real or perccived—in choosing to do business with you, and attempt to minimize them.

- **Responsiveness**—The speed with which you respond to customer requests is a sign of how much you value them; the faster the response, the greater the personal validation.

- **Tangibles**—Customers want something more than just the product purchased or the service requested; thank you notes, special mailings, and other printed materials show your interest in their business.

On average, it takes $10 of new business to replace $1 of lost business. Using the fact that businesses typically lose 15–20 percent of their customers each year, you can more than double your company's growth rate by focusing on cutting customer losses in half.

In the *Harvard Business Review*, management consultants Frederick Reichheld and Earl Sasser suggest that "companies can boost profits almost 100 percent by retaining just 5 percent more of their customers." They argue that this applies whether you are as large as Microsoft or a small mom-and-pop operation.

This makes sense, especially in light of the fact that a full 68 percent of customers will stop doing business with you simply because they feel ignored or unappreciated. To keep a majority of your customers, simply show them how much you care. Keep in touch with them, respond quickly and appropriately to any complaints, and take note of any particular preferences so that you can better serve them in the future.

It's important to also note that operating costs decline as your customers use your services more. Their increased familiarity with your business and products translates into fewer questions, speedier transactions, and better response rates to any materials you mail to them. All of this spells higher sales and lower operating costs.

In recent years, calculating the lifetime value of customers has come into vogue. Instead of looking at a customer in terms of the potential revenue from a single transaction, businesses are valuing customers based on their total potential purchases during their lifetime. In doing so, businesses place appropriate importance on pleasing current customers.

The key to maximizing the lifetime value of each customer is in continually strengthening your relationship with him or her. Take time to really get to know your customers' business needs. The best way to accomplish this is through a regular program of communication.

Some of the opportunities for customer communication include:

▪ **Newsletter**—Stay in touch by keeping customers informed about the operation of your

> **"**
> If you've never calculated the lifetime value of a loyal customer, try this formula: average sale × number of sales per year × years expected to be in business × lifetime value of customer.
> —Grace Butland, author of *Everything I Need to Know About CRM . . . I Learned at the Craft Shops*
> **"**

Moneysaver
Have notecards printed up with your company's logo on the front, which can be used for virtually any occasion. You'll save money by using them for multiple purposes in place of commercially available thank you cards, which are extremely expensive per piece and don't reinforce your company image the way customized notecards will.

company and reminding them of the pleasant experience they had in doing business with you. You can also use this opportunity to inform customers of other products or services they may be interested in. Many customers don't buy all they can from you simply because they don't know the scope of your products or services; use a newsletter to communicate this information.

Also keep in mind that a newsletter can be provided in a number of different formats—as a mailed printed piece, as an electronic document sent via e-mail, or as a fax transmittal.

- **Thank you note**—Immediately after making a sale, be sure to express your appreciation to your customer for his or her business.

- **Follow-up evaluation**—Two to four weeks after the sale, mail out a questionnaire/evaluation for customers to let you know how you're doing at meeting their needs. Use the feedback you collect to further improve your operations.

  Don't limit your follow-up to current customers either. Contact former customers to learn why they no longer do business with you; what caused them to go elsewhere and what can you do to win their business back. It's often not difficult to regain their patronage.

- **Survey thank you**—After receiving a completed survey, let your customers know that you've heard their suggestions and are taking steps to implement them. No one likes feeling like he or she provided information for nothing.

- **Suggestion box**—Install a comment or suggestion box in your store or office to give customers a way to anonymously give you feedback.

■ **Birthday card**—Everyone enjoys feeling special. Make note of your customers' birthdays and take the time to send a card.

■ **Holiday card**—Some companies send out the traditional holiday card before New Years' day to thank customers for their support during the year. However, those businesses that don't want their cards to be lost often elect to send a remembrance at a slightly different time of year—such as with a Thanksgiving card or a New Year's greeting.

■ **Notes and letters**—Whenever you come across an article or piece of information that you think might be of interest, send it along. It demonstrates that you're keeping your customers' needs in mind at all times. Remember that all your correspondence is a reflection on your business, so be sure that you're presenting your best image. Use e-mail whenever convenient for your customers, so that you stay in touch using the technology they prefer.

Responsiveness

The speed with which you respond to customer communications is also a sign of how much you value their business. When you respond quickly, you demonstrate that you care about keeping them satisfied. And when you dawdle, you tell them that they are less important than other customers. Keep this in mind as you respond to

■ Phone calls

■ Mail

■ Comment or evaluation cards

■ E-mail

Unofficially . . .
According to the Federal Office of Consumer Affairs, 95 percent of all dissatisfied customers never bother to complain to the seller.

- Service calls
- Product returns

Well-known retailer and mail order powerhouse L.L. Bean was one of the first companies to guarantee every product it sold. If customers *ever* had a problem or complaint, L.L. Bean replaced it at no charge. Even years after a product had been purchased from the company, the guarantee was still in effect. Unfortunately, L.L. Bean's policy has become somewhat more restrictive in recent years, but the company was the forerunner of such policies.

A relative newcomer to the mail order industry, television shopping channel QVC seems to have taken up where L.L. Bean left off. Despite the enormous potential for returns and complaints, QVC responds quickly to any customer concern, offering to replace any item appearing defective.

Part of the key to such policies is that employees are authorized to satisfy customers on the spot. Whether a guarantee exists or not, employees need to be able to correct a customer's problem. Nothing is more annoying to customers than to be told, "That's not my department," or "You'll have to see the manager."

Ensuring that return policies for products are prominently placed at the register or featured on packing materials is one way to reduce altercations over returns. Similarly, stating the terms under which services will be provided also helps to reduce miscommunication.

Unless the request from a customer is unusual or suspicious, consider authorizing employees to immediately do whatever is required to satisfy the customer. Employees will feel empowered and more responsible for customer satisfaction, and

Bright Idea
Offering a money-back guarantee is smart. Not only will it encourage customers to buy from you, but also few people will ever actually return something. The cost of a guarantee is negligible, but the added sales can be substantial. In addition, you enhance your credibility as a business by standing behind the products and services you offer.

you'll build goodwill with any customer who has a problem.

However, in smaller companies, it's always nice to demonstrate to customers that you are personally involved in handling their business. For that reason, you may want to follow-up any complaint or discussion between employee and customer with a personal note or phone call. This will show your customers that you're well aware of the goings-on in your business and the value you place on their business.

The way the owner of Mario's Restaurant in upstate New York handled a recent customer complaint is an example of how such incidents should be dealt with. When a young family visited the Italian restaurant for a casual dinner one weekend, they were forced to deal with a laundry list of gaffes by the waiter. In addition to failing to provide some of the meal's basics—water, bread, and silverware—one of the dishes served was incorrect, and all were extremely delayed.

After weathering the experience, they sent a letter to the owner detailing the horrible experience they had been subjected to. Although the food had been delicious, they reported, the service tarnished their evening. The day that the owner received the letter, he called, apologized profusely, and offered a $20 gift certificate toward a future meal. He then sent it with a personal note expressing his appreciation for their communication.

The diners report that they would feel very comfortable returning to Mario's given the prompt follow-up the owner provided; had he not, however, they would have considered boycotting.

Since we have implemented our 100 percent unconditional satisfaction guarantee, our business has grown every year an average of 15 to 20 percent. We can't say that it is all due to the guarantee, but we believe it plays a big part.
—Keith and Wendy Rockcastle, owners of Rockcastle Florists

Unofficially . . .
Depending on
the dollar value
of their prob-
lems, only 9–37
percent of
unhappy cus-
tomers who do
not complain will
do business with
the offending
company a sec-
ond time. But
50–80 percent of
those who *do*
complain and
have their com-
plaint resolved
report they will
buy again from
that company.
Source: The
Technical
Assistance
Research
Programs
Institute 1986
study

Learning from complaints

A complaint from a customer is a sign that he or she cares about his or her relationship with your business; it is a cry for help, of sorts. Companies that hear that cry and respond accordingly, going above and beyond what was necessary to make the situation better, can turn those complaining customers into extremely loyal ones. How the company resolves the problem is a sign of how much they value that individual customer; it is a test that customers take very personally.

When customers express their dissatisfaction with some aspect of your business, whether it is product quality, parking availability, or staff attitude, you need to take immediate action to rectify the situation. Telling customers that you'll "look into it" just isn't enough to have them consider ever doing business with you again. Take their complaint as a sign that they want to continue to do business with you. If they didn't care, they would just go elsewhere.

To do your best to keep complaining customers, try this four-step process, adapted from Ron Willingham's book, *Hey, I'm the Customer:*

1. **Understand the problem from the customer's point of view.** First, let your customer vent his or her frustration about the problem, if necessary, and then ask about the specifics. Gather as much information as possible so that you fully understand what the customer is unhappy about, and use this to develop a solution. Restating what the customer has told you is a smart way to confirm that you've heard him or her correctly.

2. **Identify the cause of the problem.** Using the information provided by the customer, discuss

what may have caused the problem. You may be able to immediately identify the source, or you may have to do some independent research. You'll want to do this for two reasons: to understand why this customer was dissatisfied and to root out the cause to ensure other customers aren't impacted.

3. **Propose potential solutions to the customer.** In the end, the customer cares less about the source of the problem and more about the solution. Brainstorm what action would satisfy the customer, compensating him or her for the inconvenience caused. Ask what the customer thinks is fair as a solution if your suggestions don't seem to hit the mark.

4. **Agree on an acceptable solution.** After reviewing potential options, decide what action will best satisfy the customer. Tell the customer how the solution will be implemented and how quickly the situation will be resolved. Then make sure you do it!

Since most customers don't take the time to complain or state their dissatisfaction, a lot can be learned by staying in touch with people who haven't bought from you recently. Keeping tabs on them will alert you to a previous problem, giving you the opportunity to try and rectify the situation. Without tracking activity, however, you may never notice lost business.

For years I faithfully visited a particular hair stylist every 4–6 weeks. Although I was very pleased with her work initially, over time I began to feel that she wasn't listening to my requests. Several times it was difficult to notice any change in my appearance following a $35 cut. So I decided not to schedule an appointment after leaving the last time.

Given that I had been a regular customer for several years, I anticipated that I would receive a call from the stylist or her scheduler within a week or two to ask about my next appointment. Expecting this, I was ready to explain how dissatisfied I had become and that I hadn't planned on returning.

To my surprise, I never received a call. No one ever asked why I stopped coming to the salon. Despite the fact that they had received more than $2,500 from me during the last five years, I never heard from them. Needless to say, they also stopped receiving referrals from me.

Now, had I received a call, I might have been persuaded to come back. That's the lesson to be learned. Never let a customer fade into the distance.

Ask and ye shall receive referrals

Referrals are a sign of trust from customers—trust that you have served them well and that you will treat their friends or colleagues the same way.

When you have a good experience with a merchant, don't you want to tell all of your friends and encourage them to do business there, too? That's exactly how the process of referrals works. When you have confidence in a particular supplier, you want to support them with additional business and lead your friends and colleagues to a reputable business. You help both parties when you make a connection for them.

Learning to say "no" to customers

Although more is generally better when it comes to customers, there are instances when it makes more sense not to do business with a particular person or organization.

Bright Idea
A week after resolving a complaint, send along a note thanking the customer for his or her business. Enclose a gift certificate or coupon to encourage the customer to quickly buy from you again.

- You know you won't be able to provide the quality level the customer demands.

- You can't meet the schedule or deadline the customer has requested.

- The customer has a history of slow payment.

- You or your employees have had difficulty satisfying the customer in the past.

- The company is not in sync with your company's image or ethical standards.

- Colleagues or fellow business owners have warned you about dealing with this particular person or entity.

I have been in the situation where I've been warned about the potential pitfalls of accepting a particular company as a client; perhaps they pay slowly or didn't pay at all, frequently forgot the instructions they had given, were extremely picky, or always need work done in a rush.

In one situation several years ago, I had been contacted by a temporary help firm for marketing consulting. Although I was forewarned by friends who had had bad experiences in being paid by the firm, I plunged ahead. After a complete re-write of the company's brochure because the president "changed his mind about the approach" and repeated telephone calls to try and gather information needed to complete the project, I was told I wouldn't be paid in full because the work wasn't done. Nevermind that they were the hold-up, I wasn't going to be paid.

The lesson to be learned is that when you hear from others about bad experiences, consider whether it's really worth your time to take the risk. Perhaps their experience was the exception—but

Bright Idea
Implement a frequent buyer program to encourage customers to buy more from you and to reward those who do. By initiating such a program, you'll collect a great customer mailing list and give incentives to your "regulars" to buy high-profit items or to buy during slower periods.

do you really want to find out? Running a credit check or calling current suppliers isn't difficult and can provide a wealth of information about a company's business practices. Decide whether it's worth the chance of a very negative outcome, and if so, then refer them somewhere else. Some customers are just not worth having.

Of course, you'll need to be tactful when turning down business so that customer pride is never damaged or feelings hurt. Gracefully turning a customer away can protect your reputation while supporting your mission to deal with more desirable customers. For some businesses, "desirable" customers may be large, Fortune 500 corporations. For others, wealthy women over age 50 may be the target.

Remember the scene in *Miracle on 34th Street*, where the Santa at Macy's refers a mother to Gimbel's for a toy that Macy's didn't have? Although his superiors were aghast, customers were impressed—and thrilled—that someone would truly have their best interests at heart. Referring people to other businesses when you know you can't give them exactly what they want can earn you a reputation for honesty and helpfulness. While you won't make that sale, you'll encourage the individual to come back to you again in the future. You'll also build a bridge to your competitors that may yield business referrals back to you.

Two copywriters I know had traveled in the same circles for years, bidding on the same projects from time-to-time. When one became overloaded with work one summer, he referred the extra work to the second copywriter, who was only too happy to pick it up. So when the second writer needed to refer some business away later that fall, he was only too happy to turn it over to his colleague and competitor to show his appreciation for the earlier referral. This congenial referring back and forth has continued, to the benefit of both.

Such a relationship isn't unusual and is becoming even more common with the increased emphasis on teaming and collaboration.

You take control of your company's growth and expansion when you clearly define which customers will help you achieve your goals—and then elect to do business only with them.

Some suggestions for turning down business:

■ State that you're too busy to take on more customers right now and provide the names of two or three colleagues.

■ Provide a price quote that is considerably higher than what you normally charge. If they choose not to proceed, you're off the hook. And if they accept, the additional money should compensate you for the irritation you anticipate.

■ Explain that the customer's request is not your specialty and recommend two or three people who can meet the customer's needs.

Over time, as customers gain an understanding of the products and services you provide, the quality of customers should improve. However, it is in the best interest of your business to proactively decide which types of customers to target.

Just the facts

■ Customer relationship management is much more than just responding to customer wants; it's about anticipating and meeting their needs.

- Complaints are expressions of loyalty from customers; resolve them quickly and thank the customer profusely for caring enough to alert you to a problem.

- Be prepared to ask for referrals; don't assume that your good job will be enough to automatically generate them.

- Selecting your customers carefully is critical to the growth of your business; learn to say no to those who don't fit your definition of a desirable business relationship.

GET THE SCOOP ON...
Finding corporate clients ▪ Doing business with
▪ Uncle Sam ▪ Creating killer proposals ▪ New
business sources

Pursuing Big Business

S ecuring a corporate or government customer is frequently a sign of a small business's coming of age. When a Fortune 500 corporation or blue-chip company places its trust in your business, other smaller companies will feel more comfortable doing so as well. Not only is there the prestige of being able to claim an IBM or Procter & Gamble as a client, it can translate into many more business opportunities for you. Most smaller businesses pursue corporate customers because they generally have

- Larger budgets.

- Knowledgeable professionals and technicians.

- An ongoing product or service need.

- Less price sensitivity.

- Exciting/cutting edge product or service needs.

Additionally, because corporations make purchasing decisions based more on qualifications and capabilities than price alone, many corporate relationships are long-term, loyal, and profitable.

In many cases, it makes sense to gain experience and a satisfied customer base first by working with smaller companies. Taking the step up to the corporate arena is easier with a solid base of satisfied customers to serve as testimonials. At that point an investment in top quality marketing materials will be required; be sure your image is in line with the customers you are trying to win.

The same is generally true for pursuing government business. Government purchasing agents expect that potential suppliers will demonstrate experience, quality, and technical expertise. And while the federal government has a reputation for slow payment and higher administrative costs, contracts are typically larger and longer-term than most business relationships.

The major challenge for small businesses interested in doing business with the federal government is deciphering the purchasing process. Once that is learned, there is a virtually unlimited market for a company's offerings. The bottom line is that becoming a supplier for a corporate project or government contract takes research, patience, and some luck. Since it can sometimes take up to a year before the contract is awarded, you definitely want to have alternate sources of revenue before you tackle this type of endeavor.

Corporate clients

The process for wooing corporate customers is much the same as competing for the business of smaller firms. The main difference is in the quantity and quality of information required by larger companies.

Larger companies typically have more involved purchasing processes with longer decision cycle

> 66
> Only 1 percent of all small businesses currently sell to the nation's largest corporations. This is astounding—and unfortunate, because several million entrepreneurs offer products and services that corporate America needs.
> —Jeffrey Davidson and George-Anne Fay in *Selling to the Giants*
> 99

times. There may be more intermediate steps required as well, from additional face-to-face meetings to oral presentations to additional proposals.

Finding corporate opportunities

One way to get closer to corporate contacts is to identify some of their existing suppliers and propose a collaboration or alliance. If your products or services complement those that the existing supplier already provides, there may be a win-win opportunity to expand the scope of offerings.

An arrangement with collaborating suppliers is typically called subcontracting, where the corporate client or government agency has awarded a contract to a company—the contractor. In many situations the contractor will need to rely on other suppliers— subcontractors—in order to meet the terms of the contract. If the turnaround time is tight or the scope of the project broad, the contractor may recognize that it will be virtually impossible to do all the work alone, which is where subcontracting opportunities arise.

One source of information that is easy to access is the corporate annual report. Most corporations make them available free of charge through their investor relations or public relations office. Just call the 800 directory at (800) 555-1212, find out the company's main number, and then request that an annual report be sent. You'll gain an appreciation for the scope of products and services available and the future direction the company may be taking.

Look for organizations you can join that will put you in touch with corporate purchasing decision makers. Paul Smith, chief operating officer of A-1 Professional Property Services Inc., a $7.5 million exterior maintenance service firm in San Mateo,

Calif., won a $1.5 million annual janitorial services contract with Kaiser Permanente through his membership in the Northern California Supplier Development Council. Even though it wasn't easy, an emergency gave Smith an opening. "It took 11 months of performing janitorial services to satisfy Kaiser Permanente. We bid with 20 other companies—some that were very large prime contractors—and won based on our quality performance," Smith said. A little luck, being in the right place at the right time, and lots of persistence and hard work paid off for A-1.

Watch Out!
Be careful not to become too reliant on corporate clients. When one company accounts for more than 10–20 percent of your total revenues, you're at risk of a major upheaval if you ever lose their business. Try to prevent more than 80 percent of your business being generated by less than 20 percent of your customer base.

Try a soft-sell approach, says Joset Wright, vice president of procurement and property services for Ameritech in Chicago. "Know about my business . . . know what to offer and what we need," she says. Wright, who oversees $5 billion in procurement ($131.3 million with minority firms), was impressed by one woman who sent information once a week about her company, as well as articles she thought would interest Wright. "She showed a willingness to be persistent and persevere," says Wright.

The federal government's listing of bid opportunities, the *Commerce Business Daily*, also lists bid awards. Any company awarded a contract is a potential source of business and a potential foot in the door of the government agency or large corporation.

But the smartest place to start in identifying new opportunities is right in your backyard. Start with people you already have relationships with—friends, associates, clients, suppliers, and especially employees.

Alerting employees that you're on the lookout for new business opportunities is also a smart way to uncover leads. Southern New England Telephone Company rewards its non-sales employees every time they generate a lead for the sales staff. If a lead becomes a sale, the employee earns $25 in award points or a gift certificate for select stores. In 1993 the program generated $1 million in revenue.

Be careful when referring to employee incentives—it needs to be clear that any additional payments are rewards and within the sole discretion of management. Vague incentive policies can also cause misunderstanding and divisiveness if poorly tracked and managed. Companies, such as Southern New England Telephone, clearly explain the criteria required to receive the $25 award points.

Cheryl Watkins Snead, president and CEO of Banneker Industries in Lincoln, R.I., parlayed her skills in manufacturing and technology and experience working for General Electric into a $1 million company that provides supply chain management services (assembly, packaging, distribution) to companies such as Raytheon and Texas Instruments. The Raytheon contract is worth $200,000 per year, and she'll net $50,000 annually from the Texas Instruments contract. Snead is an excellent example of the several thousand African American business owners who have found success in corporate procurement.

Creating a list of target prospects is another good way to get the word out that you want to do business with these companies. Communicating that list to employees, suppliers, colleagues, and friends will help to open doors.

Bright Idea
Staying on top of where your best prospects work will be key to following them from employer to employer. Don't lose your valuable corporate contacts when they jump ship—use the opportunity to win a new customer wherever they land. ACT! and Goldmine are two useful contact management packages.

Bid lists

Many corporations maintain lists of potential suppliers, called bid lists, which they reference when in need of external products or services.

A bid list, which is compiled on an ongoing basis, saves corporate purchasing departments considerable time when a department decides to issue a request for proposal (RFP). Sending the RFP to a list of prequalified companies increases the odds of finding the best qualified supplier and negotiating the best financial deal.

Trade fairs

Corporate and government purchasing agents interested in identifying new suppliers frequently schedule trade fairs, which are similar to job fairs, but for businesses. Local trade fairs are generally focused on identifying local suppliers, while national trade fairs often provide a means for minority- and woman-owned firms to connect with corporations.

One great source for trade fair listings is *Minority Business Entrepreneur* (MBE) magazine. The back of the magazine contains a schedule of upcoming purchasing-related events. Call (310) 540-9398 or visit the publication's Web site at www.mbemag.com.

Your local newspaper may also carry trade fair information in the business events section.

Certification

To increase opportunities for minority- and woman-owned businesses to win business from corporations, the U.S. government created a process for certifying such businesses. Through the rigorous certification process, business owners are required to complete an application that documents their ownership, capabilities, and financial viability. Of particular

Watch Out!
When considering whether to exhibit at a trade fair, be sure to ask for a breakdown of past attendees from the show organizer. Such information should be readily available, so that you can make an educated decision about how well the audience matches your target customer.

importance is documenting that business decisions are actually made by a member of a minority or a woman.

Major categories of businesses that qualify for certification include:

- **Woman-owned.** Companies that are 51 percent or more owned and controlled by women can qualify for woman-owned status.

- **Disadvantaged.** Socially and economically disadvantaged individuals, who are so classified by belonging to an ethnic minority or economic group that has historically experienced higher than average unemployment, and who own 51 percent or more of a company, fall into this category.

- **Minority.** Companies that are 51 percent or more owned by individuals who are members of an ethnic minority are classified as minority-owned businesses.

Once evaluated and approved, minority- and woman-owned companies qualify for special consideration in bid situations. In some cases, certified firms receive "bonus points" that push them to the fore when a bid is awarded.

Any corporation that does business with Uncle Sam is required to set annual quotas for the amount of business they will do with woman- and minority-owned businesses. Hence, identifying certified suppliers helps them retain their government contracts.

AT&T, Ford Motor Co., IBM, J.C. Penney, and Lucent Technologies have been identified by the National Minority Supplier Development Council (NMSDC), a New York-based organization that matches certified minority suppliers with more than

Unofficially . . .
According to the NMSDC, Fortune 500 companies purchased more than $35 billion from minority suppliers in 1998, versus $86 million when the organization was founded in 1972. Even so, minorities represent only 3–4 percent of the amount corporations spend overall on procurement.

250 corporations, as having "world class" supplier development programs. These companies rated exceptional in program measurement and tracking, strategic planning, supplier sourcing and development, education, and training, among other criteria.

Ford (NMSDC's 1998 Corporation of the Year) has 300 prime minority suppliers and purchased $2.4 billion from minority suppliers last year, says Renaldo M. Jensen, Ford's director of minority supplier development in Dearborn, Mich. "We have assisted over 50 minority suppliers to date. We also provide financial assistance to help minority suppliers overcome capital needs. We now have a portfolio of $6.5 million going to 16 minority suppliers." Ameritech and Kraft Foods are two companies that now tie salaries and bonuses to how closely managers meet supplier diversity goals.

Government work

Qualifying for government work can be complicated and time-consuming, given the large number of potential agencies to approach. The first step, however, should be to register with the SBA's PRO-Net online system. PRO-Net (www.pro-net.sba.gov) is a database of 171,000 small businesses interested in being considered for federal government projects. Agency procurement officers use the database to identify potential contractors for open bids and to compile bid lists.

The SBA offers the publication *Selling to the Federal Government* to business owners who request it. Call the SBA office of government contracting at (202) 205-6460. See Appendix E for a list of other helpful government publications.

Seek out a Small Business Development Center (SBDC). It can facilitate the whole process, showing you how to contact agencies, get on bid lists, understand solicitations, get bonded, or construct a business plan to obtain a bank loan or become 8(a) certified. The government's 8(a) program is designed to help disadvantaged businesses secure government business through a multi-year mentoring program.

Understand that the government has three major processes for purchasing products and services:

▪ **Traditional Process.** Historically, government agencies issue RFPs, collect responses, evaluate proposals, and select a winner based on preset criteria within a 45-day window. Generally, no special treatment is offered to small businesses.

▪ **Simplified Acquisition.** Agencies that have been certified by the Office of Federal Procurement are permitted to use simplified purchasing procedures for contracts under $100,000, instead of full and open competition for contracts of under $50,000. This legislation also requires that purchases between $2,500 and $100,000 be set aside for small businesses.

▪ **Micro Purchases.** Contracts valued at less than $2,500 can be made by purchasing agents without obtaining competitive quotes if the agent decides that the price is reasonable. Since these purchases are typically made by government credit card, make sure you are equipped to accept Visa.

Bid lists

The best source of information regarding federal bid opportunities is the *Commerce Business Daily*, a business daily paper that lists upcoming bid opportunities valued at over $25,000.

Watch Out!
If you intend to do business with the government, be ready to do it electronically, with electronic data interchange (EDI). Agencies are beginning to require that contractors provide reports, submit invoices, and accept payment electronically. In the near future, companies that cannot transact business electronically will be completely out of the running for government contracts.

However, constantly reviewing the CBD is a reactive way of identifying potential opportunities. To be assured of receiving RFPs related to your business, you'll want to be added to an agency's bid list. Each government agency maintains a bidders' list, just as the corporate world does. To be added to the list, contact the agency of interest and submit a Standard Form #129.

In addition to placing your company's name on government bid lists, you'll also want to take steps to make contact with purchasing representatives. You may want to:

- Attend procurement conferences, trade shows, and workshops
- Attend industry expos and professional meetings
- Make appointments to meet with purchasing agents
- Advertise in trade journals read by purchasing agents

This could make all the difference in your success, as the current trend is that corporations are downsizing their supplier base, thereby cutting out the smallest companies. The silver lining in all of this is that corporations are putting pressure on their prime suppliers to implement their own diversity supplier programs that offer subcontracting opportunities for small/minority businesses through second-tier programs.

RFPs

When the government identifies product or service needs, it issues an RFP to companies on the agency's bid list and it advertises the opportunity to bid in the *Commerce Business Daily*.

Moneysaver
Anyone can gain access to the *Commerce Business Daily* online for free, by going to http://cbdnet. gpo.gov. Search current RFP announcements and learn of bid awards through this very handy system. The alternative is to pay more than $250 per year for the print version.

To learn more about what the agency requires, you need only request a copy of the RFP. Although construction bids frequently require a deposit of up to $100 to receive the paperwork, most bids are free of charge. In most cases, a written request is required to receive the RFP; faxing is permissible to speed the process.

The first thing to do when an RFP arrives is to make note of the proposal due date; work backwards from the deadline to ensure all of the necessary material is submitted.

If you decide not to bid on an RFP, send a "no bid" letter to the contracting officer before the proposal due date to notify him or her that you will not be submitting a proposal. Failure to do so will cause your company to be deleted from bid lists.

Proposals

Successful contractors follow these general guidelines when responding to an RFP:

- Follow the RFP instructions to the letter. If there are page formatting instructions or length restrictions, be sure to follow them.

- Always, always submit the proposal by the due date and time. Proposals received a minute after the deadline are considered nonresponsive.

- Use the selection criteria listed in the RFP to format your proposal. Matching your proposal to the sections the purchasing agents expect to see makes it easier for them to evaluate and ensures you'll be given full credit for the information you've provided.

- Provide samples or provide proof of work quality.

Timesaver
To quickly identify potential government subcontracting opportunities, request a copy of the *U.S. Government Purchasing and Sales Directory* from the SBA. In it you'll find a list of major government contractors potentially in need of subcontractors.

- Include graphic elements, charts, or photographs as needed.

- Make sure your proposal is packaged professionally using a quality cover and is printed on bond paper.

In addition to the specific responses to RFP questions, purchasing agents will also consider the following during the proposal process:

- Past experience on projects of a similar size and scope

- Management and technical skill set

- Capacity to complete the work required in the allotted time

- Facility size and location

- Financial strength of the firm

- Customer testimonials

- Reference checks

Moneysaver
SBA Procurement Center Representatives (PCRs) are responsible for helping agencies identify potential suppliers, as well as serving as a contracting liaison. Although they are stretched very thin, PCRs can be extremely valuable guides to the government contracting process.

The SBA has recently streamlined the procurement process for woman-owned and disadvantaged firms, awarding contracts valued at between $25,000 and $100,000 much sooner than the traditional 45-day processing period. In situations where at least one woman-owned, one disadvantaged, and at least three other firms submit proposals, procurement officers can make an award within two weeks.

Although the option to speed the process along is optional at this point, several agencies have committed to streamlining. These include the departments of Defense, Health and Human Services, and Transportation, and the General Services Administration. The new procedure is designed to award a higher percent of the $20 billion in federal contracts to woman-owned and disadvantaged firms.

Just the facts

- Although corporations may do business differently than smaller companies, the process for winning them as customers is very much the same.

- Although certification of woman- and minority-owned firms is conducted by the federal government, corporations doing business with Uncle Sam are required to do a certain amount of business with such firms each year. Certification enables that to occur.

- Asking to be placed on corporate bid lists is one quick and easy way to be alerted to contracting opportunities.

- Following government proposal guidelines to the "T" is a must if you hope to win any government contracts.

- Research companies on the Internet, and read trade magazines and newsletters such as NMSDC's *Minority Supplier News, Washington Technology,* and *Purchasing Magazine,* which identify key players and provide information on procurement opportunities.

- Seek out a mentor. Ask a successful federal or corporate supplier to help you.

Bright Idea
To learn more about past bid amounts, ask the contracting officer for previous bid information. This will help you decide if it's worth your while to pursue certain contracts. If you encounter resistance, request the information in writing through the Freedom of Information Act.

GET THE SCOOP ON...
Hiring good helpers ▪ Independent contractors ▪
Low-cost options ▪ Keeping the best and
brightest

Adding Staff

Making the decision to bring in outside help is one of the most exciting things about being in business. Reaching the point of needing assistance means that you have more work than you can personally manage, typically a sign that you're doing things right. But needing help doesn't mean that you necessarily have to rush into hiring employees. There are a number of alternatives that may actually fit your need for additional manpower better than hiring full-time employees.

You want to negotiate a tricky balance between having a skeletal staff that is stretched too thin and having too many people who are relying on you financially. Try to project into the near future and determine if the demand for your products or services will soon outstrip your personal capacity. Consider creative solutions to staffing that might work in the short term. Only add to your employee base when you feel confident that your business is stable and growing at a reasonable rate.

Chapter 12

Timesaver
Before you start trying to recruit employees, define what you need them to do. Write a detailed job description so that you'll be able to instantly recognize the perfect candidate when he or she submits a resumé for considera-tion. Tie each job description to objectives set in your annual business plan.

Once you've determined that help is needed, you'll want to begin recruiting the kind of people you want representing your business. Traditionally, companies have relied on staffing firms or head-hunters to scout out the best hiring prospects, but today you can do a lot of groundwork yourself via the Internet.

You can also research desirable perks and rewards on the Internet to improve the odds that your staff will stay with you for awhile. Losing a val-ued employee can be quite expensive, in terms of lost productivity, knowledge, and the time required finding a replacement. Given that, it makes sense to do everything you can afford to keep your workers happy with their current employer—you.

When?

Some companies need a staff in place at start-up, while others can operate successfully for years with-out any employees at all (besides the owner). It all depends on the type of business, the company's cur-rent or projected growth rate, and projected rev-enues. Manufacturing companies, for example, require more investment in equipment and man-power at the outset than service companies, such as consulting firms.

Determining when you should hire an employee—or employees—really depends on two factors: market demand for your products or ser-vices and your desire to have a staff. If you can man-age the demand for your company's offerings by yourself for the near term, you'll probably want to keep your company as profitable as possible and not add more overhead.

Your interest in having employees is an equally important issue, however. Some business owners enjoy the freedom of working for themselves and by themselves, and have no interest in having someone else around. Others look forward to the day when they can claim that 500 employees work for the business. These business owners will move more rapidly to identify and hire staff members, whether they are warranted or not. The downside is lower profitability.

The trick to maintaining profitability is to match your need for employees with demand so that you bring someone on board just as demand is increasing enough to pay his or her salary. While this is rarely possible to achieve, the best way to prepare for a sudden upturn in business is to create a pool of applicants from which you can draw. This means collecting resumés from prospective employees on a regular basis.

Keeping a file of potential employees makes it much easier to hire someone fast. It also reduces the chance of having to find someone at the last minute, when you're desperate for help. Identifying and interviewing employees should be an ongoing process, rather than a rushed operation that can be easily botched. Allow plenty of time to interview candidates, carefully check references, and review all of your options before moving ahead to make an offer.

Can you afford it?

More important than asking "Can you afford to hire someone?" is asking "Can you afford not to?" At some point in your business life, you will probably need help getting your work done. This doesn't mean that you should rush to hire an employee but

Watch Out!
Employees are becoming the competitive advantage for business in the modern world, says *The Small Business Journal*. Bad employees can cause a business to fail; mediocre employees can cause a business to break even. Good employees can make even a so-so business soar.

Unofficially . . .
The number of U.S. jobs is projected to increase 12.7 percent between 1998 and 2010, to almost 172 million, according to Woods & Poole Economics, Inc., of Washington, D.C. The majority of job growth through at least 2006 will occur in the services industry, says George Silvestri, a labor economist at the Bureau of Labor Statistics (BLS). Source: American Demographics.

that you would be smart to begin identifying sources of capacity—that is, people who can pitch in.

Consider the various ways you can bring in assistance. Several staffing alternatives to full-time employees, ranging from relatively expensive ($$$$) to relatively inexpensive($), include:

- **Part-time employees**—employees who work less than a 40-hour week and who are paid a salary or hourly wage with all employment-related taxes deducted. $$$$

- **Consultants**—like independent contractors, consultants are often brought in on a short-term or project basis to address a particular issue. $$$$

- **Leased employees**—workers who report to you but who are on the payroll of a PTO or PEO, eliminating the hassles of all that paperwork. $$$

- **Independent contractors**—workers who complete projects for you, as well as being available to other client companies, on their own terms. You don't dictate how, where, or when they get their work done, but you do specify delivery and quality requirements. $$$

- **Temporary workers**—retained through a staffing firm on a short-term basis, temporary workers can be available to support you for as long as you like in return for a higher hourly wage than you would pay an employee. $$

- **College or high school interns**—interns frequently work part-time for a semester in return for college credits; others gladly work for an hourly wage. $

While interns appear to be the most affordable option—and they usually are—be careful what tasks you assign to them. *Entrepreneur Magazine* reports that an Atlanta public relations firm learned the hard way that companies cannot "gain immediate advantage from the interns' work." This is one of six criteria that the Department of Labor uses to distinguish interns from employees:

1. The business offering the internship must not receive direct advantage from the work of the intern. Interns cannot be assigned to do client-billable work, for example.

2. Interns must receive on-the-job training and experience similar to what they would receive in a vocational school. Assign them to man the copier or run errands and the Labor Department may require that wages be paid.

3. The main purpose of the internship should be to provide training. While interns can also perform work duties, the activities should be related to their training.

4. Interns should not be paid for their training and should be closely supervised.

5. The internship should not be a precursor to a job, although interns can be offered jobs after graduation. Just be sure the internship is not pre-job training.

6. The intern should not be brought in to replace an existing employee or to do the work an employee once did.

If you're unsure of what you can afford to pay, take a look at your financial projections for the year and calculate what the various options will cost to implement. Then subtract the cost of each option

Moneysaver
If you hire someone who has recently been on welfare or who belongs to a special target group, your company can receive tax credits from welfare-to-work and work-opportunity programs. Ask your accountant about what percentage of your employee's wages can be taken as a credit.

Bright Idea
If your business is located close to a college or university, look into the availability of work-study funds to partially pay for a part-time student employee. Some colleges have co-operative education programs that place students in full-time, short-term work situations as part of their curriculum. Northeastern University in Boston and Rochester Institute of Technology in Rochester have two prominent co-op programs.

from your bottom line to compare the impact of each approach.

Who do you need?

Just as important as the decision to add workers is the determination of what they will do for you. Carefully evaluate what role you need filled and what types of skills and experience should be expected.

Start by defining all of the possible functions within the company. Typically they can include:

- Financial.
- Marketing.
- Sales.
- Operations.
- Production.

However, as your company grows, those functions can become more specialized. The financial manager, for example, could offload responsibility for accounting and bookkeeping to someone else, retaining the long-term financial management duties. Or the sales manager could assign responsibility for customer retention, new business development, and customer service to three separate people if the company were growing quickly.

If you're unsure of how to begin developing an organizational chart for your company, don't be shy about bringing in a human resources consultant to help you. Investing time and money to build the infrastructure for your company is money well spent and will certainly save you plenty later.

Be careful not to tailor a position to a particular individual. If you've defined what the company needs in the way of knowledge and experience, it is in the best interests of the business to find someone matching that description. To settle for someone else is shortsighted.

Where can you find talent?

Despite the dearth of good employees, there are a number of resources to turn to for names of prospective employees. Start in your own backyard—which will save you the time and expense of relocating an employee—and expand your search from there. Begin by checking

- Job banks of local trade and professional associations.

- Competitors.

- College and university placement offices.

- Alumni job banks.

- Your local paper for news of high achievers.

- Local career placement services.

- Unemployment offices.

- Internet job banks.

Networking with friends and colleagues is another smart way to direct potential employees your way. Send letters listing the job openings you are trying to fill, call friends who are well connected, and post job announcements in the newsletters of organizations to which you belong. In a nutshell, get the word out.

How to keep them once you have them

Competition for good employees is so fierce these days—and especially in high tech fields—that some companies are treating workers like volunteers. According to Matt Weinstein, author of *Managing to Have Fun*, "Employees know they could work anywhere, so companies need to create an environment

Watch Out! The IRS maintains fairly restrictive guidelines on which types of employment relationships can be categorized as independent. Review the IRS's checklist to determine whether you have an employee or an independent contractor; you'll find it on their Web site at www.irs.ustreas. gov. Guessing wrong can cost you back taxes and penalties, which you don't have to pay for independent contractors.

where people feel appreciated and recognized."
Larger companies with larger budgets have fewer
problems investing money in retention programs,
but start-ups strapped for cash must be a bit inven-
tive.

Giving key employees and managers ownership
in the company is one incentive that frequently
works to keep them around. If you're considering
using equity as a sign-on incentive or as a retention
strategy, carefully work through how you will use this
now and in the future. You'll need to establish criteria for determining who will qualify and who doesn't,
at what point they will be eligible, and under what
circumstances they lose that equity, if any. Being fair
to other employees is just as important as providing
a reason for top staffers to stay.

Some of the proven low-budget, high-impact
employee benefits reported on the Delphi Business
Strategies Web site include:

- **Recognition.** The least expensive perk is simply
  remembering to say "thank you" to employees
  who have done a good job. Honoring workers
  publicly is priceless to those being honored.
  Award programs, bonuses, and "employee of
  the month" honors are a great place to start.

- **Free food.** You don't need to match Microsoft's
  company-subsidized cafeterias, but you could
  consider providing free meals, just as Zweig
  White & Associates of Natick, Mass., does. The
  consulting and publishing firm's 37 employees
  receive free food and drink year-round.

- **Free entertainment.** The seven employees of
  Seattle public relations firm Firmani &
  Associates go to the movies during work once a
  quarter. Employees of Born Information

Timesaver
One of the quick-
est and most
efficient ways to
identify potential
employees is to
turn to the
Internet.
America's Job
Bank allows
employers to
post job listings
free of charge
and to search the
resumé database
for candidates.

Services—the Minneapolis information technology consulting firm—share free tickets to local athletic games in the company's skybox. Employees of Hot Topic, a music-related apparel-and-accessories store in Pomona, Calif., go to rock concerts free, in return for a written report on what the band and audience were wearing as input for future merchandising ideas.

- **Casual dress code.** Sharon Anderson Wright, president of Dallas-based Half Price Books, asks that her employees wear clothing that is "clean, untorn, and free of offensive slogans or graphics."

- **Flexible scheduling.** Flextime, telecommuting, and four-day workweeks are all options companies have offered their employees to increase their productivity and job satisfaction.

- **Advancement opportunities.** Employees appreciate understanding the specific criteria for future promotions and raises. Firmani & Associates provides a well-defined career track, as well as specific criteria for raises and advancement. Employees that bill 1,200 hours a year and make two new business contacts know exactly how much their salary will increase at the end of the year.

- **Paid community service.** Allowing employees to invest their time in charitable causes or community organizations says something good about both your company and its employees. Autumn Harp, the Bristol, Vt., skin care manufacturer, gives employees two days a year in paid community service time.

Moneysaver
Who better to identify quality employees than your own quality employees? Establish an employee referral program that provides a financial incentive to employees who refer talented candidates your way. You'll save more than enough money on recruiters to cover the cost of the referral bonuses.

Unofficially . . .
The Bureau of National Affairs states that turnover rates for U.S. employees average around 12 percent.

▪ **Great vacations.** CEO Rick Born of Born Information Systems invested in lakefront property in a Minnesota resort area and allows staff members to take turns bringing their families to the six company-owned houses. In return, he's earned valuable employee loyalty. One employee told him, "I couldn't leave [the company] if I wanted to; my family would divorce me." This perk is probably why his company's turnover rate is one-third his industry's average.

If you're unsure of how to begin, turn to your most valuable assets—your employees—for input regarding what would make your company an even more desirable place to work. Money may be the great equalizer for some, while for others, vacation time, flexibility, or recognition may mean the difference between a short- and long-term employment relationship.

Just the facts

- College interns can be an excellent source of support during busy times, but be sure the focus of their assignment is training or the Labor Department may require that they be paid wages.

- Create job descriptions before beginning the hiring process to ensure that new employees truly meet the needs of your organization.

- Examine projected revenues and expenses to determine whether you can afford to bring on an employee; be sure that increases in revenues from the hiring will increase long-term profitability.

- Employee benefits programs that demonstrate how much you value your employees can help reduce costly turnover and make your company a more fun place to work.

GET THE SCOOP ON...
Asking for help ▪ Allying yourself with a winner
▪ Avoiding poor partners ▪ Alternatives to a
board of directors

Advisors and Partners

N o business can operate totally independently—without interaction with other businesses and individuals—and be successful. By its nature, business involves developing relationships with employees, customers, suppliers, advisers, shareholders, neighbors, and anyone else impacted by a company.

The truth is that collaboration and cooperation with others generally improves the quality of a company's products and services. Pooling the knowledge and know-how of a group of individuals or businesses, not to mention its network of relationships, can only serve to inform and aid a business owner. Accessing expert assistance can be achieved through a relationship with a consultant, a business coach, a mentor, your own advisory board, or by forming a strategic alliance.

Many companies are beginning to see that forging alliances can help them reduce product development cycles, create totally new products and services, open new markets, and leapfrog the competition. Working together, two or more companies can frequently make progress in an area that may

Watch Out!
Collaborations or alliances with poorly documented expectations can cause more problems than the collaborations themselves are worth. Clearly delineating the boundaries can avoid confrontations and miscommunication.

have stymied the individual entity. Another reason for the increasing popularity of alliances is that they can be temporary in nature; once a particular goal is achieved, there is no ongoing obligation between the organizations. Each party is free to reevaluate whether continuing the alliance is in its best interest.

Forming alliances aren't just a good idea—they may be your key to survival.

How external advisers can help

Many entrepreneurs are reluctant to admit that they don't have all the answers; some are uncomfortable seeking out business experts for guidance when faced with a difficult challenge. If this describes you, get over it and ask for help before it's too late! Smart business owners recognize their weaknesses and are comfortable compensating for them by retaining outside help. Gaining an external perspective may be all that is needed to see the problem in a whole new light. Your reluctance to do this could stunt the growth of your company, or even kill it. Remember—more often than not, people enjoy sharing their advice and consider it a compliment that you think they can help you.

External advisers, such as consultants and coaches, have the advantage of being able to view the performance of your company from a variety of perspectives. Whereas you may be too close to the situation to be able to identify your company's strengths and weaknesses, threats and opportunities, an expert's emotional detachment enables him or her to see what you are missing. And experts can help you refocus your efforts.

Who you can turn to

If you're like most business owners, you have a circle of trusted friends you frequently turn to for advice. Such a group is a wonderful source of encouragement and help, but in many situations the expertise of your colleagues may be limited to their industry or their job function. To be successful, you need to stretch beyond the familiar to new sources of information.

To keep costs down, you'll want to turn to the government for help first. A multitude of agencies and offices have been established specifically to help business owners like you find answers to problems that crop up.

SBA/SCORE

Uncle Sam wants you to succeed in starting a business; he's even created agencies with the sole objective of supporting your efforts. Given that your tax dollars are already being spent on this support, why not take advantage of any free counseling you can get?

The first place to start is the Small Business Administration (SBA). The SBA, in partnership with local colleges and universities, provides free counseling to small business owners and would-be entrepreneurs through Small Business Development Centers (SBDCs).

SBDCs are great places to turn for free problem-solving help, as well as for referrals to other expert professionals.

Likewise, some business owners have found the Service Corps of Retired Executives (SCORE) to be a valuable resource. SCORE volunteers serve as mentors and trouble-shooters for small business owners at no charge.

Unofficially . . . A recent *Entrepreneur Magazine* article reported that businesses participating in alliances outperformed businesses that didn't. Forty-nine percent of the pro-alliance ventures reported more growth, 21 percent reported higher than expected revenues, and 38 percent achieved increased productivity.

Watch Out!
One of the keys to benefiting from SCORE's consulting is to identify a member/mentor who has had past success in your industry. Some volunteers may not know enough about your market to be of assistance, and others may know your industry but have failed in their own businesses. Although the time SCORE volunteers spend with you is free, your time is valuable—don't waste it if you don't have a good fit.

SBDCs and SCORE are only the tip of the iceberg, however. The government has thousands of employees in place to help you with a myriad of business situations.

Need market research on export opportunities in Kenya? The Export Assistance Center in your area can support you with the information you need, introduce you to critical contacts within the country, and escort you on a trade mission to establish new relationships.

Need financing to help you expand your business and hire new employees? The Job Development Authority and the Economic Development Department in your city are two great organizations that have the authority to grant lucrative loans and incentives.

These are just a few examples of how your local and federal government can provide you with invaluable assistance and information. Don't overlook available, no-cost help when faced with a business challenge.

Advisory board

Public companies rely on the input and guidance of their prestigious board of directors, who also ensure that the corporation's management is achieving their objectives. For smaller companies, however, advisory boards generally make more sense. The reason? Control.

While boards of directors have fiduciary responsibility to the shareholders, as well as being shareholders themselves, advisory boards offer a wealth of constructive suggestions on an informal basis. If the owner disagrees with the feedback or direction provided by the advisory board, he or she is not bound to follow any of it. The relationship is similar to that of a consultant and client. That said, don't establish an advisory board if you aren't willing to be candid about company operations or aren't open to making changes recommended.

An advisory board can help a business owner in a number of ways, including:

- **Problem solving**—helping the owner develop solutions to existing or potential threats to the business

- **Networking**—connecting the owner with potential customers, employees, or sources of information

- **New business development**—sometimes the only way into a new organization is through existing relationships; advisory board members can smooth the way for you

Be prepared to pay the six to eight advisory board participants for their time and counsel, just as you would pay a qualified consultant. An hourly fee of $75–$200 is reasonable, or you can offer a fixed honorarium for their participation in quarterly meetings. Most advisers are not in it for the money, but since you get what you pay for, you'll want to be generous.

To keep your costs down, carefully choreograph each session to take best advantage of your members' time and attention. If possible, send out agendas and assignments prior to each meeting so that you can avoid rehashing old information. Try and keep the discussion focused on problem-solving rather than information sharing and you'll get better value for your money.

Consultants

Turn to consultants when you need expert advice. Use them on a short-term basis to surmount a

Watch Out!
Be careful about asking paid consultants to serve on your advisory board; doing so may create a conflict of interest. Participation in an advisory board may give consultants a forum to gain support for their recommendations.

Moneysaver
Many MBA programs at prestigious universities have on-campus consulting organizations that provide quality services at bargain rates and are overseen by a top-notch faculty member. Consider hiring a student consultant to tackle a particular project.

challenge, make progress towards a goal, or to establish new processes and procedures for the future.

Finding a consultant best qualified to assist you is best done by collecting referrals. Ask fellow presidents and CEOs for recommendations and then investigate each consultant carefully. And then check references in all cases, to improve the odds that you'll find someone supremely able to help.

Be wary of becoming too reliant on a consultant, however. An ongoing relationship without an end date or designated completion point can be extremely expensive and set up a dependency you can't afford. Hire an employee if you identify an ongoing job function.

Coaches

While consulting has been an age-old profession, coaching is a relatively new phenomenon in the business world. Business coaches serve as part advisers, part cheerleaders, helping the business owner to recognize what he or she needs to do to accomplish goals.

Unlike consulting relationships, which are typically short-term and project-oriented, coaching relationships may span several years. Having someone to bounce ideas off of and who knows your goals and your thought process can be extremely helpful.

Vendors/suppliers

Sometimes your best sources of information are people already on the inside at the competition or your target customers. Companies with whom you already have a business relationship, such as vendors and suppliers, have a vested interest in helping you succeed. With your success comes increased business with them.

Vendors and suppliers can be excellent sources of information about new contract opportunities, staffing shake-ups, and problems within companies that could mean opportunity for you, as well as feedback on how to improve your own operations. As vendors and suppliers to a range of companies, they are in a good position to advise you on how you can improve your own operations. For this reason, vendors and supplier representatives are often welcome participants on advisory boards.

Industry roundtables

Many trade organizations have built-in mechanisms for bringing industry participants together for the purpose of sharing information. At trade shows, conferences, seminars and expositions, there are often opportunities to mingle with other companies in your industry. Joining a committee is an excellent way to network, establish yourself as a leader, and to learn from fellow members who may have more experience.

Such discussions or regular meetings provide an invaluable opportunity to brainstorm, share war stories, and collect advice on dealing with new challenges that a colleague may have already surmounted.

Organizations like the Young Entrepreneurs Organization (YEO) bring together fast-growth companies run by owners under the age of 40, helping them to grow their enterprises. Functioning like a roundtable, participants are encouraged to share challenges, solutions, tips, and cautions with fellow young entrepreneurs.

Where consultants frequently provide input regarding a particular organizational function, such

Timesaver
If you'd like to explore the benefits of retaining a personal or business coach, start by contacting Coach University at (800) 48COACH or www.coachu. com for a referral. In this new, unregulated industry, unqualified coaches are running rampant. Save time and money by narrowing your search to someone who has been trained to function as a coach.

Moneysaver
If you're a solid public speaker and you're interested in being part of an expensive industry pow-wow at no charge, inquire about speaking opportunities at the upcoming meeting. If selected, you'll speak in front of influential industry participants—which is a valuable opportunity in and of itself—in addition to gaining free admission to all the other sessions during the conference.

as finance or marketing, industry roundtables offer the chance for companies to share inside information regarding goings-on in their trade. Such meetings can also create new opportunities for alliances by giving participants the chance to get to know each other.

Alliances may be the answer

Where advisers can aid a business owner in addressing a particularly puzzling problem or tackling a challenge that seems to have no answer, alliances help companies overcome their weaknesses by partnering with companies possessing complementary strengths.

An alliance refers to any relationship established to benefit two or more organizations. These might include:

- Competitors
- Suppliers
- Customers
- Geographically diverse companies in the same industry
- Professional organizations
- Trade associations
- Organizations that have previously had no ties or contact

When partnering is smart

Entrepreneur Magazine reported the top reasons companies form alliances:

- Joint marketing—54 percent
- Joint selling or distribution—42 percent
- Joint production—26 percent
- Design collaboration—23 percent

- Technology licensing—22 percent
- Research and development—19 percent
- Outsourcing—19 percent

Despite the seeming range of purposes filled by aligning two or more companies, the common factor is weakness. Where one company is weak, its partner is strong. Bringing together complementary skill sets and capabilities results in benefits to all involved.

Joining forces can also increase a company's ability to compete with larger entities. Integrated Suppliers Alliance of Wisconsin (ISAW) was formed by a group of 10 smaller tool distributors as a means of increasing the clout and strength of its member companies. With larger manufacturers beginning to limit their relationships with smaller distributors, the 10 companies decided to pool their resources and offer a complete range of products. In doing so, they made themselves much more attractive to manufacturers as a potential supplier.

When considering a partnering relationship for yourself, evaluate your company's strengths and weaknesses as a guide to the capabilities you need to find in your match. Then use your list of strengths to persuade your desired partner to collaborate for joint gain.

Who to partner with

Smaller companies can benefit most from alliances with market leaders because such organizations can create new opportunities, offer vast resources, and position them for further growth.

The co-owners of Uniformity LLC, a Los Angeles manufacturer of high school uniforms, approached Macy's West and proposed that the two companies

“
For some small companies, alliances are a matter of survival. It's becoming too complicated and expensive to develop expertise, and market access is becoming much too hard to come by.
—Robert E. Spekman, professor of business administration, Darden School of Business at the University of Virginia, in a recent issue of *Entrepreneur Magazine*
”

❝
Economic advantages may be created by any person who surrounds himself with the advice, counsel, and personal cooperation of a group who are willing to lend him or her wholehearted aid in a spirit of harmony. This form of cooperative alliance has been the basis of nearly every great fortune.
—Napoleon Hill, author of *Think and Grow Rich*
❞

form an alliance to market Uniformity's products. Having not yet entered the clothing market for public school uniforms, Macy's West responded with interest. Just a year later, Uniformity's product line debuted in the Baldwin Hills, Calif., store with plans for expansion into 10 more Macy's locations.

With a limited marketing budget and little industry clout, it would have taken Uniformity much longer to create a name for itself without the support and involvement of a retail powerhouse like Macy's. On the other hand, Macy's knew nothing about the high school-uniform market at the outset, and relied on Uniformity's considerable expertise to launch a new product line. By first recognizing their individual deficits and then combining the strengths of both organizations, both companies benefited.

In evaluating potential partners, look for

- Companies that are market leaders, rather than runners-up.

- Companies that are weak where your company is strong, such as with knowledge of a market, proprietary technology, or customer base.

- Companies that have a similar corporate culture; mismatched cultures has been the downfall of many otherwise beneficial relationships.

- Companies within the same range of your own; too great a disparity can cause trouble and unrealistic expectations on the part of both organizations.

Identifying potential partners

Before entering into an alliance, recognize the inherent differences between the cultures of smaller businesses and corporate giants, advises Richard

Hagberg, Ph.D., corporate psychologist and president of Hagberg Consulting Group:

- Internal politics impact much of what corporate employees do and which initiatives they support.

- Corporate employees will probably be more task-focused than relationship-focused.

- In larger companies, conformity is key.

- The pace of progress in larger companies is much slower; find out how decisions are made and what a reasonable timetable is.

- Working with a larger company will probably require a loss of control; be sure you're comfortable giving that up—even temporarily.

Alliances are prone to misunderstandings and failure because of soured management relationships. Developing a plan for your partnership complete with objectives, goals, and defined responsibilities will help avoid issues. Resolve to have frequent, honest communication and to act promptly to resolve any disputes. Because of the accounting, tax, and legal ramifications of an alliance, seek out the advice of your own attorney and accountant.

Just the facts

- Advisors, mentors, coaches, and consultants are excellent resources for problem solving and idea generation.

- Partnering with organizations that have complementary skill sets and capabilities has the greatest potential to benefit all involved.

- When aligning your organization with larger corporations, be aware that the difference in corporate cultures can create problems.

Unofficially . . .
A recent Pricewaterhouse-Coopers study indicates that 48 percent more alliances exist among America's fastest-growing companies today than just a few years ago. The study suggests that the number of alliances per company is also increasing. Of the firms surveyed, 61 percent are participating in an average of four strategic alliances, compared with 55 percent involved in an average of three alliances in 1993.

■ The best partners are market leaders with substantial resources, where the association significantly enhances your image and/or capabilities.

■ Balance getting professional advice with rolling
up your sleeves and doing some research yourself. Your local library and the Internet are free
and invaluable sources of information.

■ To feel good about the partnership, both sides
need to feel they are gaining something. Having
a plan for how things will work can go a long
way toward avoiding a disastrous alliance. If you
can't agree on that, call it quits.

Other Types of Businesses

GET THE SCOOP ON...
Operating from home ▪ Equipping your
enterprise ▪ Overcoming zoning opposition ▪
Avoiding the home-based stigma

PART VI

Home-Based Business Basics

Chapter 14

E very day, thousands of Americans start home-based businesses. Some are full-time, replacing traditional jobs, while others are part-time, supplementing income from other employment relationships. In the *Business Start-Ups Home Office Guide 1999*, the National Association of Home-Based Businesses estimates that there are between 12 million and 15 million people operating full-time home-based businesses in America today.

Home-business gurus Paul and Sarah Edwards estimate that by the year 2000, one out of every two households will have someone working from home. Although that figure includes telecommuting workers who are employed by other companies, the statistic drives home the increasing prevalence of home-based ventures.

The total number of home-based businesses today is approximately 25–30 million, say the Edwardses.

Zoning issues

When home-based businesses became popular during the early 1990s, many communities were initially fearful of the impact that such operations might have on the character of residential neighborhoods. In response, some towns passed restrictive ordinances specifically preventing for-profit ventures based in residential communities. The primary concern of such zoning boards was the potential for noise and inconvenience.

Your first step should be to learn the zoning laws for your community. Call your local planning department and ask, but it's probably best that you not identify yourself for the time being. If your local zoning laws restrict home-based business, ask about filing a "variance" with the zoning board, which is a waiver or exception to the law.

According to Beverley Williams, founder of the American Association of Home-Based Businesses (www.AAHBB.org), zoning restrictions continue to plague her association's membership nationwide. "We haven't had the complaints from home-based business owners [recently] that we've had previously. So it's very positive—it's just slow-moving," she commented in a recent *Home Office Magazine*. One sign of progress is the pro-home-based business zoning legislation slated for approval by the state of Maryland.

Townhouses, coops, and condos may also restrict home-based activity by banning it from the premises. Since the business owner is agreeing to abide by the rules of the community, operating without approval can put continued residence at risk. If in doubt, quietly investigate before signing any contract.

Watch Out!
If you decide to proceed without first checking things out (or despite what you learn), you need to know that if neighbors complain about business activity and you're operating in a restricted area, you could be out of business with little recourse.

Even if your area does not discriminate against home-based companies, you would be smart to avoid

- A constant stream of clients filing into your house for appointments. Clearly labeling your house or apartment will help reduce the number of customers who knock on the wrong door.

- Having deliveries made by semi-tractor trailers. Instead, consider renting a self-storage warehouse.

- Cars frequently lining your driveway. Some business owners rent driveways from their neighbors in times of great activity; it involves them in the business and dispurses the car load on the street.

- Creating a lot of noise that neighbors can hear.

- Customers that drop by during non-business hours.

Entrepreneur Magazine has rated the following cities as the best for small-business growth and entrepreneurial activities:

- Best Bets for Small-Business Growth
    1. Charlotte/Gastonia/Rock Hill, N.C./S.C.
    2. Norfolk/Virginia Beach/Newport News, Va./N.C.
    3. Memphis, Tenn.
    4. Cincinnati, Ohio
    5. Raleigh/Durham/Chapel Hill, N.C.

Cities that appear to strongly encourage and support new businesses include the following five:

- Best Bets for Entrepreneurial Activity
    1. Monmouth/Ocean, N.J.

Unofficially . . .
The number of home office households will grow six times faster than general U.S. households, according to International Data Corporation (IDC)/Link.

2. Las Vegas, Nev.

3. Salt Lake City/Ogden, Utah

4. Austin/San Marcos, Tex.

5. San Antonio, Tex.

Establishing a professional image

One of the biggest challenges home-based business owners face is being taken seriously by customers and prospects. Instead of viewing such business owners to be smart and cost-effective, some individuals see home-based business owners as less serious about their work and less professional in how they conduct business. Although this is clearly not true for the majority of home-based businesses, it is the unprofessional exceptions that make it more difficult for others.

Whether you work from home or in commercial office space, you'll want to be sure to follow these rules of thumb in how you present yourself and your company to the outside world:

▪ Install a separate business phone line and instruct other family members not to answer it—that's what voice mail is for.

▪ Make yourself available to customers during normal working hours. Working after hours is fine, but don't make it inconvenient for people to do business with you.

▪ Establish work hours that conform to your clients' schedule. If your customer base is international you may find that setting work hours that start before or extend beyond the typical U.S. work day works best. You'll certainly set yourself apart from the competition in terms of accessibility.

Bright Idea
Individuals and small businesses can now get the long distance (LD) rates once reserved only for large corporations. LD brokers offer real savings, without gimmicks or hidden charges, at rates never before possible. For more information, call USATel (800) 390-6891 or go to the Supermarket of LD Services at LD.net on the Web to shop for the lowest cost long distance programs available.

- Be sure to dress appropriately for every meeting with customers and prospects, whether that meeting is in your dining room or at their headquarters. If it's customary for customers to stop by during the day you'll want to be professionally dressed at all times; one incident of greeting someone in your bathrobe is one too many.

- Likewise, present your company ultra-professionally by using high quality marketing materials, including professionally designed letterhead, envelopes, and business cards, as well as a corporate brochure. Investing minimally in your marketing reflects on how you approach business relationships in general.

- Don't price your goods and services much below market rates; doing so only gives the perception that your quality or service must also be cut-rate.

- Invest in office equipment that positions your company as current or leading edge. Using out-of-date technology also reflects poorly on your business standards.

Consider becoming a member of the American Home Business Association (AHBA). One of its newest member services involves making it safer for you to accept checks. With the Internet and AHBA software, you have electronic checking capabilities. Checks are processed almost immediately and members receive payment without worry of bad checks or C.O.D. delays, not to mention collection nightmares.

Another AHBA membership perk is the ease of obtaining merchant account status—the association waives application and set-up fees for new merchant account members. Contact the AHBA at

Moneysaver
If you need childcare during the day but can't afford a daycare center or nanny, consider approaching neighbors about exchanging babysitting services. They care for your kids when you have important meetings scheduled and you reciprocate during evenings and weekends.

Bright Idea
Providing customers with several payment options, including credit cards, is an excellent way to boost sales. There are a handful of firms that work with home-based companies and have reasonable processing fees. ECHOtel is one such company, currently recommended by Mothers' Home Business Network. Get more information at www.homeworking-mom.com/echo.

(800) 664-2422 or www.homebusiness.com for more information.

Equipment

Although the term "industry standard" changes practically every day when it comes to office equipment, investing in obsolete technology costs you money and credibility. Look to your customers and prospects for the best sense of what is considered good quality and what is behind the times.

If, for example, you generally see laser-printed correspondence, buying a cheap dot matrix printer will certainly not impress your prospects. Strive to have equipment that is at least as good as that of your customers.

You've probably heard the advice that to succeed, employees should dress like people who already have their dream jobs. Apply that same thinking to your investment in office equipment. Buying the next level up in equipment quality will demonstrate your commitment to the business, as well as positioning your company as a market leader.

To be sure that you're getting just what you need, and to avoid potential performance problems down the road, refer to popular references such as *Consumer Reports* or *PC World*. Such guides pinpoint potential problems other consumers have had, and that you're likely to encounter. Magazines like *Home Office Computing* are also helpful, as they frequently review the newest hardware and software products.

Investigating your supplier is also smart. After you've determined which model PC or copier will work best for you, don't buy from a questionable supplier; doing so will only put your warranties at risk. Yes, you may be able to negotiate a great price through an Internet site, but how much after-sale support will you want? Can they realistically and conveniently provide it?

Depending on your familiarity with the equipment, you may want to spend a tad more and gain access to a company with 24-hour support, a technical support line, and local technicians. This advice also applies to any software you invest in; the more complicated the application, the more support you may want. Be sure you're not cutting yourself off from technical help by buying from a cheap outlet store.

Home-based businesses are extremely technologically savvy—perhaps more so than many corporations. The reason? Home-based companies must use technology and equipment in order to compete with other businesses that have more financial resources; the right equipment can even the score.

IDC/Link has found that 65 percent of home-based businesses are equipped with computers. IDC statistics indicate 19.7 million U.S. home offices will access the Internet in 1999; that figure will skyrocket to 30.2 million by 2002 as a direct result of the expanding home-office population. This is expected to near 50 million by 2002, with the number of home offices with PCs approaching 38 million by then. It is therefore not surprising to also find home offices equipped with fax machines, computer scanners, etc.

The technological advancement of home-based business capabilities has, in turn, enhanced home-business respectability. Home-based businesses are no longer something to be hidden or to make excuses for. In some ways, home-based business owners are entrepreneurs on the cutting edge.

But almost as important as computer technology is the telecommunications technology you put to

Bright Idea
Use Internet discussion forums, called the Usenet, to get immediate feedback from fellow consumers with opinions about your brand or model of office equipment. The Usenet can be accessed via a Newsgroup reader or with a Web based search engine like www.dejanews. com.

work. With accessibility being so important to customer relationships today, providing customers with a number of options for reaching you is critical. Think about all the ways you can enable customer communications:

- Business phone line(s). Having more than one line is smart, especially if you're running a dedicated fax and want constant Internet access.

- Voice mail

- 800 phone line

- Pager

- Cellular phone. Some cellular plans are so reasonably priced these days that you might even consider using a cell phone as your main business phone line. Be sure and test the quality of the signal from inside your office before making that commitment; some electronic equipment creates interference.

- E-mail. If you anticipate that your e-mail usage will be high, look into upgrading from a standard modem to a cable modem or ISDN connection for faster speed.

- Fax

- Video conferencing

One business owner I know has failed to recognize the impression her telephone system makes on customers and prospects. On a typical day, trying to reach her is virtually impossible—and extremely frustrating—for several reasons.

Since she uses a personal line for incoming calls, her business is not listed in the phone book; good luck finding her phone number if you don't know her last name or address! When callers phone her, they frequently hear an answering machine message meant for callers to the home. Or, if her children are home, they may answer the phone with a "hello." When this occurs, callers are often asked to phone the business owner in her car, so another call is made, only to be greeted with the standard cellular message that the person is not available.

This business owner has obviously not thought about making it convenient—or even possible—for callers to get through to her. And those who do are surely fed up with the inconvenience. Can this be good for business? Certainly not.

Make sure you think about how easy it is for your customers to reach you and what kinds of telephone greetings they hear every time they call.

If you decide to rely heavily on a cellular phone for customer communication, be sure and add the voice mail feature so that callers never hear that annoying "The cellular customer you are trying to reach . . . ."

Prospects and customers should not need to know where you physically do your work, and if you appear to be completely professional, the issue may not ever come up. However, some home-based operations make it plainly clear by the equipment they use that they are not professional.

Of course, there is no special equipment required to run a home-based business. The equipment list in Chapter 6, "Setting Up Shop," should provide guidance in purchasing exactly what you'll need. Unfortunately, setting up a home-based business is no less expensive than establishing a business located in commercial space, with one big exception—you don't have to pay rent.

One cost you may not have considered, but should, is taking out a separate business insurance policy in addition to the one you maintain for your

Moneysaver
Paying for a cellular phone, to which calls can be forwarded when you're out of the office, improves communication with customers and reduces your need for personnel. Handling more calls yourself is certainly cheaper than hiring someone else to do it for you.

home. Some homeowner's policies offer extended agreements—called riders or endorsements—to include home-based businesses, but coverage is often limited. Your insurance agent should be able to provide an affordable, comprehensive package to cover your equipment (property liability), your clients (general liability), and any other specific areas of risk your home-based business may encounter. If not, don't hesitate to shop elsewhere for coverage; it's crucial to protect your business. Many trade associations offer group insurance at discounted rates; check with yours for availability and price.

The National Insurance Consumer Helpline ([800] 942-4242) offers free information about home-based business insurance. The Insurance Information Institute's (III) brochure, *Insuring Your Home Business*, provides information about home business insurance and lists phone numbers for state insurance departments. For a free copy, send a #10 SASE to III at 110 Williams St., New York, N.Y. 10038. Anyone with customers who come to their business—no matter where it is located—should have insurance in place.

Home life issues

When individuals tell me that they want to start a home-based business in order to spend more time with their children, I become very concerned. The sad truth is that business and children rarely mix well. Yes, a home-based business will give you the flexibility to set aside more time to spend with your kids, but it's very risky to try to do both at once. Few people have succeeded at doing both well. Those that generally have older children and were able to light their entrepreneurial spark by finding small, useful jobs they could do and paid them for their help. Jane Applegate, award-winning syndicated business columnist and owner of The Applegate Group, has found this worked well.

Arranging for childcare during working hours is the only way that most home-based professionals can get any work done. Some take their children to daycare or a family member's house, while others hire a nanny. The solution that you choose is not important as long as it is healthy for your child; you must be able to focus on business when you need to and not be distracted with concern for your child's well-being.

In addition to juggling parental responsibilities and business ownership, selecting a physical location within your home is another important consideration. To get the biggest tax advantages from being home-based, you'll want to set aside a workspace totally dedicated to your business; the IRS requires that the workspace be used "exclusively" and "regularly" for business. Although a separate room is best to meet that criteria, some businesses use partitions or equipment to delineate a private work area.

Companies not confined to a particular room or workspace are not eligible for the home-office tax deduction, which can yield hundreds or thousands of dollars in deductions each year. Each year, the cost of the space devoted solely to generating revenue (expressed as a percentage of the total annual mortgage) can be deducted, as well as the pro-rated cost of utilities. IRS publication #587, "Business Use of Your Home," can give you the specifics of taking the deduction, providing a list of which expenses are deductible and which are not.

Unofficially . . .
A 1998 survey of Canadian workers by Ekos Research Associates revealed that 33 percent would choose working from home over a 10 percent raise.

The best way to reduce the chance of the IRS questioning your taking of that deduction is to set aside a room of your home solely for business use. Everything in the room should pertain to or be used by the business; a daybed used from time-to-time by out-of-town guests is a no-no, for example. Likewise, business should be conducted in your office and nowhere else. If you begin completing work anywhere but in your home office, that deduction becomes suspect; your home office is where the great majority of your work should be completed.

Keep in mind that just taking the home office deduction opens you to potential audit; it's one of the red flags that the IRS looks for. That reason alone scares some business owners from taking the deduction, even when it is clearly permitted.

To substantiate your claim of eligibility, you'll want to keep everything business-related within your work space. You'll also want to calculate the total square footage of your living space and determine what percentage is comprised of your office. That percentage is the pro-rata figure you can use to calculate what percent of your homeowners insurance, for example, can be deducted.

Whenever client meetings are held at your home, conduct them in your office—that's what it's there for. Conducting them anywhere else in your home brings your office into question. If you need to hold them elsewhere, due to space constraints or distance from the client's office, there are a number of options. Hotels frequently have conference or meeting rooms which can be rented, as do country or social clubs.

When selecting an alternate meeting space, cost will certainly be a factor, but don't forget about the image you present based on your choice. Meeting at a diner may be less expensive and convenient, but it lacks the professionalism that a private club's meeting room provides. Weigh the cost with the classiness of the space to determine what will be the best option for you.

And whatever you do, don't use the business computer for personal work. Files relating to personal checkbook management, for example, have been used by the IRS to show that the home office was not used exclusively for work.

Another reason to have a separate and exclusive work space is to avoid burnout. Some home-based owners find it easy to shift from business to home life, while others, like me, do not have the discipline to shut down the business at the end of the day. For these owners, the business is never closed—and work is done continuously. These individuals are prime candidates for early burnout, because there is never a break from work.

And a third reason for confining work to one area is that you'll be more organized and less cluttered. While clutter and disorganization may not bother you, it can give a negative impression to any customer who arrives unexpectedly on your doorstep.

Pros and cons

Operating a business from home can be a very cost-effective way to set up a new venture. But over the long term there are some limitations you'll want to be aware of:

Here are the pros:

▪ **Lower start-up costs.** Instead of investing in commercial space, you can reallocate that

Bright Idea
When a large conference room is needed for a client meeting or presentation, look to your customers and suppliers. Negotiate to use their space from time to time. Other options include public libraries, colleges and universities, and the Small Business Development Center.

Timesaver
Many home-
based profession-
als rely on the
services of a rea-
sonably priced
courier service to
take care of cus-
tomer deliveries
while they keep
working. By
building in a fee
for deliveries up
front, you spend
time working on
important pro-
jects rather than
racing around
town making
deliveries your-
self. That's not
something your
larger clients
would do, so why
should you?

money to equipment purchases or marketing materials.

- **Home life flexibility.** Being home to meet your child's school bus everyday is a real possibility when you're home-based.

- **No commute.** You'll have more time to spend on work when you don't have to drive to the office.

- **Tax advantages.** You can deduct the portion of your home dedicated to running your business, as well as a percentage of utility costs. Keeping business and personal finances completely separate also assists you in proving your home office legitimacy. Some business owners write a business check for the pro-rated portion of the mortgage due for their work space; the balance is paid from the personal account. This certainly keeps things separate.

But there are also cons:

- **Limited expansion possibilities.** Unless you're willing to put on an addition to your house or renting a second apartment, there may come a time when you simply can't continue to operate from home. Moving can be very costly.

- **Employees in your personal space.** If you hire employees, be prepared to adjust to having them in your living space. Privacy and solitude are much more difficult.

- **Assumed unprofessionalism.** Past experiences with unprofessional work-at-homers may lead some customers to be less willing to deal with a home-based supplier.

- **Feeling isolated.** Ask yourself how you will feel about not being in direct contact with others on a daily basis. In a regular office you can chat with a co-worker over a cup of coffee, bounce ideas or problematic situations off of them, or grab a bite of lunch together, but not at home. To get the same kind of feedback and information sharing, home-based business owners must make a special effort.

■ **Staying focused.** How good are you at setting a schedule and sticking with it without becoming distracted? Your success will depend on your ability to separate yourself from household/ outdoor chores that need to be done. However, one of the benefits of being home-based is that you can often adjust your schedule to fit the needs of your clients; working extra hours in the evening isn't as much of an inconvenience as it would be to a corporate employee stuck at the office.

Just the facts

■ Many customers and prospects will be skeptical of the professionalism of a home-based business.

■ Your communications equipment is the most important investment you can make; be sure customers can reach you quickly and easily.

■ Although a home-based business may become unwieldy when you bring on employees, it's a cost-effective and convenient place to get started.

■ Trying to run a business and care for children simultaneously will only lead to lost business and unhappy kids; arrange for childcare during the day so you can get work done.

GET THE SCOOP ON...
The best Web businesses to start ▪ Designing a
killer site ▪ Web versus bricks-and-mortar ▪ Web
success stories

Setting Up a Web-Based Business

A decade ago, few market analysts would have predicted the impact the Internet would have on business and the number of opportunities it would create. Through use of the Internet, global business relationships are a reality rather than a goal. New customers are found in a matter of keystrokes. And the pace at which business occurs has been significantly hastened, thanks to 24-hour e-mail.

Communication capabilities provided by the Internet are extremely conducive to researching opportunities, keeping in touch with customers and colleagues, and creating new business relationships. Some of the newest Web-based companies are perfect examples of what is possible on the Internet.

Autobytel.com, the Web-based automotive marketplace started in 1995, processed a total of 345,000 purchase requests for cars through its site in 1996, generating $1.8 billion in auto sales. Near the end of 1997, the Web site was processing more than

100,000 purchase requests each month and generating $500 million a month in sales.

Keep in mind, however, that not every Web business is a stunning success. The ever-increasing number of Web sites creates clutter that interferes with a company's ability to attract customers to its business. With competitors around every corner, lowest price is the name of the game. The Web has enabled customers to get increasingly detailed, accurate, timely, and inexpensive information. With just a few keystrokes, your company and its offerings can be compared to all your competitors, so carefully consider what it is you have to offer the Internet user. Creating and maintaining strong customer relationships will be the only way to beat your online competitors.

Thanks to the Internet, Bear, Stearns & Co. analyst Rich Scocozza says, "Companies will need to be more adaptive to the needs of their customers." To this end, a number of companies are trying to establish themselves as leaders in the emerging market for Enterprise Relationship Management (ERM) software solutions. These applications are intended to address the impersonal aspect of doing business via the Internet.

Since making customers feel individually served will determine the long-term profitability of any Web-based business, software that can make thousands of Web customers feel a personal, one-to-one connection with your company will be invaluable.

Why the web?

Some of the major advantages of starting and running a Web-based business are:

- **Ease of set-up.** Inexpensive Web design software, such as Microsoft FrontPage, is virtually all you need to get up and running. Some sites will even walk you through the process. Be aware, however, that as the average Internet user becomes more sophisticated, the basic Web page will no longer be sufficient to compete; visitors to your site will increasingly expect rich content, eye-catching design, and online, secure ordering. Although you can begin using a simple page design, if you're serious about e-commerce, you'll want to identify and hire a professional Web designer.

Moneysaver
There are companies, such as NetFruits.com, that will design and promote your Web site for free, in return for a commission on the sales generated on the site. Not a bad way to get up and running with no up-front design and development costs!

- **Low capital investment.** Besides having a Web page designed and selecting a hosting company, there are few major expenses required to establish a Web business. Keep in mind, however, that although start-up expenses may be minimized, the long-term success of your online business will depend on your investment in marketing your site. And, unfortunately, marketing can be quite costly.

- **Flexible hours.** Unlike a bricks-and-mortar business, which requires scheduled hours of operation, a Web-based business can be operated virtually at the owner's convenience. Updates, additions, and order processing can be completed at any time of day.

- **Flexible location.** Since a Web-based business is located in cyberspace, not a fixed geographic location, the owner can operate from any city with Internet access—Paris, France, or Paris, Tex.

- **Significant growth rate.** Some 159 million people worldwide are now online. By 2003, International Data estimates 510 million people will be online worldwide. Clearly, as Internet usage increases, so do opportunities for Web-based sales. Currently the growth rate of Internet businesses far exceeds most traditional businesses. Traffic on the Internet has been doubling every 100 days, says INTECS, Inc.

▪ **Unrestricted sales territory.** Unless you intend to represent products sold through distributors with assigned territories, your geographic service area is international. With no additional cost to reach international customers, you can easily do business outside your home country. Until recently, expense concerns prevented Network Associates in Santa Clara, Calif., from marketing its anti-virus software outside the United States. A recent *Business Week* article explained how the Internet has changed that; in 1998, Network Associates' first sale of a new help-desk software product came from a bank in Spain, which downloaded it and ordered a 30-seat license. "That's the marketing power you get online," says division manager Zach Nelson. "Instant sale. No cost."

▪ **Potentially lower marketing costs.** Relying on the Internet to promote your business is often much less expensive than traditional marketing methods. Web hosting fees, e-mail distribution costs, and order processing charges are minimal in comparison to traditional direct marketing expenses.

A business unto itself

For many established businesses, the Web is just another channel of distribution, expanding their potential revenue sources by one more mechanism. No matter whether a Web site will be one of many distribution channels, or the sole means of selling your goods and services, you'll need a distribution strategy. Ensuring that your various channels don't overlap or compete will significantly boost your profitability and reach.

One of the nation's largest book retailers, Barnes & Noble, launched an online bookstore (www.barnesandnoble.com) in 1997 to expand its distribution channels and to compete with the likes of Internet bookstore Amazon.com, which sold $148 million worth of books in 1997 and $610 million in 1998.

In the consulting world, The Expert Marketplace is another great example of a stand-alone Web business that is raking in the bucks. Its PEN (Premier ExpertNet) Group generates more than 1,250 online leads a month for consulting services and forecasts annual revenues of $6 million, on $250 million in project fees this year.

PEN gets a commission on consulting projects, ranging from 5 to 15 percent, that it refers to its 650 affiliate firms, who pay an average of $2,400 to join the network. Although the company's revenues represent a small piece of the $62 billion management consulting industry, its affiliate members tend to have more experience and generally charge less than Big Five firms. It is possibly due to these two reasons that PEN is experiencing exponential growth; annualized revenue is expected to hit $75 million by 2002.

These companies, and those that are fully reliant on Web sales, have identified advantages the online medium provides and have leveraged them. Major advantages include:

- Speed of response
- Low overhead cost
- Customized communications

Popular products/services

The primary types of products and services available on the Web include:

- **Commercially available products,** such as cookware, clothing, and auto accessories, which can also be found through other distribution channels.

- **Custom products,** such as custom-fitted golf clubs or CDs prepared with the customer's music selections.

- **Services,** such as market research, grocery delivery, and travel reservations.

- **Information,** such as online newspapers, special reports, and books.

- **Consulting,** such as online guidance and coaching.

Of course, when the Web was first used commercially, most revenues generated were from advertising fees. Companies seeking to advertise their products and services through other Web sites paid fees for advertising space on those sites. Although advertising fees still comprise a significant revenue source for some companies, it is not the most common form of Web business. And with the amount of competition now on the Internet, establishing an advertising fee-based business would be more challenging than a decade ago.

The Expert Marketplace, for example, was originally started using an ad-based revenue model, where affiliate consultants were expected to pay for banner ads and directory listings. But the founders soon learned that the ad-based model just wasn't working, and switched to the consulting referral approach. Consulting firms now pay for the ability to access consulting assignment want ads placed by corporations worldwide. The Expert Marketplace is now a placement firm of sorts, providing a marketing outlet for smaller consultants.

Web site design

While almost anyone can design and establish a Web site, the quality of the finished product will vary depending on how much experience the designer has. As with anything else, there are nuances that only a professional will be privy to. Have an expert set up your site, but then minimize ongoing site maintenance expenses by learning to make changes to it yourself.

On the SmallOffice.com Web site, the editors of *Home Office Computing* and *Small Business Computing* advise readers on seven steps to take before launching a Web site:

1. Determine what your objectives for having a Web site are.

2. Register a domain name for your company's site.

3. Check out the winners of the *Home Office Computing*/U.S. Robotics Best Small Business Web site contest to see what great Web sites look like.

4. Read up on the subject of Web site design.

5. Map your site and its information content on paper.

6. Research Internet Service Providers (ISPs) and the associated costs.

7. Select a hosting company.

Unofficially . . .
Consumers spent an estimated $2.7 billion on travel, books, music, and other retail items over the Internet during 1998. By 2002 that figure is expected to grow to $65 billion, says Pegasus Research International.

Timesaver
Before retaining
a consultant or
designer to lay
out your Web
site, take the
time to visit the
Web sites of
competitors as
well as sites
from other indus-
tries. The more
time spent visit-
ing existing
sites, the better
direction you will
be able to pro-
vide your own
designer regard-
ing the look and
functionality of
your company's
site.

After investing time in setting the goals and objectives for your site, you are ready to begin the design process.

Taking orders online

The U.S. Department of Commerce forecasts that by the year 2001, an estimated $300 billion in commerce will be done via the Internet. The two biggest obstacles to Internet sales are:

- consumer fear regarding the security of their credit card account numbers and
- the reliability of the cyber merchant.

Although that fear has been somewhat allayed by the addition of secure servers, in many cases customers may decide to place their orders via more traditional routes. For this reason, you risk losing sales if your site does not include a downloadable order form and/or toll-free number for phone/fax orders.

In January 1999, BBBOnLine, a subsidiary of the Council of Better Business Bureaus, announced a Privacy Program offering a graphic image of a seal that signals to businesses and consumers that this Web site is an ethical electronic business using credible online privacy practices. This trustmark will no doubt be quickly adopted by the more than 2,000 e-commerce businesses that already carry the BBBOnline Reliability Seal.

Establishing an online merchant account

In order to accept credit or debit card payment via a Web site, you will first need to establish a merchant account. Just like a brick-and-mortar shop, you will establish such an account with a local bank who in turn contracts with a third-party clearinghouse, called a "merchant processor," to handle the transactions.

Once a merchant account and third party processor have been selected and established, an online merchant can begin to accept credit card payments. You will be charged a fee of 1.5 to 3.0 percent for the opportunity to accept credit or debit card payment. Negotiate the lowest rate possible, as it can add up to substantial savings over time.

Because of the nature of the Internet, added steps must be taken to provide for secure transactions and authentication of both buyer and seller. To increase customer confidence, select a processor like First Data, Paymentech, or Bank America Merchant Services that process transactions via secure servers.

The major industry players, including Netscape and Microsoft, have worked to develop security encryption technology and safeguards to eliminate customer concerns about placing credit card orders on the Net. The importance of addressing privacy and security issues is driving the development of even more sophisticated encryption technologies and standards that will no doubt offer customers even more confidence in making online purchases.

Interestingly, although online credit card processing is a key concern for Internet users, credit card numbers are more likely to be learned through telephone orders placed using a cordless phone. Anyone with a scanner can hear conversations over a cordless phone, including those precious Mastercard and Visa account numbers. Perhaps as more users become comfortable with the Internet, online ordering will not be seen as any more risky than telephone transactions.

Malls

Electronic malls were one of the first places consumers could spend their money online.

Commercial services such as CompuServe and America Online established online areas where companies could feature their products, just as in traditional malls. However, malls have not garnered the sales growth that individual Web sites have, suggesting that they may be on their way out.

An article not too long ago in *The Financial Times* supports this contention, stating that "Analysts believe that online shopping malls fail to combine the front office with the back office operations of a retailer," and that large companies would derive more benefits from establishing their own Web site. The article also mentions that IBM has closed down its World Avenue online mall and that Shopping. com has experienced some difficulties.

Clearly shoppers are not shopping less; they're just not using the online malls. But even physical malls are feeling the pressure of the increasing number of commercial Web sites. Greenfield Online (greenfieldonline.com) reports that 39 percent of shoppers with Internet access are visiting bricks-and-mortar stores less often.

And the success of online superstores, such as Amazon.com, seem to bear out the popularity of specialization rather than generalization when it comes to product promotion.

Outsourcing fulfillment

The immediacy of the Web is what pushes some customers to order products and services online; they want it now, and they are willing to pay extra to get it quickly. Shipping the correct items and responding to their orders quickly will determine if you keep them as long-term customers. This doesn't mean that you personally need to be the one to ensure their order is processed and shipped ASAP. Relying on a fulfillment service may improve your turn-around time and ease your headaches.

Fulfillment services offer a range of services, from answering the phone, to receiving and processing Web orders, to shipping products you have stored in their warehouse. Keep in mind that the more responsibility the fulfillment service takes for getting your order out, the higher the cost.

Adding on to an existing business

Many smart companies are taking the new capabilities that the Web provides and creating new products and services to supplement their existing business. CareerPath.com is one example of a complementary—yet new—service offered by six major newspaper publishing companies.

CareerPath.com is one of the top Web sites for job seekers and employers. Culling help wanted ads from the member newspapers and from the Web sites of leading employers, CareerPath.com provides a new venue for job seekers and employers to turn to.

Essentially, it takes information already provided through daily newspapers and repackages it for the Web, putting to use the search capabilities unique to the Web. This repackaging has created a new revenue source for the papers, as well as a new print benefit to offer potential advertisers. Job seekers can literally have jobs come to them by simply signing up to receive daily e-mail job leads that match parameters they've selected.

Taking existing information and repackaging it in many forms is what Martha Stewart does like no other marketer. Introduced in 1997, the Martha Stewart Everyday brand rang up $800 million in sales at Kmart in 1998. According to the *Democrat*

Bright Idea
If you are distributing products manufactured by another company, ask about dropship arrangements, where you provide the name and address of a customer and the company ships the product directly from its warehouse. You avoid involving a fulfillment service and the product is shipped from the source quickly.

and Chronicle, an estimated 30 million people a week come into contact with some form of Martha Stewart marketing. Starting with her books, Martha has rechanneled her information into a syndicated newspaper column, a monthly magazine, *Martha Stewart Living*, a TV program, a radio program, a Web site, and a mail-order catalog.

Web as new distribution channel

One-stop shopping from a home or office is one of the advantages the Web has to offer, both to business owners and customers. Instead of traveling to a store, making a phone call, or sending in a card or order, customers can log into the Internet and gain access to a wide range of product and service options. Odyssey L.P., an independent market research firm, reports that 47 percent of online households have purchased something over the Internet within the past six months.

With numbers like this, knowing how to use e-mail as a sales development tool will be an increasingly important skill in order to succeed as an online marketer. Definitely build into your site a way to interact with your customers by creating your own opt-in e-mail list. Go to www.webpromote.com to get this tool free. Also investigate software programs that allow you to personalize e-mail, such as www. digital-impact.com and www.guesttrack.com.

For many companies, the Web is creating new sales opportunities. For others, the Web is cannibalizing existing sales from traditional channels.

Dell Computers has been a popular computer seller, one of the first to eschew retail outlets and go direct to the consumer. So the Web was a perfect add-on to their direct approach, just using a different communication medium. Using Dell's Web site,

Bright Idea
"Try before you buy" is becoming more commonplace via the Web, say CNET founders Headapohl and Barzun, with companies creating "wrappers" for software, for example, that give customers a certain number of days before payment must be received. After that point, the product is shut down. Think about how you can build in "try before you buy" to your site.

customers configure their own PC online and have the ability to then track its assembly and shipping status. With this kind of customer service orientation, it's no wonder that sales for the build-to-order pioneer are still growing 38 percent a year, more than double the industry's 15 percent average.

In December 1997, reports INTECS, Inc., Dell experienced sales of $6 million in a day several times that month, up from less than $1 million a day only a few months before. Cisco Systems, another information technology company, saw its Web-based business jump from $100 million in 1996 to $3.2 billion in 1997. While these revenue levels are impressive, keep in mind that the Internet is just one of several profit centers for these successful ventures.

Although most companies built their traditional distribution channels first, then their Web site, that doesn't mean that you need to follow the same business model.

In fact, too few Web-based companies have expanded beyond their Internet community. Some smart marketers are beginning to explore how to leverage their online presence to create new customer relationships—The Onion is one example. The Onion Web site has published a book based on its community, *Our Dumb Century: 100 Years of Headlines from America's Finest News Source*, thereby extending its relationships into traditional retail book outlets.

Look for ways to penetrate all of the various distribution channels open to you. While the Web may be the best place for you to start, don't limit your growth solely to the Internet.

Improving communication and collaboration

In addition to building sales, the Web can aid in improving relationships with existing customers,

66

Use the Web to build the loyalty of existing customers, then think about using it to find new customers . . . . Create a Web site that's filled with useful information—fact sheets . . . (are) a mechanism for customers to ask questions and get answers as quickly as possible. An online newsletter is another possibility . . . .
—Mary J. Cronin, author of *Doing Business on the Internet*

99

suppliers, and employees. In turn, these can have a positive impact on the bottom line:

- **Collaboration**—Information sharing via e-mail, message boards, and chat rooms helps improve customer service, morale, and quality of deliverables.

- **Online project management**—Secure servers enable customers to check on the status of their orders, even going so far as to allow customers to view work-in-progress.

- **Training**—On-demand training via the Internet can improve both process and product.

Building non-web sales

Some manufacturers use the Web to increase sales from their existing sales channels. Rather than cut out the middleman, smart businesses are supporting their supplier relationships with a site that refers business to their distributors, in addition to offering online ordering.

Rainbow Play Systems' Web site (www.rainbowplay. com) provides visitors with a search engine and map that pinpoints the dealer closest to the customer's location. Consumers can also view the various possible combinations of the company's modular playground systems and check pricing. But to order, the consumer must visit an authorized dealer.

Likewise, national companies are creating joint venture opportunities that benefit all participants. ValuPage (www.ValuPage.com) is an online couponing system that alerts consumers to weekly product specials that can be earned at participating local grocery stores. After selecting the coupons of interest, the consumer simply prints them out on a printer and brings them into the store.

ValuPage earns a fee from the participating consumer products companies, who pay for the advertising space, and the participating grocery store benefits from consumers directed to their location through the program.

Web sites create the opportunity to do business with customers, as well as serving as a marketing tool that can supplement and strengthen existing channels of distribution.

Ongoing maintenance

After your Web site is functioning like a well-oiled machine, providing information, processing orders, and building long-term relationships with new customers, you'll want to be sure you don't drop the ball. Just as in traditional businesses, make sure you provide top notch online customer service. This includes:

- Responding immediately to any e-mail inquiries. Software programs that immediately send a follow-up receipt confirmation are a smart way to let visitors know that you've heard them and will get back to them soon.

- Confirming receipt of orders via e-mail.

- Asking for feedback regarding the customer's satisfaction with your operations via an online survey.

- Constantly updating and improving the existing site, giving visitors a reason to return frequently.

- Providing a mechanism, such as an ezine or weekly mailer, that reminds prospects and customers of your business.

Last but not least—disadvantages

Yes, the Internet is *the* place to be right now and will be for years to come. But there are challenges that

may impede your making a million dollars in sales
the first year. Those challenges include:

- Credit card security, as mentioned before.

- Total reliance on your Web hosting firm for continuous access to your cyberbusiness.

- Low barriers to entry, providing little or no protection from new competitors jumping into
  your market tomorrow.

- Designing an easy-to-load, friendly site that is
  inviting to new visitors, interesting to read
  through, and speedy to move through. Slow-to-
  load sites, often overloaded with images, frus-
  trate new visitors and discourage orders.

Just the facts

- Establishing a Web-based business is one of the
  least expensive means of starting a business.

- A Web site can create new customer relationships, as well as solidify and improve existing
  ones.

- Web malls have not caught on as quickly as individual company Web sites, suggesting that you
  should consider marketing your products
  online yourself.

- Relationship management and e-mail software
  solutions are critical components of successful
  online marketing.

GET THE SCOOP ON...
Franchising fundamentals ▪ MLM misconceptions
▪ The realities of part-time ownership ▪
Sidestepping scams

Investing in a Business Opportunity

Chapter 16

Business systems, such as franchises and multilevel marketing opportunities, provide would-be business owners with valuable guidance and support. Such businesses have tried-and-true policies and procedures in place, significantly shortening the potential franchisee's learning curve and increasing his or her profit potential.

Instead of having to learn some of the basic rules of business on their own, franchisees are brought up to speed quickly under the careful tutelage of the franchisor.

Franchises are an excellent way for individuals to be in business for themselves, but not by themselves. Franchisors provide a proven method of doing business that significantly increases a business owner's probability of success.

Franchising

Buying an established franchise is the preferred method of starting a business for many people, especially those who have some corporate experience but little in the way of small business know-how.

229

Franchises provide the purchaser with more than just an established name. In addition, franchisees also gain:

- Established policies and procedures
- Operations training
- Assistance in site selection
- Marketing and advertising support
- Quality control standards
- Prenegotiated supplier relationships
- Management support
- Brand name and trademark usage rights
- Significant opportunities for growth

While the advantages of franchising are established policies and procedures, the disadvantages are reduced flexibility in how the company is operated. With quality control processes come expectations regarding how the business will function. For some business owners, operating guidelines are just what they're looking for, and for others, the control from a central office defeats the purpose of being an entrepreneur.

Watch Out!
Securing an exclusive territory can be a requirement for success in most franchises. Be sure to ask whether you are being offered rights to an exclusive geographic area during your negotiations.

Finding the opportunities

There are currently franchise opportunities available in virtually every industry. According to Andover Franchising, Inc., an Atlanta consulting firm, the following business categories are contenders for the top 10 franchises of the twenty-first century:

- Diaper Retailing ($35,000–$50,000 investment)
- Upscale Deli Restaurant ($150,000 and up in malls; $250,000 and up freestanding)
- Painting Contractor ($40,000–$60,000 investment)

- Restoration Services ($100,000–$150,000 investment)

- Specialized Manufacturing and Customized Remodeling ($65,000–$90,000)

- Advertising Company ($50,000–$250,000, depending on market size)

- Gift and Furnishings Store ($150,000–$175,000)

- Home Inspection ($20,000–$40,000)

- Maid Service ($20,000–$30,000)

- TV Satellite Dish Installation ($27,000–$40,000)

- Internet Marketing (typically less than $10,000)

However, those entrepreneurs interested in the hot franchise systems may want to scan the list of *Entrepreneur Magazine*'s top 10 franchise brands:

1. Orion Food Systems

2. Matco Tools

3. Computer Renaissance

4. Surface Doctor

5. Ace America's Cash Express, Inc.

6. House Doctors

7. Candy Bouquet

8. Big Apple Bagels

9. Curves for Women

10. Wetzel's Pretzels

When evaluating a franchise opportunity, gather as much information as you can about the market you are considering entering and the franchisor. Don't just investigate the franchise parent—you may miss significant changes in the industry or market that could impact your chances of success. Specific market indices you'll want to check are

Bright Idea
Potential franchisees in need of start-up financing should consider applying for funding through the SBA's Franchise Registry (www. franchiseregistry. com), which has prequalified at least 39 franchises for such help. Applying through the Registry reduces the review process, improves the odds for approval, and cuts the processing time to weeks instead of months.

Bright Idea
If a franchisor states that you can expect to make a certain amount of money or that current franchisees are making a certain income, request written substantiation. The Federal Trade Commission (FTC) requires that of franchisors.

- Industry growth rate.

- Target market/demographic changes.

- Competition.

- Success of similar businesses in your local area.

In looking at the information provided by the franchisor, carefully review:

- **Financial statements**—How quickly have sales been growing? How healthy is the balance sheet? Compare an individual franchisee with the "typical franchisee" to see if the franchisor's projections are realistic.

- **Franchise agreement**—What are the requirements of franchisees? How long is the agreement in force? Do you have a right to terminate the agreement? Are there penalties? What are they?

- **Record of bankruptcies**—Have any of the franchisees or principals of the franchisor filed for bankruptcy?

- **Lawsuits**—Have any lawgsuits been filed against the company?

- **Fees**—What fees are due in addition to royalties, if any? How are they calculated? Are they paid regardless of profit?

Of greatest importance are discussions with current or former franchisees. Meet or talk by phone or e-mail with franchisees, asking at least the following questions:

- How is your business doing? Is it doing as well as the franchisor indicated it would?

- What do you think are the keys to success in this particular business?

- How valuable is the franchise name and support to your business?

- What, if any, problems have you had in dealing with the franchisor? Have they been resolved to your satisfaction?

- Has the franchisor done everything to support your business that it promised it would?

- Knowing what you know now, would you go with the same franchisor? If not, why?

Steering clear of the scams

Oversight by the Federal Trade Commission (FTC) has clamped down on scams within the franchising industry. With the various disclosure documents now required, few franchisees are duped.

The same is not true of the less-regulated multi-level marketing (MLM) industry, where scams continue to do a brisk business with people in search of fast wealth. Take a look at the list of MLM scam signals later in this chapter.

Pros and cons of buying a known commodity

While the major strength of a franchise is that the business model has been proven successful for prior franchisees, there are downsides to such a system. Here are the pros:

- An established product or service

- Improved probability of success

- Technical assistance from the parent organization

- Better financing odds

The cons include:

- Less upside potential in building an equity position in the business that can be sold.

Timesaver
Using franchising Web sites, such as FranNet (www.frannet. com), you can conduct self-evaluations to determine which franchises may best meet your financial resources, personal skills, and interests. You can quickly rule out franchises that do not fit your personality or resources, saving you hours of time.

- Ownership restrictions.

- Higher service costs.

- Franchise agreements typically run for 15–20 years but are not automatically renewed.

- Royalty or other fees may be required even if/when the business is not generating revenues.

Multilevel marketing

Multilevel marketing (MLM), also called network marketing, is a type of business that involves networking to make sales. People who join the network use their personal connections to introduce friends, neighbors, family members, and business associates to the products or services they represent, rather than referring them to a retail store or catalog.

However, participants not only sell products or services, they also recruit other salespeople to further expand the distribution of the product. As more people join the sales network, a hierarchy is created. Those at the top of the hierarchy share in whatever profits are generated from the sales of those below them. These profits are what would traditionally be paid to a distributor, but which are, instead, paid out to individual distributors.

The part-time opportunity

Although franchises are typically purchased for full-time operations, many MLM participants begin as part-timers. In fact, many operate out of home offices during non-working hours. The fact that many networking and training meetings held by MLM companies are scheduled during evening and weekend hours is a sign that many people are not full-time salespeople.

Those who do well in an MLM may elect to become full-time salespeople at some point in the future. It is this flexibility that attracts many people to such programs. For some, however, the flexibility is a disadvantage. Many participants drop out after several months, perhaps due to lack of structure.

Evaluating the opportunities

With so many MLM companies out there, it's hard to know which ones are legitimate and have the potential to yield significant revenues, and which ones will be featured on *60 Minutes* as the scam of the year. Worldwide Information Systems recommends carefully evaluating five aspects of each MLM you are considering:

1. **The product.** Is it unique? Does it provide superior performance to an existing product? Products that can be easily found at a local discount chain are not good MLM prospects.

2. **Your upline.** How many people are between you and the founder? If there are more than eight, the people at the highest rungs of the organization do not have a vested interest in your success.

3. **Upline support.** How accessible is your sponsor? Are successful people in your upline willing to share information and to provide guidance and advice? Do you have their phone numbers?

4. **The company.** Is the company heavily invested in manufacturing its product? Do the principals have business experience beyond the MLM industry? Since few MLMs last longer than seven years, you want a company with staying power.

Timesaver
For an A–Z list of low-cost network marketing opportunities, check out www. entrepreneurmag. com. *Entrepreneur Magazine* has compiled a list of 65 MLM opportunities, all of which can be started for less than $3,000.

5. **Inventory purchases.** What are the requirements regarding inventory purchases and what are the return policies?

Due to changing consumer demographics, some of the best MLMs to be in right now include:

- Nutrition
- Homecare and personal care products
- Telecommunications

The SBDC indicates that an MLM may be a pyramid scheme—a company totally dependent on new recruits, rather than product sales, to fund its growth—if it

- Guarantees extremely high earnings.
- Charges high entry fees or requires huge investments in inventory.
- Does not offer to buy back unsold product.
- Pays bonuses or fees for new recruits.
- Has only some participants actually selling products.

Understanding how they work

MLMs provide several means of generating income, according to counselors at the San Joaquin Delta College Small Business Development Center:

- **Personal sales**—commissions paid on products and services that you sell, at a set rate
- **Residual income**—commissions paid to you when a customer makes a repeat purchase
- **Group bonus**—bonuses paid based on the total sales generated by your network
- **Usage bonus**—bonuses paid based on a percentage of the network's usage level

■ **Leadership bonus**—bonuses paid when you help one of your sponsors reach a higher level in the organization.

Do you have the personality?

One skill essential to success in multilevel marketing is sales. If you are considering investing in a MLM opportunity, evaluate whether you truly feel comfortable doing the following tasks:

■ Cold-calling prospects, and the accompanying rejection that will occur time and again

■ Making sales presentations

■ Following up with customers by phone

■ Recruiting potential new salespeople

■ Keeping track of sales records and contact information

Another factor critical to your success is perseverance. Your willingness to stay committed to an MLM network will significantly improve your odds of success. Few people stay involved with an MLM network very long; if you are willing to work hard and take a long-term view, you will have the advantage over others who are expecting quick riches.

Just the facts

■ One of the major advantages of franchising—standard policies and procedures for every aspect of the business—may be too restrictive for some entrepreneurs.

■ Franchises provide a trademarked image and a method of operating, training, and management support that have resulted in extremely low failure rates.

Moneysaver
Protect your money by first going to the Better Business Bureau (www.bbb.org) for a reliability report. The Multilevel Marketing International Association, (714) 622-0300 or www.mlmia.com, can tell you if the company is a member in good standing. Also, the Federal Trade Commission (FTC), (202) 326-2222 or www.ftc.gov, has information on any complaints.

- Only consider joining an MLM network with a unique, superior product or service that has a history of success.
- To be successful in an MLM network, you must be willing to make a long-term commitment to the venture; the reputable companies are not get-rich-quick schemes.

GET THE SCOOP ON...
A company's true assets ▪ Paying as little as
possible ▪ Winning negotiating strategies ▪
Sealing the deal

Buying an Existing Business

Chapter 17

Although starting a company from scratch can be an extremely satisfying achievement, many would-be business owners are happy to buy the immediate cash flow and experience of an existing business. In doing so, they miss the trials and tribulations of the start-up struggle—not to mention the considerable time and money that are also required. The reality is that taking a business from start-up to profitability can take years—and many never reach it. Purchasing an existing company means that instead of starting at the bottom of the learning curve, you'll start at the middle and quickly progress, usually with the help of the previous owner.

The hardest part of buying a business is settling on a purchase price that satisfies both parties.

Pros and cons

There are four major advantages to buying an existing business, according to Gary Schine in *How to*

Unofficially...
According to ASI, approximately 50 percent of the businesses sold annually are food-related, 15 percent are retail businesses, 15 percent are service businesses, and the remaining 20 percent are in distribution, manufacturing, and construction.

Avoid 101 Small Business Mistakes, Myths, and Misconceptions:

- An existing customer base
- Established procedures
- A recognized name and reputation
- Easier financing

Other advantages to consider include:

- Existing inventory and equipment
- Experienced employees already on staff
- Training and mentoring that may be available from the seller
- Easier and more plentiful financing options

Whereas a true start-up has an unproven track record, unknown potential for financial gain, and relatively poor chance for long-term success (just look at the small number of companies still in existence after five years), an existing business available for sale has frequently already achieved success.

After being in business for a few years, a company has a sales history that can be shared with a potential buyer. And, most importantly, it has a financial history that can be a good indicator of future potential.

Of course, there are always downsides. The same track record that some buyers would pay dearly for can sometimes be a liability. A poor location, obsolete equipment, lackluster reputation, or ineffective marketing program can have a lasting impact on a new owner.

Just because a business has been operating one way doesn't mean that it's the right way or the most profitable. But few people without start-up experience would be able to recognize the signs of trouble.

One solution is to rely heavily on the expertise of advisers, such as a business broker, attorney, and accountant that you have retained. Of course, doing so can get expensive, but as expensive as starting from scratch? Probably not.

Where to find businesses for sale

With several hundred thousand businesses being sold each year, finding available companies will not be a problem. There are a number of sources of information regarding businesses currently on the market. These include:

- Newspaper classified ads.
- Trade journals and national magazines.
- Business owners in the industry you are targeting.
- Real estate agents.
- Suppliers to the industry you are interested in.
- Attorneys.
- Business brokers.

Business brokers can be a very useful resource for identifying potential local acquisition candidates. Remember, however, that these professionals have been retained to find a buyer, much like a Realtor is hired to match buyers and sellers of buildings. Your local yellow pages should have listings of several business brokers.

Make an appointment to sit down with the broker to discuss the type of business you are interested in and what he or she may currently have on the market. Be prepared to divulge

- Types of businesses you are interested in.
- Past employment experience that may be of use in a purchased business.

Watch Out!
If you try to identify acquisition candidates by telephone or direct mail, realize that you risk overpaying for the business. Since you are contacting businesses that are not currently for sale, the owner has little incentive to sell beyond obtaining a high sale price. Businesses already on the market are there because the owner is interested in selling and may be ready to make a deal.

- Past experience as an entrepreneur or business owner.

- Your timetable.

- Amount of funding available as a downpayment.

If you would consider moving to a new area for the right opportunity, you'll want to expand your search. Consider turning to the Internet for input. Some good sites to start with include:

- Business Resale Network—www.br-network. com

- *Inc.* Magazine—www.inc.com

- BizQuest—www.bizquest.com

- Business Broker Web—business-broker.com

- BizBuySell—www.bizbuysell.com

- SmallbizNet—www.lowe.org/smbiznet

- American Express Small Business Exchange— www6.americanexpress.com/smallbusiness

- Deloitte & Touche Online—www.dtonline.com

Negotiating a deal

As you consider putting an offer on an existing business, first put a value on the various aspects of the company:

Tangibles

- Existing profits/earnings from operations

- Customer lists and existing contracts

- Equipment

- Building (if owned) or lease

- Fixtures

- Inventory and supplier agreements

- Office supplies and materials

- Marketing literature

Unofficially...
Each year there are 750,000 new businesses started in the U.S., says business broker Jeff Jones, yet less than 15 percent survive beyond five years. On the other hand, approximately 200,000 existing businesses are acquired each year with over 75 percent continuing to be successful after five years.

- Patents and trademarks
- Mortgages, liabilities, and other debt

Intangibles

- Reputation
- Established policies and procedures
- Brand equity
- Proprietary processes and unprotected intellectual property

Next, you'll want to review the following pieces of information to get a complete picture of a company's health and potential:

- **Contracts and agreements.** These would include contracts with customers as well as with employees, suppliers, and/or distributors.

- **Legal documentation.** Carefully examine the articles of incorporation or DBA filings, trademark filings, patent applications, and copyrights, as well as any documents related to litigation.

- **Financials.** The past five years' tax returns, profit and loss statements, balance sheets, and cash flow statements should all be shared. Also ask about personal use of the business's assets, which can lower a company's reported earnings; it's not permitted, but some owners do it anyway. CPA-audited statements carry more weight, so ask if they have such documentation available. Make sure your accountant reviews all of the financial and accounting records, too.

- **Sales records.** Examine sales by month and by customer for at least three years. Pay particular attention to the percentage of sales accounted for by the largest customers; how diverse is the customer base and how stable?

Watch Out!
Although there is value in a business's established relationships with its customers, some relationships are more easily transferred to a new owner than others. You will lose a large percentage of personal service customers, for example, and keep a larger percentage of customers with product or service contracts.

Timesaver
During the nego-
tiating process,
as you agree on
terms of the
sale, confirm
everything by
way of a brief
letter. Not only
will this save
you time when it
comes to draw-
ing up the offer
to purchase, but
it avoids rehash-
ing issues later
that have already
been resolved.

▪ **Business plan.** The strongest businesses have a written plan that guides the company's operations. The business plan should include a marketing plan, which should be carefully evaluated. The financials in the plan should enable the buyer to reasonably project sales for the next three years.

▪ **Organizational chart.** Take a look at who's on the payroll, what they do, and what they are paid.

▪ **Insurance.** What level and type of insurance does the company carry? Find out if there are additional riders that should be in place for this type of business.

A business has different values to different people. Someone new to an industry will probably be willing to pay more for a company because of its established reputation and procedures than a competitor, who may only want the business for its earnings. To the neophyte entrepreneur, the business has several assets of interest; to the competitor, the earnings may be all that are of value.

There is no one way to value a business, and eventually it comes down to "How much do you want to pay now to own the revenue of the company in the future?" Obviously, the more potential you see for increasing sales or decreasing expenses in the current operations, the greater the value to you.

Some of the more common approaches to valuing a company include:

▪ **Balance Sheet Method**—this value is based simply on the value of the company's net assets. Book value is calculated by subtracting total liabilities from total assets. The advantage is that the numbers are easily available. Its drawbacks are that it isn't fair market value so much as a historical value.

- **Earnings multiplier**—by evaluating the sales of other companies in the same industry and working out a ratio of selling price to sales, a conversion figure is determined that is multiplied by gross sales or earnings.

- **Gross sales**—some manufacturing businesses simply go by the company's annual sales.

- **Profits**—especially in service businesses, where there are few hard assets, the company is only as good as its earnings.

One key concept to keep in mind as you try to determine a company's value to you, the potential buyer, is that the business should be able to support itself. If paying the former owner will reduce your profits to nothing for an extended period of time, carefully consider whether this is the best use of your money. You may be able to invest it in a mutual fund for 10 years and get a better return; investing in your own business should potentially yield higher returns. You should also be able to pay the former owner out of operating earnings and not have to go deeply in debt to make the deal happen. If the company can't support such payments, is it a viable enterprise for you? Only you and your advisers can decide for sure.

In business negotiations, agreeing on a purchase price is just the first stage to finalizing a deal. After settling on the total amount, you'll need to negotiate what will be paid and when; that is, how much will be paid as a downpayment, how much will be paid out over time, and how long is that pay-off period? Typically, the seller's objective is to receive as much as possible up front, with the remainder

Moneysaver
Some sellers will try to price the business according to its potential profitability under new ownership, warns Ira Nottonson in *The Secrets to Buying and Selling a Business*. However, the seller is really only entitled to a purchase price based on what he or she has done to build the business.

paid in short order; the buyer seeks the exact opposite scenario. Finding middle ground is where sales occur.

But agreeing on the terms of the sale is just the beginning of the transfer of ownership. After settling on purchase price and terms of the sale, a nonbinding letter of intent or offer to purchase is drawn up to that effect. At this point, either the buyer or seller can walk away.

With the offer to purchase submitted, the buyer has a limited period of time to conduct due diligence—the process of confirming the information supplied by the seller, such as by having the financials audited and intellectual property (patents, trade secrets, copyrights or trademark rights) verified. Once due diligence is completed, the sale is then confirmed—if everything is as the seller said it was—and a closing date set. The closing, just as in real estate transactions, is the date on which ownership officially transfers to the buyer. The last step in the process is writing a list of assumptions on which the buyer is completing the sale; if the representations made by the seller prove untrue, the buyer can renege on the deal.

The trouble with turnarounds

For some entrepreneurs, bringing a company back from the brink of bankruptcy is even more exciting than starting a new one. Implementing new procedures, initiatives, and programs to turn a company around can be very fulfilling. Unfortunately, turnarounds are tricky business.

Yes, you may be able to negotiate a low purchase price for a company in dire straits, but do you have the expertise and financial resources to fix all of its problems? While turnarounds have the potential for

> ❝
> There is a general misconception that only businesses in trouble are for sale. The truth is that unprofitable businesses are very difficult to sell. Most acquisitions involve profitable businesses where the owner is willing to sell due to retirement, ill health, partnership problems, family problems, burnout, desire to go into another profession, or undercapitalization.
> —Jeffrey D. Jones, ASA, CBA, CBI, president, Certified Appraisers, Inc. and chairman, Certified Business Brokers
> ❞

significant financial gain if their troubles are corrected, the investment necessary to bring them to that point may be more than starting over.

The fact is that there are well-funded turnaround specialists that buy up hurting businesses with the hopes of saving them and reselling them. Yet even these experts don't always make money on their acquisitions.

On the other hand, turnarounds can be immediately lucrative if there are liquid assets that can be quickly resold for more than the asking price. For example, if there is office equipment, furniture, or accounts receivables that are readily accessible, they can be sold off to yield a profit immediately. Of course, there is no business left after the assets have been disposed of, but there is the potential for profits.

Before you invest in an existing business, decide for yourself what your goals are, why an existing company is of greater value to you than starting from scratch, and what your criteria are for selecting a potential acquisition. With that information, you are in a stronger negotiating position with sellers because you know what you want.

Moneysaver
Don't pay full price for a company's accounts receivables if they are more than 90 days past due. Since the likelihood of collecting on them is reduced, ask the seller to guarantee them and charge back those that are uncollectible to the purchase price.

Just the facts

- Buying a business takes less time than starting from scratch and has the added advantage of having a track record.

- Unprofitable businesses are difficult to sell; most companies for sale are on the market because the owner needs to make lifestyle changes, not because of poor financial performance.

- There is no standard formula for valuing a business, nor is there a single selling price that is applicable to each buyer; a business has different values to different people.

- Even more important than purchase price to a seller is the size of the downpayment and the payment period; the seller wants more money now, while the buyer wants to pay as little as possible up front.

There's More to Life Than Work

PART VII

GET THE SCOOP ON...
Avoiding burnout ▪ Blending work and family ▪
The key to longevity in business ▪ Success on
your own terms

Balancing Your Life

A chieving a healthy balance between work, family, and community activities requires daily effort and constant vigilance. Differentiating between what you want or what others want for you—money, success, recognition, creative stimulation—and what you truly *need* to be happy can be complicated. Shifting the percentage of time you invest in the various aspects of your life is a gradual process that can only happen little by little; few people can afford to cut back on several areas of responsibility overnight.

Balance requires that the proportion of time spent on each area of your life reflects the value you place on it. When the time investment does not jibe with the value of the activity, we feel emotional, physical, and mental stress. The only solution is to better align the two.

So, if your highest priority is being available to your family, the amount of time you spend with family members should be greater than any other activity. If it isn't, that's a signal that you need to make some changes.

251

Those business owners who are the most successful—according to their standards and ours—are more well-rounded, balanced individuals. Work and business are not the center of their lives, simply one element. Making sure that your business doesn't become your sole focus is critical for your own long-term success and happiness. This is especially true if you start a home-based business. Your ability to set aside time that is just for work or just for family will be crucial to avoiding burnout and family misunderstandings.

Keeping a personal life

Our lives consist of many areas of responsibility, each of which provides a level of fulfillment and enjoyment. However, some require more energy and effort than they provide in positive results. Working 100 hours a week, for example, may provide a bigger paycheck, but if it's at the expense of everything else in your life, is it truly worth it? And if you yearn to invest more time in community work but can't because of professional commitments, your life is not as fulfilled and satisfying as it could be.

Making trade-offs between activities is the only way to do more of what you love and less of what you hate (or perhaps would simply prefer not to do). Surprisingly, those trade-offs are actually easier to make than you may realize.

Start by making a list of your daily and weekly responsibilities. Being aware of where your time goes is taking the first step towards being able to realign your activities so that they better reflect your priorities.

Timesaver
Want to know how balanced your life is? For a quick and easy assessment, complete the "Wheel of Life" exercise at the SBA's Online Women's Business Center (www.onlinewbc. org).

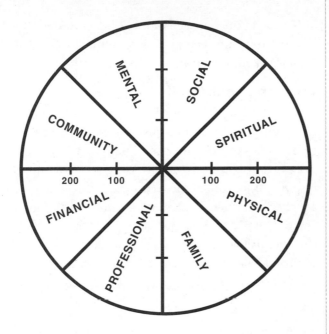

← Note!
Tools like the Wheel of Life can help you identify where your time is concentrated right now, and where you need to shift some attention.

The SBA defines eight major areas of our lives:

- **Financial**—All activities and feelings surrounding the earning and spending of money

- **Family**—Activities that involve spending time with family

- **Social**—Time spent with friends and colleagues

- **Spiritual**—Time spent reflecting on or praying to a higher power

- **Physical**—Activities focused on physical health and appearance

- **Professional**—Non-income-generating activities that impact a career

- **Community**—Time spent on improving the neighborhood or community

- **Mental**—Time spent in contemplation or relaxation

I know that in the final analysis, workaholics are not business successes. I try to create an environment in which people know that it's OK not to be a workaholic—in which they get ahead because of their contribution, not because of the number of hours they log. I let people know that balance is important—for them and for us.
—Patti Manuel, former president and COO, long distance division, Sprint Corp. as quoted in *Fast Company*
99

Investing time in each of these categories in proportion to their value to you is the ultimate measure of how balanced your life is.

Involving your family

If you're feeling that your life is already out of balance, fortunately, as the business owner, you can take action to remedy the situation. Consultant Robert Moskowitz advises, "Long-term, a good response is to work at the structural factors that create the imbalance: organizational policies, lifestyle choices, and day-to-day job activities. You can also shift the balance more toward your family by using tried-and-true time management techniques:

- Concentrating on top priority responsibilities
- Delegating
- Avoiding time-wasting meetings and phone calls
- Limiting out-of-town travel
- Making family events, activities, and responsibilities a top priority.

One way to bring family and financial aspects into harmony is to merge the two, or at least let them mingle. Involving spouses and children in the business can be a tremendous boost. You, the business owner, can connect with your family during business hours, as well as sharing with them how the company functions. Family members can gain satisfaction from contributing when needed, such as by helping out with odd chores. Allowing children to spend time at the business, participate in minor aspects, and learn about what Mom or Dad does during the day can significantly improve communication, not to mention strengthening the family bond.

Bright Idea
Use technology as much as possible to get work done and stay in touch in those in-between intervals. Cellular phones are great for catching up on phone calls, while e-mail helps reduce phone tag by communicating online during non-meeting hours. Personal digital assistants (PDAs) help keep appointments, to dos, and notes close-at-hand, so that you can take action from anywhere.

Of course, this does not mean you want to become overly reliant on family members who can pitch in from time-to-time. Teaching your children about what you do is very different from expecting them to be able to stuff envelopes each weekend. Or asking them to become your business receptionist. Don't overload your personal and family life with business activities.

Bringing work home doesn't qualify. Achieving balance calls for making a break from work in order to focus completely on the other aspects of your life. Simply relocating your work activities doesn't count as spending time away from the company. In Jane Applegate's *201 Great Ideas for Your Small Business*, Marcy Carsey, a successful television producer of shows like *Roseanne, Cybill, The Cosby Show, Third Rock from the Sun* and many others, is an admitted workaholic. Recognizing that she "needed the ability to balance my life", she "drop[s] work the minute I leave the office."

Learning to say no

Before you decide to invest your heart and soul, not to mention your life savings, in starting a business, decide what your definition of success is. What are you striving to achieve? Is it professional celebrity? Financial wealth? Growth of an organization you've created?

Setting goals will help you to prioritize all of the elements of your life and establish some boundaries. This in turn should show you where you need to place some limits on how you currently invest your time. By restructuring your priorities, you've developed a road map to finding balance in your life, and achieving balance is probably the most challenging and elusive goal of all.

Unofficially...
Seventy-four percent of women and 48 percent of men value the ability to work a flexible schedule. "Men still aren't making as many trade-offs as women," says Tara Levine, Catalyst's director of research and advisory services, but they are "indicating a need for companies to help them balance work and home." Source: Parenting Magazine Online, 1999

Susan Podziba, a public-policy mediator and mother of an eight-year-old girl, often worked late on weeknights and during weekends. She slowly came to realize that she didn't need to agree to every demand made of her. "Now I negotiate with clients for deadlines that won't require me to twist myself into a pretzel," she says in a recent *Parents Magazine* article. "I really needed to disconnect from the office and be with my family. Giving myself the right to do that was the best thing I ever did."

Part of the notion of placing limits on activities and responsibilities involves learning to choose between alternatives. Recognizing and accepting that you actually can't do everything begins to focus your attention on those activities that really matter. Instead of being restrictive, however, setting limits can be very freeing, say people who've tried it. Less actually is more.

Elaine St. James, author of *Simplify Your Life*, suggests limiting your workday. By scheduling her day to end an hour earlier, she immediately cut her workday by 10 percent. Later, she cut her workday by another hour and found that her productivity actually increased.

She also learned to say no to commitments that didn't match her priorities. St. James and her husband, Gibbs, developed a list of reasons for belonging to any organization. They then resigned from those organizations that did not jibe with the following three statements. They advise staying involved only when

1. Membership is a professional imperative.

2. You actually enjoy the meetings.

3. You're proud to be a member.

Although learning to say no is awkward at first, mastering this skill will begin to free up time you can then reallocate to other, more satisfying endeavors.

In addition to setting limits on the activities you participate in, you should also seriously evaluate what you want your business to look like as it grows. How large do you want it to become in five years? What about in 10 years? How many employees do you hope to have? How many product lines or service capabilities will you offer? And how many hours a week will you be working at that point?

Before you begin to build a company that fits someone else's definition of success, carefully consider how your business can support and enhance your life. Some business owners will only be satisfied if they create the next Microsoft, and they are willing to sacrifice the other categories of their life to achieve it. Other owners have no desire to manage a huge staff and intend to keep their companies small but profitable. Where are you on the business success continuum?

Delegating

To be a successful business owner, you'll need to adjust to the fact that you can't do it all yourself and still do everything well. Instead, most high achieving business people rely on specialists whom they retain to take care of pieces of their lives. These specialists may assist in managing some aspect of the business, or they may support management of the home, or they may ensure that community and civic responsibilities are handled. The point is that you can find people who will make it easier for you to achieve your goals. And they will prevent you from having a nervous breakdown along the way.

Bright Idea
Sometimes changing work hours can make a world of difference in productivity, enjoyment, and sanity. Night owls may benefit from starting work later in the morning, while early birds may want to consider starting and leaving earlier to take advantage of the hours when your mind is most alert. As the business owner, you have the power to make that decision.

Bright Idea
Establishing ritu-
als that rejuve-
nate your spirit
can help main-
tain balance in
your life. Make
regular fun dates
with family and
friends, such as
Friday night din-
ners out or
Saturday break-
fasts with the
girls, to give
yourself a
change of pace
and a fresh per-
spective on life.

Jennifer White, president of the JWC Group, a Cincinnati success coaching firm, and author of *Work Less, Make More*, points out in a recent *Home Office Magazine* article that "If you focus on what's important to you—regarding your business and your personal life—you'll get more pleasure out of and be more successful with both."

White calls her group of specialists her "support team" because they are supporting her to allow her to focus on her top priorities. She says, "If you spend 80 percent of your time focused on things you do well and enjoy, your business will be profitable . . . . When people stick to that ratio, they have no prob-lem integrating their home and personal lives with their businesses."

Look for ways to buy services that will free up your time for what really matters to you. Check ads in neighborhood newspapers or on community bul-letin boards to find out who is offering services that you might want to try. Ask friends for recommenda-tions, too. Teenagers or college students anxious to earn extra cash are performing many common around-the-house services. Consider these areas as you try to find what fits your lifestyle needs and bud-get:

- **Childcare services.** Some business owners retain part-time nannies, others pay for round-the-clock child assistance, while others rely on day-care providers.

- **Errand Service.** Hire someone to pick up dry cleaning, take the car for repair or inspection, go to the bank, wait in line for theater tickets, return library books and videos, at a cost of $12–$20 an hour.

- **Grocery Services.** Some supermarkets will deliver groceries that are ordered by phone, fax, or on the Internet, usually for an additional fee of $8–$13.

- **Meal Services.** If you get tired of pizza and Chinese deliveries, in some communities you can pay a service to bring a different ready-to-eat meal to your door each weeknight. A five-night dinner plan can be purchased for $30 per person, which is less than it would cost to eat out.

- **Home Organizers.** These folks help you make sense of unkempt closets, file drawers, storage spaces, basements, home offices, and kids' rooms. Prices range from $25 to more than $100 an hour. Some charge a fixed fee for a particular job. To find one, check the yellow pages or call the National Association of Professional Organizers at (512) 206-0151.

- **Cleaning Services.** Someone who comes to your home to help keep things at least sanitary can be a major friction reducer and timesaver, even if those visits are once a month.

If your budget won't allow you to purchase many services, you may be able to trade tasks. For example, you may find some senior citizen neighbors who'd be happy to have your children stay with them for an hour in exchange for a nominal amount of groceries. Don't overlook technology as a solution. Almost anything you can buy in a store, you can buy online.

- **Computer support.** When your computer begins acting up, do you have someone you can turn to immediately to straighten things out?

Unofficially... Locating child-care takes 10 hours away from work initially and an additional 10 hours each time an employee switches child-care providers, according to Families and Work Institute of New York City. In addition, 77 percent of women and 73 percent of men with children under 18 say they deal with family issues during work.

Computer downtime can be one of the most expensive and disruptive types of problems.

■ **Accountant.** As your business grows, you'll want to hand off management of your books to someone who specializes in accounting or bookkeeping. This doesn't mean that you'll turn over your check writing authority, just that you'll have someone ensure that payments are being deposited in a timely manner and bills are paid on time.

■ **Assistant.** Hiring someone to help manage your business or personal activities can be a lifesaver for many busy executives. Business assistants can handle scheduling, filing, phone calls, and more, while personal assistants can do your entire errand running.

Of course, the major benefit of delegating is the reduction of your workload. By relying on others to complete work that is your responsibility or that you need done in order to progress towards your goals, you also reduce the stress in your life. The more in control you feel about your daily activities, the more satisfying your work and your relationships will feel.

For those of you who can't see your way to delegating right now, at least try some of these stress reduction ideas. Writer Kristen Bruno provides the following five "quick fixes" on the Women's Wire Web site (www.womenswire.com):

■ **Breathe.** Deep-breathing exercises help to increase blood flow throughout your body, relax your muscles, and soothe your nerves. It also brings oxygen to the brain, so that you can think more clearly.

- **Treat your feet.** Foot massages can be one of the quickest ways to relax your entire body. Soaking your feet or having them massaged can significantly reduce your blood pressure.

- **Move.** Take a break during the day to move around the office, or around the block. Physical exercise helps relax you, not to mention burning unwanted calories.

- **Hydrate.** Drinking six to eight glasses of water throughout the day is also recommended, primarily to reduce any chance of dehydration, which can interfere with mental acuity. You can almost never drink too much water, suggests researchers.

- **Aromatherapy.** Scented candles or potpourri in your office can help keep your nerves calm under pressure by providing pleasant stimuli.

- **Pets.** Spending time petting a dog or cat is another form of relaxation therapy. Just having animals nearby can also help reduce stress.

Taking time for yourself can help reduce your stress, allow you to focus better on work, and keep your healthy for those you care about. If you're having trouble making a decision, get away from work for a bit to clear your mind; take a walk, read the paper, or go to the movies, for example. Getting away from the issue or problem for awhile will help you view it from a new perspective when you come back to it.

Set aside any feelings of guilt and make it a point to reward yourself; it will be the best investment you can make.

Just the facts

- Setting priorities is the key to achieving balance and the means to shifting how time is invested in the various areas of our lives.

- Redirecting activities to other people—hiring out services or trading services—can enable you to stay focused on your priorities and not get sidetracked by draining activities.

- Learning to set restrictions or to pull back from some activities is one sure way to realign your activities in pursuit of balance.

- Stay healthy mentally, physically, and emotionally by periodically setting aside private time for yourself.

- Taking advantage of technology to streamline activities is an easy and cheap way to add time to your day and reduce stress.

Glossary

accounts payable   Amount owed to suppliers for work performed. Also refers to a function within the accounting department responsible for paying bills from suppliers.

accounts receivable   Amount owed to a company from its customers.

accrual accounting method   The accounting method used by companies with significant inventory, which allows a product's production costs to be directly associated with any revenue derived from its sale.

advisory board   A group of consultants, advisors, mentors, and/or colleagues who provide a business owner with input and recommendations regarding business strategies. Unlike a board of directors, there is no fiduciary responsibility or liability; the owner has no obligation to carry out their suggestions.

alliance   An agreement between two or more organizations to collaborate on a project or series of projects, for the benefit of all involved. Unlike a merger, the partnership is temporary.

263

amortization Dividing an amount owed by the repayment time frame to determine the monthly payment amount.

angel investors Silent investors who fund start-ups without getting involved in the day-to-day management of the venture.

assets Anything of value that a company owns.

bid list Lists of potential suppliers maintained by corporations and government agencies.

bookkeeping Activities associated with accounting and financial management that involve tracking incoming and outgoing cash on a regular basis.

break-even analysis A financial tool that enables business owners to calculate how many units of their product or service must be sold before the business starts making a profit.

business plan A 40–50 page document used to determine the viability of a business concept. It is also used to persuade investors to finance the company.

buy/sell agreement An agreement reached between family members typically, where one partner agrees to buy out the other under certain circumstances.

cash flow The inflow and outflow of cash on a monthly basis. Also refers to a tracking document—a cash flow statement.

cash method of accounting The simpler accounting method, cash basis reports all cash received in a tax year, as well as all cash paid for expenses.

certification The process that minority-owned, women-owned, and disadvantaged businesses can apply for, enabling them to qualify for corporate and government business.

copyright The mark and record of ownership of a creative product, such as fine art, music, or a book.

corporate culture The personality and atmosphere evident within a company that often comes to define the business' image.

cost-plus pricing A pricing strategy based solely on the cost to produce a product or service, plus an industry standard profit percentage.

debt A type of financing in which the business receives a loan—often in the form of a mortgage, line of credit, or note—which must be repaid by the company within a set period of time.

depreciation The accounting procedure by which the value of a piece of property, plant, or equipment is reduced according to its expected life.

doing business as (DBA) A form completed registering a business under an assumed name, rather than the given name of the business owner. Not needed if the business name is the same as the individual owner's name.

downline The group of people in a multilevel marketing participant's organization that contribute to his or her earnings. A downline is everyone below you.

e-commerce Using the Internet as a company's sole means of marketing and distributing its products and services.

economic development zone (EDZ) Special geographic areas within a city that are targeted for business investment. Companies willing to relocate in such areas can potentially benefit from tax incentives, low-interest financing, and grants.

electronic data interchange (EDI) The process of sharing information electronically, rather than in hardcopy form. Government agencies are increasingly requiring their suppliers to be EDI capable—that is, that they are able to process work and payments without the use of paper.

equity   A type of financing that does not need to be repaid; the investor buys an ownership interest in the company in return for the potential gain if the company succeeds.

equivalent ad value   A means of valuing editorial coverage that entails calculating what it would have cost to purchase the same amount of space as an advertisement.

errors and omissions   A type of insurance purchased to guard against the possibility of inadvertently—rather than negligently—omitting key pieces of information when advising a client.

factoring   A cash flow tool where a company sells its accounts receivables at a discount in return for cash now; an expensive means of financing a business.

Federal Trade Commission (FTC)   This government agency is responsible for monitoring the activities of U.S. franchise operations.

Federal Unemployment Tax Act (FUTA)   Tax paid to the government equal to 8 percent of the first $7,000 earned each year.

fixed cost   All costs associated with running a business or producing a product that do not vary with the quantity produced.

franchise   The right to use a company's name, brand, trademark, and processes for a specified period of time, in return for an up-front and ongoing payment.

general contractor   The company primarily responsible for the completion of a project or contract. The general contractor frequently pulls in other vendors to help out; these are considered subcontractors.

gross lease   The landlord or building owner pays all operating costs. The lessee pays just for the space being rented. These leases are generally much more desirable.

incubator   Commercial office space made available to start-up businesses at a below-market rate in order to foster entrepreneurism.

independent contractor   An individual free to work for a business or businesses on an as-needed basis. The lack of an ongoing work relationship excludes these workers from employee status.

intellectual property   A company's information assets.

liabilities   The total amount owed by a company for what it owns.

limited liability company (LLC)   A type of legal structure available to a business that shields the owners from legal liability while providing more operating flexibility than a corporation.

line of credit   Debt financing that allows a company to draw against an available pool of money as needed; revolving debt.

logo   A symbol or mark that represents a business or its products and services.

margin   The percentage difference between the retail and wholesale price, divided by the wholesale price.

market-based pricing   A pricing strategy that takes into account what the market players are currently charging as well as how the company wants to be positioned against its competition.

mentor   An experienced business adviser willing to share information on a regular basis.

merchant account   The ability of a business to process credit card transactions for its customers, with the proceeds being deposited into this type of bank account.

mezzanine financing A type of second-stage financing secured to enable a company to significantly expand.

mission statement A brief write-up expressing what a company stands for, is striving for, or aims to be.

multilevel marketing (MLM) A type of business opportunity in which an individual both sells a company's products or services and recruits new participants to join their sales organization.

network marketing See *multilevel marketing*.

nondisclosure agreement A statement signed that indicates the signer will not reveal information regarding their client or contact.

outsourcing The practice of assigning responsibility for a particular task or function to someone other than an employee.

patent Government-issued protection against copies of an invention for a period of 17 years.

perceived-value pricing A pricing strategy based on what the market will bear. This is typically an opportunity to significantly increase prices temporarily during a sudden demand surge.

price point The price at which a certain category of products are sold. For example, cereals above a $4.00 price point don't sell as well as those below $3.00.

procurement center representative (PCR) Government employee responsible for assisting small business owners in winning government bids.

Professional Employer Organization (PEO) Leasing companies that will hire your employees and lease them back to you, taking responsibility for paying their wages, tax withholding, and benefits in return for a monthly fee.

profit The amount of money left over after the cost of producing a product or service is deducted from the selling price.

public relations A marketing tool that involves communicating with a company's customers, employees, shareholders, etc., through special events, publications, and the media.

publicity A form of public relations that uses the media to communicate a company's news to the community at large.

request for proposal (RFP) A bid opportunity issued by a government agency or corporation that requires a written proposal in response.

royalty fees Fees paid by franchisees to the franchisor based on gross sales.

small business innovation research (SBIR) grant Government grants awarded to encourage research and development activities within U.S. businesses.

serif font A typeface that has extra nubs on each letter, making it easier for the eye to read. The opposite of sans serif.

slogan A brief sentence that summarizes what a company does, its product benefits, or a reason to do business with the organization.

small office/home office (SOHO) A market category consisting of smaller businesses and home-based professionals.

sole proprietorship A legal business structure in which there is one owner. All sales and expenses are processed as personal income and expenses for tax purposes.

subcontractors Companies retained by a general contractor to assist in the completion of a large corporate or government project.

substitute products Products and services currently being used in place of the product in question; the U.S. Postal Service was a substitute product for fax transmissions before the technology was adopted.

SWOT analysis A business tool in which a company's strengths, weaknesses, opportunities, and threats are evaluated.

trademark Legal record of a company's right to use a particular mark or brand for a specified period of time.

triple net lease All operating costs are borne by the lessee (the business renting the space). These include property taxes, electricity, heat, maintenance fees, and repairs.

UFOC Uniform Offering Circular; a franchise prospectus document required of franchisors. Franchisees must be provided with this offering document following the first official meeting with a franchisor.

undercapitalized Not enough money.

variable cost The costs associated with a business that vary as production of goods or services increases; electricity would be one example of a variable cost.

variance A request made of a zoning board to allow an exception to be made to standard zoning laws.

venture capitalist (VC) An individual or firm that makes money by investing it in high growth companies for a period of 3–5 years with the expectation of at least doubling the investment during that time.

white space The area on a printed piece of paper where there is no copy.

withholding The amount set aside for federal income taxes at each pay period.

workers compensation Insurance required by law to be made available to any employee who injures him or herself on the job.

working capital Money used within a company to fund its everyday activities.

List of Businesses to Start

Contacts/resources

American Association of Minority Businesses
222 S. Church Street, Suite 220
Charlotte, NC 20202
(704) 376-2262
www.website1.com/aamb

American Subcontractors Association
1004 Duke Street
Alexandria, VA 22314-3588
(703) 684-3450
www.ASAonline.com

American Women's Economic Development Corp.
(NYC)
71 Vanderbilt Avenue, Suite 320
New York, NY 10169
(212) 692-9100

Business Information Centers (BICs)

For information about the BIC closest to you, call (202) 206-6665. New ones are opening monthly. Existing centers are located in the following cities:

Albany, NY	(518) 446-1118
Baltimore, MD	(410) 605-0990
Boise, ID	(208) 334-9077
Boston, MA	(617) 565-5615
Charleston, SC	(803) 853-3900
Charlotte, NC	(704) 344-9797
Chicago, IL	(312) 353-1825
Chiloquin, OR	(541) 783-2219
Chula Vista, CA	(619) 482-6375
Denver, CO	(303) 844-3986
El Paso, TX	(915) 534-0531
Fairmont, WV	(304) 366-2577
Ft. Worth, TX	(817) 871-6001
Grand Ronde, OR	(541) 879-2478
Helena, MT	(406) 441-1081
Honolulu, HI	(808) 522-8131
Houston, TX	(713) 845-2422
Kansas City, MO	(816) 374-6675
Lewiston, ME	(207) 782-5355
Los Angeles, CA	(213) 251-7253
Nashville, TN	(615) 749-4000
Newark, NJ	(201) 645-6049
Oklahoma City, OK	(405) 232-1968
Omaha, NE	(402) 221-3606
Providence, RI	(401) 528-4688

Randolph Center, VT	(802) 828-4518
St. Louis, MO	(314) 854-6861
Salt Lake City, UT	(801) 364-1331
San Diego, CA	(619) 557-7252
Seattle, WA	(206) 553-7311
Spokane, WA	(541) 353-2630
Warm Springs, OR	(541) 553-3592
Washington, DC	(202) 606-4000, ext. 266
Wilmington, DE	(302) 831-1555

Chambers of Commerce

International Franchise Association
1350 New York Avenue, NW, Suite 900
Washington, DC 20005-4709
(202) 628-8000
www.franchise.org

Minority Business Development Agency
14th Street & Constitution Avenue, NW, Room
    H6708
Washington, DC 20230
(202) 482-5061
www.mbda.gov

Minority Business Development Centers (MBDCs)

For the location of the MBDC nearest you, contact the headquarters office at:

Minority Business Development Agency
Department of Commerce
14th and Constitution Ave., NW.
Washington, DC 20230
(202) 482-3237

Minority Business Information Centers
15 West 39th Street, 9th Floor
New York, NY 10018
(212) 730-6390
e-mail: nmsdc1@aol.com

National Association of Purchasing Management
2055 E. Centennial Circle
P.O. Box 22160
Tempe, AZ 85285
(602) 752-6276
www.napm.org

National Business Incubation Association
20 E. Circle Drive, Suite 190
Athens, OH 45701
(740) 593-4331
www.nbia.org

National Federation of Independent Business
1121 L Street, Suite 1000
Sacramento, CA 95814
(916) 448-9904

National Minority Supplier Development Council
15 W. 39th Street, 9th Floor
New York, NY 10018
(212) 944-2430
e-mail: nmsdc1@aol.com

National Small Business United
1155 15th Street, NW, Suite 710
Washington, DC 20005
(202) 293-8830

One-Stop Capital Shops (OSCSs)
Visit the SBA's Web site at www.sba.gov/services, where you can search the databases of national OSCSs to find the one nearest you.

Service Corps of Retired Executives (SCORE)

Visit the SCORE Web site at www.score.org to locate the office nearest you, or to receive free online counseling.

Small Business—www.burnabybc.bc.ca/busresor. htm—provides a listing of comprehensive business sites to those who are just starting a business or in some phase of growth.

Small Business Administration
409 3rd Street, SW
Washington, DC 20416
www.sbaonline.sba.gov

Small Business Development Centers (SBDCs)
www.sbditc.org/

State Economic Development Agencies
Check the blue pages of your phone book to locate your state's economic development agency.

U.S. Business Advisor (www.business.gov)

U.S. Small Business Administration
409 3rd St. S.W.
Washington, D.C. 20416
(800) U-ASK-SBA
www.sba.gov

SBA Online (www.sba.gov)

Office of Women's Business Ownership
(www.sba.gov\womeninbusiness)

U.S. Export Assistance Centers (USEACs)

Atlanta
Ray Gibeau
(404) 657-1961

Int'l Trade Specialist
U.S. Export Assistance Center
(404) 657-1900

OFFICE
285 Peachtree Center Avenue, Suite 213
Atlanta, GA 30303
e-mail: Raymond.Gibeau@sba.gov
Territory: Kentucky, Tennessee, Georgia, Alabama

Baltimore
Patrick Tunison
(410) 962-4582
Deborah Conrad
(410) 962-4581

Int'l Trade Specialists
U.S. Export Assistance Center
(410) 962-4539

OFFICE
World Trade Center
401 East Pratt Street, Suite 2432
Baltimore, MD 21202
e-mail: Patrick.Tunison@mail.doc.gov
e-mail: dconrad@mail.doc.gov
Territory: Maryland, Virginia, West Virginia

Boston
John Joyce
(617) 424-5953
Int'l Trade Specialist
U.S. Export Assistance Center
(617) 424-5990

OFFICE
World Trade Center, Suite 307
Boston, MA 02210
e-mail: John.Joyce@mail.doc.gov
Territory: Maine, Vermont, New Hampshire,
Massachusetts, Connecticut, Rhode Island

Charlotte
Dan Holt
(704) 344-6561
Int'l Trade Specialist
U.S. Export Assistance Center
(704) 344-6563

OFFICE
521 East Morehead Street, Suite 435
Charlotte, NC 28202
e-mail: Daniel.Holt@sba.gov
Territory: North Carolina, South Carolina

Chicago
Paul Kirwin
(312) 353-8059
Jack Nevell
(312) 353-8065
Int'l Trade Specialists
U.S. Export Assistance Center
(312) 353-8040

OFFICE
Xerox Center
55 West Monroe Street, Suite 2440
Chicago, IL 60603
e-mail: Paul.Kirwin@sba.gov
e-mail: John.Nevell@sba.gov
Territory: Wisconsin, Illinois, Indiana

Cleveland
Patrick Hayes
(216) 522-4731
Int'l Trade Specialist
U.S. Export Assistance Center
(216) 522-4180

OFFICE

600 Superior Avenue East, Suite 700

Cleveland, OH 44114-2650

e-mail: PKHayes@sba.gov

Territory: Ohio, Western New York, Western
Pennsylvania

Dallas

Rick Schulze

(214) 767-0533

Int'l Trade Specialist

U.S. Export Assistance Center

(214) 767-0543

OFFICE

World Trade Center

2050 North Stemmon Freeway, Suite 170

P.O. Box 420069

Dallas, TX 75342-0069

e-mail: Richard.Schulze@sba.gov

Territory: Oklahoma, Texas

Denver

Dennis Chrisbaum

(303) 844-5652

Int'l Trade Specialist

U.S. Export Assistance Center

(303) 844-6622

OFFICE

1625 Broadway Avenue, Suite 860

Denver, CO 80202

e-mail: Dennis.Chrisbaum@sba.gov

Territory: Wyoming, Utah, Colorado, North
Dakota, New Mexico

Detroit

John O'Gara

(313) 226-3670

Int'l Trade Specialist

U.S. Export Assistance Center

(313) 226-3650

OFFICE

211 West Fort Street, Suite 2220

Detroit, MI 48226

e-mail: John.Ogara@sba.gov

Territory: Michigan

Long Beach

(562) 980-4557

Joe Sachs

Director

(562) 980-4550

OFFICE

U.S. Export Assistance Center

One World Trade Center, Suite 1670

Long Beach, CA 90831

e-mail: Joseph.Sachs@sba.gov

Territory: Southern California, Nevada, Arizona, Hawaii

Miami

U.S. Export Assistance Center

(404) 526-7425

OFFICE

Trade Port Building

5600 NW 36th Street, Suite 617

Miami, FL 33159-0570

Territory: Florida

Minneapolis
Nancy Libersky
(612) 348-1642
Int'l Trade Specialist
U.S. Export Assistance Center
(612) 348-1638

OFFICE
Plaza VII Tower
45 South Seventh Street, Suite 2240
Minneapolis, MN 55402
Nancy.Libersky@sba.gov
Territory: Minnesota

New Orleans
Delta U.S. Export Assistance Center
(504) 589-6702

OFFICE
One Canal Place
365 Canal Street, Suite 2150
New Orleans, LA 70130
Territory: Arkansas, Louisiana, Mississippi

New York
Herbert Austin
(212) 466-2958
Int'l Trade Specialist
(212) 264-1356
U.S. Export Assistance Center
(212) 264-0600
6 World Trade Center, Suite 635
New York, NY 10048
e-mail: Herbert.Austin@sba.gov
Territory: Western New York, Northern New Jersey,
Puerto Rico

Philadelphia
Robert Elsas
(215) 597-6110
Int'l Trade Specialist
U.S. Export Assistance Center
(215) 597-6101

OFFICE
1 Independence Mall
615 Chestnut Street
Philadelphia, PA 19106
e-mail: Robert.Elsas@sba.gov
Territory: Eastern Pennsylvania, Southern New
Jersey

Portland
Inge McNeese
(503) 326-5498
Int'l Trade Specialist
U.S. Export Assistance Center
(503) 326-3001

OFFICE
121 SW Salmon Street, Suite 241
Portland, OR 97204
e-mail: inge.mcneese@sba.gov

San Jose
U.S. Export Assistance Center
(408) 271-7300

OFFICE
101 Park Center Drive, 10th Floor
San Jose, CA 95113
Territory: Northern California

Seattle
Pru Balatero
(206) 553-0051
Int'l Trade Specialist
U.S. Export Assistance Center
(206) 553-5615

OFFICE
Westin Building
2001 6th Avenue, Suite 650
Seattle, WA 98121
e-mail: Pru.Balatero@sba.gov
Territory: Northern Washington, Alaska, Northern Idaho

St. Louis
John Blum
(314) 425-3304, ext. 228
Int'l Trade Specialist
U.S. Export Assistance Center
(314) 425-3304

OFFICE
8182 Maryland Avenue, Suite 303
St. Louis, MO 63105
e-mail: John.Blum@sba.gov
Territory: South Dakota, Nebraska, Iowa, Kansas, Missouri

Women's Business Centers (WBCs)
(www.onlinewbc.org)

Home-based Business (www.smartbiz.com)

Home Office Association of America
(www.hoaa.com)

Businesses you can start for less than $1,000, $5,000, $10,000

Less than $1,000

Business/personal coach

Cleaning service

Credit counselor

Dog walker

Gift basket maker

Image consultant

Medical transcription

Personal fitness trainer

Personal shopper

Professional organizer

Restaurant delivery

Less than $5,000

Bookkeeping

Business broker

Business plan/grant writer

Computer repair

Consulting

Copywriting

Daycare provider

Financial planner

Information broker

Lawncare

Mediator

Public relations firm

Recruiter

Seminar promoter

Temporary help agency

Trainer

Writing and editing

Less than $10,000

Advertising agency

Courier

Graphic design

Secretarial support

Video production

Web site design

Important Documents

Appendix C

Business Plan Outline
Executive Summary

Write this section last, so you can give a good 1–2 page overview of the plan as a whole.

Industry Analysis

Assume the banker or investor reading this plan knows nothing about your industry and try and give them a mini-education in this section; what are the opportunities, what's going on in the market, who are the big players, how have they succeeded.

Market Analysis

After giving a macro view of your industry, talk specifically about what's happening in your geographic market. What are the opportunities, who is the competition, how can you differentiate yourself, how will you succeed, given market demands and trends.

Business Description

Describe your business, how long it's been in operation, what the legal structure is, who the owners are, what your short-term and long-term goals are, and why you need money now (is it for expansion, marketing equipment purchase, debt reduction?)

Competitive Advantage

In order to convince potential investors to put money in your business, you need to clearly explain how your business is better than the competition and why it will succeed.

Marketing Plan

Who are your current customers, who would you like to have as customers, why will they be interested in buying from you, what is your pricing strategy, how are you distributing your product, and how are you promoting your business.

Organization

After describing how your business operates, describe who is responsible for making it work. Write a brief paragraph about each of your top managers, detailing their expertise and background. Convince the investors that these are the people most capable of making your business a success. Include an organization chart and describe your plans for adding or subtracting staff members.

Operations

This section is most important in manufacturing operations, which have many different pieces of equipment and operations processes that need to be described. For service businesses, describe how your business is being run, what the departments are within the business, and how you will be able to expand (by hiring, buying equipment, moving location, outsourcing production, etc.)

Funding Needs

Explain the total amount of money needed and how it will be used, such as for marketing materials, working capital, hiring, equipment purchase, and why that is the right way to spend it.

Financial Statements

This is where the past three years' balance sheets and income statements should be placed. In addition, five years of projections should also be developed; balance sheets, income statements, and a 5-year cash flow with monthly projections for the first 3 years and quarterly projections thereafter.

Appendix

This section should be used for important reference information that need not appear in the body of the plan. For instance, a summary of a recent contract you won, a map of planned sites, resumé of key managers, or marketing literature.

© Marcia Layton Turner, Layton & Co., Inc. 1993.

A Sample Business Plan
Table of Contents

Company Description

Kundo, Inc., a Massachusetts based company, will operate Abonda, a single unit, medium-size restaurant serving healthy, contemporary style food. The restaurant will be located at 645 Deacon Street in Cambridge, Massachusetts.

Mission Statement

The company's goal is that of a multi-faceted success. Our first responsibility is to the financial well-being of the restaurant. We will meet this goal while trying to consider: 1) the effect of our products on the health and well-being of our customers (and our staff), 2) the impact that our business practices and choices will have on the environment, and 3) the high quality of attitude, fairness, understanding, and generosity between management, staff, customers, and vendors. Awareness of all these factors and the responsible actions that result will give our efforts a sense of purpose and meaning beyond our basic financial goals.

Development & Status

The company was incorporated in September of 1995 and elected sub-chapter S.

The founders are Jack Morton and Wilma Mason. Jack is the President and Wilma the Vice President. There are a total of 10,000 shares of common stock issued. Wilma and Jack each own 3,000 and the remainder are retained by the company for future distribution. In addition they have loaned the company $25,000 of their own money for research and start-up costs.

A suitable site for the first restaurant was found last month and lease negotiations are in the final stages. The location will be on Deacon Street, just outside Harvard Square and close to a dense population of the target market. When the lease is signed there will be three months of free rent for construction and in that time the balance of the start-up funds must be raised. With that phase completed, Abonda Restaurant can then open and the operations phase of the project can begin.

Future Plans

If the business is meeting its projections by month nine, we will start scouting for a second location and develop plans for the next unit. Our five-year goal is to have 3 restaurants in the greater Boston area with a combined annual profit of between $500,000 and $1,000,000.

Industry Analysis

Although the restaurant industry is very competitive, the lifestyle changes created by modern living continue to fuel its steady growth. More and more people have less time, resources, and ability to cook for themselves. Trends are very important and

Abonda is well positioned for the current interest in lighter, healthier foods at moderate to low prices.

The Restaurant Industry Today

The food service business is the third largest industry in the country. It accounts for over $240 billion annually in sales. The independent restaurant accounts for 15% of that total. The average American spends 15% of his/her income on meals away from home. This number has been increasing for the past seven years. In the past five years the restaurant industry has out-performed the national GNP by 40%. The reasons given by the Folkney Report (November 1994) are 1) lifestyle changes, 2) economic climate, and 3) increase of product variety.

There are 600 new restaurants opening every month and over 200 more needed to keep pace with increasing demand.

Future Trends & Strategic Opportunities

The predicated growth trend is very positive both in short- and long-term projections. Folkney states again that as modern living creates more demands, people will be compelled to eat more meals away from home. The DMR Industrial Report (April 1995) estimates this as high as 30% over the next five years.

In 1988 The National Restaurant Association released the Food service Industry 2000 report that forecasted how the industry might look in the year 2000. Some highlights from the panel's findings:

- "Consumers will spend a greater proportion of their food dollar away from home.
- Independent operators and entrepreneurs will be the main source of new restaurant concepts.

- Nutritional concerns will be critical at all types of foodservice operations, and food flavors will be important.

- Environmental concerns will receive increased attention."

Products & Related Services

Abonda Restaurant will be offering a menu of food and beverages with a distinctive image. There will be three ways to purchase these products: table service at the restaurant, take-out from the restaurant, and delivery to home or office.

The Menu

The Abonda menu (see appendices) is moderate sized, and moderate-low priced offering a collection of ethnic and American items with a common theme—healthy (low-fat, low cholesterol, natural ingredients), flavorful, and familiar. Our goal is to create the image of light satisfying and still nutritious food.

There has been an increased awareness of nutritional and health concerns in recent years and a growing market of people who now eat this style of cooking regularly.

Production

Food production and assembly will take place in the kitchen of the restaurant. Fresh vegetables, meat, and dairy products will be used to create most of the dishes from scratch. The chef will exercise strict standards of sanitation, quality production, and presentation or packaging over the kitchen and service staff.

Service

There will be three ways a customer can purchase food. They may sit down at one of the 54 seats in the dining room and get full service from a waitperson. A separate take-out counter will service those who wish to pick up their food. Most take-out food will be prepared to order with orders coming from either the telephone or fax. Delivery (an indirect form of take-out) will be available at certain times and to a limited area.

Future Opportunities

There is a market segment that prefers to eat this type of cooking at home although they do not have the time to cook. There are already caterers and even mail order companies that provide individuals and families with up to a month's supply of pre-prepared meals.

This opportunity will be researched and developed on a trial basis. If successful, it could become a major new source of income without creating the need for additional staff or production space.

The Target Market

The market for Abonda's products covers a large area of diverse and densely populated groups. Although it will be located in a downtown urban setting, it is an area where people travel to eat out and one that is also frequented by tourists. It is also an area known for and catering to the demographic group we are targeting.

Market Location & Customers

The Harvard Square area is one of the most desirable retail locations in New England. The Mass. Chamber of Commerce rates it as the third best retail market in the state. There are more than 400 businesses in a $1/4$ square mile area with average sales of $330 per square foot.

The customer base will come from 3 major segments:

- **Local population**—the city of Cambridge with a year-round population of 145,000 is centrally located in the Boston area and is within 15 minutes drive of 8 major suburbs.

- **Colleges and Universities**—Harvard alone has 6 different schools within walking distance of Deacon Street and a seasonal population of 22,000. In addition 5 more colleges near the square have large student bodies.

- **Tourism**—between hotels, motels, bed & breakfast rooms and inns, there are over 8,500 rooms available. Last year they were at 92% occupancy.

- **Local businesses**—The Cambridge Chamber of Commerce lists over 900 businesses with an average of 12 employees in the Harvard square area.

The food concept and product image of Abonda will attract 3 different customer profiles:

- **The student**—more and more young people have developed healthy eating habits. Some also go through a "health food phase" while in college.

- **The health conscious person of any age or sex**—this includes anyone on a restricted or prescribed diet or those who have committed to a healthy diet.

- **Curious and open-minded**—"if you try it, you will like it." Through marketing, publicity, and word-of-mouth, people will seek out a new experience and learn that nutritious food can be tasty, fun, convenient, and inexpensive.

Market Trends & The Future

The population and demographics of Harvard square have remained steady for the last 14 years. Tourism has increased 24% over the last 3 years and is predicted to keep growing. Local businesses are increasing at a rate of 18% yearly.

The idea of a health consciousness through nutritional awareness and dietary change has been slowly building for the last 7 years. The extensive government studies and new Food Guide Pyramid have given everyone a new definition of a balanced, healthy diet. This is not a fad but a true dietary trend backed by the scientific and medical community, the media, the government, and endorsed by the big food manufacturers. As the Foodservice 2000 report stated, this trend would be even more important by the turn of the century.

As people want to stay home more and cook less our strategy of delivering prepared meals on a weekly or monthly arrangement may be a widespread accepted new way of eating.

The Competition

There are over two dozen restaurants in the Harvard Square area that sell food at similar prices. Although this presents an obvious challenge in terms of market share, it also indicates the presence of a large, strong potential. The newest competitors have made their successful entry based on an innovative concept or novelty. Abonda will offer an innovative product in a familiar style at a competitive price. Our aggressive plans of take-out and delivery will also give us an advantage to create a good market share before the competition can adjust or similar concepts appear.

Competitor's Profile

Competing with Abonda for the target market are these categories of food providers:

- Independent table service restaurants of similar menu and price structure
- Chain
- Commercial foodservice companies serving students directly

Independent operators include Grendel's Den, Iako, Bombay Club, Iruna, and The Border Cafe. Most are ethnic based and will carry at least two similar menu items. Grendel's and Iruna are long-standing businesses while the others are fairly new. They all are doing very well.

The major chain restaurants are House of Blues, Chili's and Bertucci's. All are relatively new but well established and profitable. They have big resources of marketing and/or a specialty product or attraction (House of Blues is also a live music club). Ogden Foods and Cysco both service 24,000 Harvard students but their product is not appealing enough to prevent students from eating out 5 to 7 meals a week. In addition, there are two local catering companies that deliver prepared meals daily to offices.

Competitive Strategy

There are three major ways in which we will create an advantage over our competitors:

- product identity, quality, and novelty
- high employee motivation and good sales attitude
- innovative and aggressive service options

Abonda will be the only restaurant among all the competition, which focuses the entire menu on healthy, low-fat cooking. Each of the competitors offers at least one "healthy" selection on their menu. Grendel's Den even has an entire section called "On the Lighter Side" but in all cases they are always seen as alternatives to the main style being offered. The target market will perceive Abonda as the destination location for healthy, low-fat cooking.

Once they have tried the restaurant, their experience will be reinforced by friendly, efficient, knowledgeable service. Return and repeat business will be facilitated by accessible take-out and delivery options. At the time of this writing all of the competitors offered take-out but only two (Bertucci's & Chili's).

Marketing Plan & Sales Strategy
Market Penetration

Entry into the market should not be a problem. The store has high visibility with heavy foot traffic all day long. The local residents and students always support new restaurants and the tourists do not have fixed preferences. In addition, $10,000 has been budgeted for a pre-opening advertising and public relations campaign.

Marketing Strategy

Focusing on the unique aspect of the product theme (healthy, tasty foods) a mix of marketing vehicles will be created to convey our presence, our image, and our message.

- **Print media**—local newspapers, magazines and student publications
- **Broadcast media**—local programming and special interest shows
- **Hotel guides**—concierge relations, Chamber of Commerce brochures

- **Direct mail**—subscriber lists, offices for delivery
- **Misc.**—yellow pages, charity events

A public relations firm has been retained to create special events and solicit print and broadcast coverage, especially at the start-up.

The marketing effort will be split into 3 phases:

1 **Opening**—An advanced notice (press packet) sent out by the PR firm to all media and printed announcement ads in key places. Budget—$10,000

2 **Ongoing**—A flexible campaign (using the above media), assessed regularly for effectiveness. Budget—$10,000

3 **Point of sale**—A well-trained staff can increase the average check as well as enhancing the customer's overall experience. Word-of-mouth referral is very important in building a customer base.

Future plans and Strategic Opportunities

Catering to offices (even outside of our local area) may become a large part of gross sales. At that point a sales agent would be hired to directly market our products for daily delivery or catered functions.

Operations
Facilities & Offices

The restaurant at 645 Deacon Street is a 2400 Square foot space. It was formerly a restaurant and needs only minor structural modifications. The licenses and codes' issues are all in order. New equipment and dining room furnishings will be purchased and installed by the general contractor. Offices of the corporation are presently at Jack Morton's home but will be moved to the restaurant after opening.

Hours of Operation

The restaurant will be open for lunch and dinner 7 days a week. Service will begin at 11:00 AM and end at 11:00 PM. The restaurant will be closed Christmas, Thanksgiving, and the Fourth of July.

Employee Training & Education

Employees will be trained not only in their specific operational duties but also in the philosophy and applications of our concept. They will receive extensive information from the chef and be kept informed of the latest information on healthy eating.

Systems & Controls

A big emphasis is being placed on extensive research into the quality and integrity of our products. They will constantly be tested for our own high standards of freshness and purity. Food costs and inventory control will be handled by our computer system and checked daily by management.

Food Production

Most food will be prepared on the premises. The kitchen will be designed for high standards of sanitary efficiency and cleaned daily. Food will be made mostly to order and stored in large coolers in the basement.

Delivery & Catering

Food for delivery may be similar to take-out (prepared to order) or it may be prepared earlier and stocked. Catering will be treated as deliveries.

Management & Organization
Key Employees & Principals

Jack Morton, President. Jack Morton is also the owner and manager of Grains & Beans, a local natural food wholesaler and retail store. Since 1977 his company has created a high-profile mainstream image for natural foods. In 1992 Grains & Beans opened a small cafe within the retail store that became so popular and profitable, he decided to expand the concept into a full service restaurant.

Jack brings with him a track record of success in the natural foods industry. His management style is innovative and in keeping with the corporate style outlined in the mission statement.

Compensation & Incentives

Abonda will offer competitive wages and salaries to all employees with benefit packages available to key personnel only.

Board of Directors

An impressive board of directors has been assembled that represents some top professionals from the area. They will be a great asset to the development of the company.

Consultants & Professional Support Resources

At the present, no outside consults have been retained, excepting the design department at Best Equipment.

Management to be Added

We are presently searching for a general manager and executive chef. These key employees will be well chosen and given incentives for performance and growth.

Management Structure & Style

Jack Morton will be the President and Chief Operating Officer. The general manager and chef will report to him. The assistant manager and sous-chef will report to their respective managers, and all other employees will be subordinate to them.

Ownership

Jack Morton and the stockholders will retain ownership with the possibility of offering stock to key employees if deemed appropriate.

Long-Term Development & Exit Plan
Goals

Abonda is an innovative concept that targets a new, growing market. We assume that market will respond, and grow quickly in the next 5 years. Our goals are to create a reputation of quality, consistency and security (safety of food) that will make us the leader of a new style of dining.

Strategies

Our marketing efforts will be concentrated on take-out and delivery, the areas of most promising growth. As the market changes, new products may be added to maintain sales.

Milestones

After the restaurant opens, we will keep a close eye on sales and profit. If we are on target at the end of year 1, we will look to expand to a second unit.

Risk Evaluation

With any new venture, there is risk involved. The success of our project hinges on the strength and acceptance of a fairly new market. After year 1, we expect some copycat competition in the form of other independent units. Chain competition will be much later.

Exit Plan

Ideally, Abonda will expand to five units in the next 10 years. At that time, we will entertain the possibility of a buy-out by a larger restaurant concern or actively seek to sell to a new owner.

Financial Data & Projections

Go to Custom Modeling Packages for a set of sample (not from Abonda)

Appendices

Menus

Resumes and personal financial statements

Lease

Marketing materials

Press clippings

Budgets & schedules

Floor plan, artist rendering

Contracts

Market research study

* Business plan courtesy of virtualrestaurant.com

Brandywine Health Plans, Inc.
January, 1999

1.0—Executive Summary

Brandywine Health Plans, Inc. is a service company that will provide health plan administrative services to self-insured employers. The company will concentrate on employers with 50 to 500 employees. Many of these employers have current HMO, PPO, or major national insurance carrier health plans. While the majority of employers with 500 or more employees have at least some element of self-insurance incorporated into their health care programs, our target market is often ignored by the major national insurance companies. While more than 80% of companies with 500 or more employees are self-insured, the management of Brandywine Health Plans has identified that less than 25% of Philadelphia area companies with 50 to 500 employees have self-insured plans.

The market for self-insured and administrative services consist of those companies that are currently self-insured and companies that have other types of health plans that will be encouraged to shift to self-insurance. One factor in the transition to self-insurance is the availability of quality administrative and consultative services. Brandywine Health Plans, Inc. is led by experienced management and has formed a strategic alliance with Rockford Care Administrator, a wholly owned subsidiary of Blue Cross/Blue Shield of Delaware, for the purpose of providing first class benefits management services to its target market.

Brandywine Health Plans, Inc. will achieve revenue of more than $5 million in five years with a net profit after tax of $1.6 million. The company will turn profitable in year three with after-tax earnings of $560 thousand. As a marketing organization and service provider, margins will be extremely high with gross margins above 80% (less only sales incentive costs) and approaching 50% after all operating expenses, once market penetration has reached maturity.

The key to success for Brandywine Plans, Inc. will be the ability to attract the initial capital in order to successfully market its services in the metro Philadelphia area and in northern Pennsylvania. Adequate professional sales staffing is essential. The company must then expand a successful formula throughout Brandywine area markets. Cost control, particularly with regard to sales and marketing programs, will enable controlled expansion that is fully funded by internal cash flow.

Business Plan Highlights

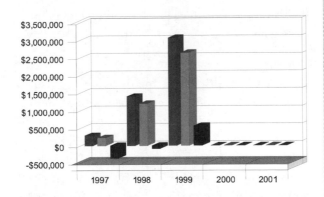

1.1—Objectives
The objectives for the company are:
1. To initiate co-operative marketing utilizing Rockford Care advertising executions with media in the Philadelphia metro market.

2. To hire sales staff both currently identified and unidentified to implement sales lead follow-up strategy.

3. To have at least 4,800 cumulative employees under management by the end of 1999.

4. To approach break-even by the end of year two (2000) holding total loss for the second year under $100 thousand while increasing market share.

5. To shift to earnings in year three (2001) and to accelerate gross margin contributions by building market maturity on top of infrastructure.

6. To expand regionally with both media and sales personnel to penetrate new markets while consolidating service capability.

7. To constantly achieve cost benefit through an expanding provider network while not compromising patient care.

8. To have more than 98,000 cumulative employees under management by the end of year five.

1.2—Mission

Brandywine Health Plans, Inc. is dedicated to providing small and mid-size employers with a comprehensive benefits administration program that will enable employers to control health benefits costs while allowing employees within the plan to have access to quality health care. By combining self-insurance with stop-loss programs and efficient plan administration Brandywine will provide to its clientele, both employers and employees, the best of health care with the minimum of restrictions and the broadest individual choice of providers. Brandywine will deliver a balance of quality care and freedom of choice at a fair price.

1.3—Keys to Success

The keys to success in this business are:

1. **Marketing.** Brandywine Health Plans will have the ability to sell both directly to employers and through independent insurance brokers and agents. It will be necessary to establish name recognition among more established programs. It is essential that media budgets be controlled and that closing ratios of at least 5% of leads per year be maintained.

2. **Product quality.** The services provided by Rockford Care Administrators are already state-of-the art among small-employer providers. The value added experience of the Brandywine Health Plans, Inc. management team and their provider networks will ensure customer satisfaction. It is a necessity that clients maintain satisfaction both with service and plan cost to minimize client erosion and to combat competition. Renewals should exceed 85% of established clients.

3. **Controlled growth.** Growth needs to be aggressive with rapid expansion to new geographic markets but also must focus on profitability. Each established market must mature as new markets develop so that growth can be internally funded. Cash flow management is essential. Both market expansion and media effectiveness must be constantly tested, and then reviewed or refined as required.

2.0—Company Summary

Brandywine Health Plans, Inc. is a service company founded by experienced medical insurance industry executives to both serve and capitalize upon the growing number of small and midsize companies that seek to control health benefits costs and manage risk by self-insurance.

The utilization of Rockford Care's existing services, products and infrastructure enables Brandywine to provide necessary service without incurring the costs of establishing proprietary programs. In addition, Rockford Care's existing provider networks enable Brandywine to serve employers with multiple locations or a widespread workforce.

Brandywine targets those employers who have from 50 to 500 employees. Services include all-encompassing benefit management programs. Rockford Care Administrators will be utilized to provide benefits management services including:

- A full array of managed care services
- Patient care management
- Local, regional, and national provider networks
- Tailored administrative services
- Flexible plan design
- Underwriting and actuarial services
- Comprehensive information management and data reporting
- Thorough stop-loss insurance administration

2.1—Company Ownership

Brandywine Health Plans, Inc. is a privately held Pennsylvania corporation. It is owned by its founders and managing partners: William Lewis, Joseph Kent, and Joyce Sutton, MD.

The company has been established with the founders' own capital. The founders have negotiated an exclusive strategic alliance with Rockford Care Administrators for certain markets in the state of Pennsylvania.

START-UP PLAN

Start-up Expenses

Legal	$0
Consultants	$12,500
Offering Expenses	$15,000
Other	$0
Total Start-up Expense	$27,500

Start-up Assets Needed

Cash Requirements	$256,000
Other Short-term Assets	$0
Total Short-term Assets	$256,000
Long-term Assets	$0
Total Assets	$256,000
Total Start-up Requirements:	$283,500
Left to finance:	$0

Start-up Funding Plan

Investment

Private Placement '96	$300,000
Other	$0
Other	$0
Total investment	$300,000

Short-term Liabilities

Unpaid Expenses	$0
Short-term Loans	$0
Interest-free Short-term Loans	$0
Subtotal Short-term Liabilities	$0
Long-term Liabilities	$0
Total Liabilities	$0
Loss at Start-up	($44,000)
Total Capital	$256,000
Total Capital and Liabilities	$256,000
Checkline	$0

The founders are now seeking to extend outside ownership interest for the first time in order to raise the funds required to execute the expansion plans of the business.

Start-Up Financing

2.3 Company Locations and Facilities

Brandywine Health Plans, Inc. currently occupies office space at 21 River Run, Suite 1100, Philadelphia, PA.

The phone number is (215) 123-4567 and the fax number is (215) 123-1234.

The current offices provide sufficient space to launch business in the Philadelphia and north Pennsylvania market. More space will be required as the Philadelphia market matures and central services are provided to other geographic markets. In addition, local sales offices will be required in other markets.

Increases in rental costs are included in the plan's pro forma as they are expected to be incurred.

3.0—Services

As health care in the United States has been changing rapidly over the past two decades, so has the way health care has been provided and how it is billed and paid. Large insurance companies and private physicians have given way to HMOs and Managed Care Plans and the TPA (Third Party Administrator) has been prospering. A TPA (like Rockford Care) exists to administer all the health care functions for a company that would have been handled by an insurance company. HMOs primarily contract for services based upon price, then re-sell those services to groups. Often, service and choice are less than satisfactory. But, most importantly, cost-effective concerns predominate. Employers are seeking to provide health care for employees at an affordable cost. A backlash has been the increase in self-insured programs administered by TPAs.

In short, a business now demands much more in the way of service and analysis than traditional support institutions have been providing to their clients. The claims processor is a case in point. Merely processing claims does nothing to help a business analyze and control its health benefits plan and to control the costs associated with the plan. And there has not traditionally been a measure for the "quality" of health care service.

Brandywine has compiled, through its own proprietary systems and an alliance of external providers, a service mix that includes Network Administration Services, Network Contracting Services, Policy Formation and Quality Assurance, and Marketing Services.

Health benefits are a fact of life for any business. The small and mid-size business is concerned with cost control and administration, just as in any other department of their business operations, except they are ill-equipped in personnel, know-how, and in systems, to administer health care internally.

Thus a full array of TPA self-insured services would include:

- Claims experience analysis and cost projections
- Plan design consulting
- Comprehensive plan analysis
- Provider network analysis
- Plan documentation
- Stop-loss brokerage and administration
- Prescription drug programs
- Vision benefits administration
- Dental benefits administration
- COBRA administration
- Short-term disability administration
- Worker's compensation services
- Custom tailored services

3.1—Competitive Comparison

Health plans for businesses and their employees comprise a multi-billion dollar industry that is highly competitive. Well known national insurance companies like Prudential, Cigna, Aetna/US Healthcare, and the regional Blue Cross and Blue Shield Companies seek the employer's dollar. A plenitude of HMOs, both regional and national, also compete. Many companies are already self-insured. Some of these companies use TPAs for outside claims processing while others use insurers or attempt to self-administer. Certain claims processors are also gravitating toward benefits management services.

Brandywine Health Plans believes that a niche exists that is both too small for concentrated coverage by large national companies and that is not well served with broad enough quality services by other TPAs. Most TPAs are still evolving toward the service mix that small and mid-size companies are demanding. By providing those quality services now, at a fair price, Brandywine believes a competitive sales advantage exists that will permit attainment of the market shares sought.

3.2—Sales Literature

Much of the sales materials and literature prepared by Rockford Care will be utilized by Brandywine. Advertising executions are included in a supplement to this plan. Direct mail pieces are being developed. A Rockford Care portfolio and videotape provides a professional presentation to prospective clients.

3.3—Sourcing

The Strategic Alliance with Rockford Care Administrators of Philadelphia, PA, provides the principal source of health plan administrative services. Brandywine will earn revenue both from enrollment sales as well as from cost advantages in the delivery of health care services.

From a product perspective, this relationship is analogous to the role of a regional dealer that sells services and brand name products within a licensed and protected geographic area. The dealer brings competence and value-added expertise to the enterprise while the source brings the credibility of brand name recognition and a substantial existing client base. This serves to reduce the risk normally associated with an early stage, unrecognized health services provider.

On the health care provider side, the sourcing of health care services is already in place from a variety of provider organizations. Brandywine management has had working relationships with Pennsylvania Baptist Health Care System, Tower Medical Group, Penn Health System, Columbia/HCA, Eastside Hospitals and other independent health care organizations.

The management of Brandywine Health Plans remains in ongoing negotiations with physician groups and hospitals to obtain the optimum mix of quality service and price for its clients. The health care providers are receptive both from the standpoint of pricing and freedom to control care. Both consumer and provider benefit from a cost/benefit mix that they find preferable to the insured HMO or Managed Care models. It is not anticipated that service sourcing will be a problem for Brandywine Health Plans. Rather, the key to success will be marketing to employers coupled with provider cost negotiation. Quality of care will not be compromised.

3.4—Future Products

Future services will include establishing both a geographic network of clients and health care providers throughout the Brandywine. As Brandywine Health Plans grows and expands it will begin to look less like a TPA and more like a Health Plan. As critical mass of clientele and medical providers is achieved, cost benefit is attained and administrative functions and services are consolidated in economies of scale. At that point of critical mass when approximately 50,000 cumulative employees are under managed care the option exists for Brandywine to develop its own proprietary heath plan. Many administrative services and functions that will be outsourced by Brandywine can be developed as internal company centers.

At that point options exist to finance the shift to a Health Plan company. Mezzanine, or Venture funding will be obtainable for a company with $5 million in revenue and $1.6 million in earnings (and no debt). After ramp-up to a $10 to $20 million dollar company an IPO is a potential. Also, the company would be an attractive target for acquisition.

4.0—Market Analysis Summary

The initial target market is the Philadelphia metro and north Pennsylvania market. The agreement with Rockford Care encompasses the following zip codes:

All three digits beginning with 199, 198, and 197.

This includes all of metro Philadelphia and surrounding counties in north Pennsylvania. At present Brandywine Health Plans holds the only strategic marketing alliance with Rockford Care in the entire Eastern United States. Both sides recognize and desire an expanded agreement after phase one goals and objectives are attained.

The critical data to establish potential customer base and market share is to sort employers within the region by number of employees, regardless of whether they are currently with an HMO, an outside insurance carrier, are self-insured, or have no insurance. All are potential clients of Brandywine Health Plans. The curve to attainment of critical mass is one of education, media, contact, and sales closure.

The market segment data is presented in the next section.

4.1—Market Segmentation

Within the targeted zip codes defined by the agreement with Rockford Care, the management of Brandywine Health Plans has identified 1,801 employers with 50 to 500 employees. Of these, 1,289

MARKET ANALYSIS

Potential Customers	Growth	1997	1998	1999	2000	2001	CAGR
Self-Insured	10%	446	491	540	594	653	10.00%
No Insurance	0%	66	66	66	66	66	0.00%
Carrier Identified	0%	1,289	1,289	1,289	1,289	1,289	0.00%
Other	0%	0	0	0	0	0	0.00%
Total	2.76%	1,801	1,846	1,895	1,949	2,008	2.76%

are known to have an identifiable insurance carrier, 446 are known to be self-insured, and 66 are known to have no insurance.

Brandywine has a clearly defined and identifiable market niche that enables highly targeted and efficient marketing of its services.

4.2—Industry Analysis

Together the national insurance carriers, HMOs, and PPOs account for 72% of the current market for employer-based health plan services. The majority of HMOs and PPOs have their own marketing and sales programs, which include company employed sales forces. National insurance companies may have company sales people or may utilize independent insurance agents. Both have strong media programs.

Neither, however, provide the mix of services that Brandywine Health Plans can provide. Nor can they provide the quality/cost ratio or the ancillary consultative and custom services of Brandywine combined with Rockford Care. Thus, Brandywine feels that this entire employer universe of 1,801 companies is vulnerable to penetration.

4.2.1—Industry Participants

Insurance carriers provide economic protection only. Such protection is at a high cost. Deductibles are increasing and the employer's ability to handle the cost burden of medical insurance coverage is diminishing. Compromises must be made in the extent of coverage, the size of the deductible, the medical services included, or often the employee is required to cover an ever-increasing percentage of the cost of his own plan as a payroll deduction. These are all unattractive options both for the employer and the individual client. The spiraling cost of health care is the culprit.

HMOs have gained substantial and significant market share over the past two decades. Their cumulative share of covered insured employees now exceeds the national commercial insurance carriers by a wide margin. However, these plans have been ruled primarily by cost containment strictures. Freedom of choice is severely limited—there is a perception that the quality of care is at an all-time low. Liability issues are beginning to surface based on compromised or neglected care due to cost parameters. Many service costs are not adequately covered under these plans and the provider base of physicians is extremely dissatisfied with compensation allowances. Many physicians complain that the freedom of decision is diminishing constantly from time and cost constraints that are imposed upon them. The ultimate client, the individual patient, is equally dissatisfied. Thus, the employer becomes dissatisfied as well.

The market niche for the quality TPA is ripe for picking. However, services must be of high quality. Many small TPAs are promising high levels of service but often don't deliver as promised because of the expense of building the internal resources required to compete effectively. Brandywine Health Plans, by virtue of its alliance with Rockford Care Administrators, already has the necessary resources in place.

4.2.2—Distribution Patterns

HMOs and Managed Care Companies are experienced and effective direct marketers. They employ media marketing and company sales forces to good effect. The primary problem they face is increasing dissatisfaction with their product. They will not be able to provide the multi-regional, customizable services that an increasing number of employers will demand. In addition, self-insurance is contrary to the buy-and-resell philosophy of these providers.

Many national insurance companies market through company sales forces and independent brokers and agents. Herein lies a potential barrier to entry into the small company market for an emerging TPA. Often the company has a pre-existing relationship with an insurance agent that may encompass a broader range of insurance services than health care. The company is, in fact, buying a "package" of varied insurance coverages that are necessary to business operation and also happen to include health care coverage. The task here is one of general education about the potential of self-insurance programs. If the insurance agent doesn't provide this alternative he stands to eventually lose the health insurance coverage. But his current "franchise" with his client can be a barrier.

It is the intention of Brandywine Health Plans both to market directly and to work through independent agents to reach their existing clients. A competitive agent compensation program is in place to accomplish this objective. It is the intention of the company to both work with independent agents who recognize the mutual value of cooperation or to sell in head-to-head competition with those who don't.

Ultimately, product, service, and price will prevail. All sales forecasts of the company recognize the time line of market penetration, and have realistic, if not conservative, market share goals.

4.2.3—Competition and Buying Patterns

Buying patterns vary by the size of the employer and according to his internal organization.

The company with 50 to 100 employers may have health care handled by the owner or a key executive. Often it is the responsibility of the Personnel Administrator as an individual (if that function is internal to the company). Also, Personnel Administration may be outsourced, but benefits may not. Sometimes an independent benefits brokerage firm handles all recommendations.

Larger companies from 200 to 500 employees may have Personnel Departments of several people. They might also employ a broker or a consultant.

Thus, it is imperative that Brandywine has flexible programs and sales and marketing efforts that are targeted to a diverse set of potential buying patterns.

It is worthy to note that customer buying patterns for health plan coverage tend to revolve around annual renewal dates. That's when competition intensifies from traditional providers. Brandywine will have an extremely significant marketing advantage since an employer may retain Brandywine for its proprietary service mix at any time. Brandywine can initiate service for a client by helping him analyze and administer his current plan. Often, such an engagement will progress to full service and to administration of self-insurance.

5.0—Strategy and Implementation Summary

With provider services already in place, the launching of sales and marketing strategies and implementation is the next task of Brandywine Health Plans. Executions include print media in targeted general business publications, direct mail programs, and sales contact follow-up.

In addition contacts and seminars directed at independent agents and benefit brokerage firms will be launched. Additional sales materials will be produced that are targeted specifically toward these intermediary "customers".

5.1—Marketing Strategy

Print media utilized will be the weekly *Philadelphia Business Journal.*

An extensive direct mail lead generation campaign will also be employed, targeted at employers, brokers, and consultants.

Both will be followed by direct sales contact by Brandywine's professional sales executives.

5.1.1—Pricing Strategy

Pricing for administrative services provided by Rockford Care is billed on a cost-per-employee basis.

Actual medical costs within self-insured programs will vary as a combination function of negotiated provider service costs coupled with the level of stop-loss (deductible) coverage.

Revenues to Brandywine Health Plans, Inc. are determined by sales commission formulas and also by cost advantages for medical services negotiated by Brandywine contracted care providers. Thus, if Brandywine provides medical service to the plan at a cost below the expected cost for the same service, differential revenue accrues to Brandywine.

In both cases there is a time lag to realization of revenue. Sales commissions are paid 30 to 60 days in arrears based upon collection from customers. Service cost revenues are based upon actual services utilized and are also paid 30 to 60 days in arrears. All revenue projections included in this plan are based upon these delayed collection premises while all expenses are treated as cash when incurred (even if paid on 30-day terms). Thus, all cash flow analyses will err on the conservative side.

According to the terms of the existing agreement with Rockford Care, Brandywine Health Plans will earn 25% of medical facility cost savings (as incurred) in years one and two and 17% in year three.

All services revenues generated by Brandywine for new clients produced for Rockford Care will be paid as sales commissions according to the formula contained in the agreement. (A copy of the agreement is available to investors).

The sales commissions are as follows:

- 11.2% of all fees in the first year of the sale.
- 2% of all fees in the second and third years.
- 5% of all fees in the fourth year and in each renewal year thereafter.
- Rockford Care administrative service costs average about $15 per month per employee covered.
- In addition, commissions on new stop-loss policies will average 15% in year one.

5.2—Sales Strategy

The sales strategy for Brandywine Health Plans is based upon concentrated targeted direct marketing with sales call follow-up. Closing ratios are estimated at only 5% of prospects to yield cumulative covered plan employees projected in the sales forecasts. Thus, higher closing ratios are potentially possible and would accelerate growth and revenue beyond the forecasts.

All forecasts are based upon per employee estimates. Dollar charges are based upon "A", "B", and

"C" size markets and the prevailing costs for medical care for those markets respectively. Back-up market data is too extensive to include in this plan.

Note: An "A" market is defined as metro Philadelphia. A "B" market is a population center over one million. A "C" market is any market below one million in population.

Annual projected revenues are illustrated in the chart below.

Monthly sales forecasts for the first year are included in the appendices.

Note: A total of 23 employer groups have already become active through Rockford Care as of November 1, 1996. Revenues based upon health care cost savings will show up in the beginning of 1997. Initial monthly revenues are based upon these employer groups, which represent approximately 1,500 employees (already 31% of the first year goal of 4,800 covered employees).

On an average annual basis, the revenue projections for health care savings revenue to Brandywine are based upon $7.40 per employee for 1997. This number is for "A" markets. "B" markets are estimated at $5.66, and "C" markets at $3.71 per employee. Rationale: Philadelphia is over-bedded and under-utilized, while in smaller markets the reverse is true.

Additional selling and retention fees are added to the above estimates to obtain total revenue numbers. In "A" markets, for example, this is set at $1.75 for new employees and at $0.75 for renewal/ retention fees.

5.2.1—Sales Forecast
The following sales forecasts are based upon the premises previously presented.

SALES FORECAST

Sales	1997	1998	1999
Sales	$288,599	$1,399,223	$3,067,966
Other	$0	$0	$0
Total Sales	$288,599	$1,399,223	$3,067,966

Direct Cost of Sales	1997	1998	1999
Sales	$57,000	$201,000	$427,500
Other	$0	$0	$0
Subtotal Cost of Sales	$57,000	$201,000	$427,500

Total Sales by Month in Year 1

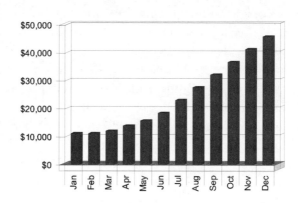

Sales

Management feels these forecasts are highly attainable.

5.3—Milestones

In addition to the primary strategic alliance with Rockford Care, Brandywine Health Plans, Inc. has already formed alliances on the health care provider network side which will provide cost advantages and thereby guaranteed revenue via Rockford Care on billed medical services.

The initial agreement with Columbia Health Care Systems will provide coverage to a substantial portion of metro Philadelphia. In addition, a second agreement is forthcoming with Independent Health Care Providers, which includes Crozer Chester Medical Center, and Wilmington Memorial Hospital System. Comprehensive availability for Philadelphia Metro will then be in place. 52% of available hospital beds will then be included. Cost savings are reflected in revenue projections on a per covered employee basis.

5.4—Milestones

Milestones already achieved:

- Founder "seed" funding of $200K to develop and research plan, secure strategic alliances, and establish initial infrastructure.

- Strategic alliances in place with Rockford Care and with Columbia Health Systems.

- 23 employer groups and 1500 employees already under managed care contracts.

- 52% of Philadelphia metro area available hospital beds under contract at acceptable cost discounts.

Upcoming milestones:

- Obtain $300K capital to staff and launch full sales and marketing executions.

- Present Rockford Care products and services to 50 of the largest employers in our target market by March 1, 1999.

- To reach stated first year goal of 4800 covered plan employees by January 1, 2000.

- To reach first year revenue goal of $288K by December 31, 1999.

- To attain break-even cash flow by the end of year two.

6.0—Management Summary

The founding management of Brandywine Health Plans has an accumulated 75 plus years of industry related experience. All are well versed in industry fundamentals, educated in the evolution of the health care services industry, and share a vision for the successful positioning of Brandywine Health Plans, Inc. within the industry.

6.1—Organizational Structure

The three founders will manage the company's growth jointly as managing partners.

All staff and sales and marketing personnel will report to them through a sales manager (heavy in industry experience) who has also been identified.

Future branch offices will each have a general manager.

6.2—Management Team

William Lewis, Managing Partner

Mr. Lewis has more than 25 years experience in sales and marketing management in employee benefits, securities, and real estate.

He has managed the marketing and sale of pension investment services for MetLife in their Western region and for CNA and Pacific Mutual nationally.

Mr. Lewis joined the MetLife HealthCare Network of Pennsylvania as Regional Director for managed care sales in 1992. He built the marketing, sales, and service organizations for the Pennsylvania network. Under his leadership, the network added 40,000 new, fully insured members over three years.

Mr. Lewis holds a BA from the University of Michigan and an MA from the University of North Carolina.

Joseph Kent, Managing Partner

Mr. Kent has more than 25 years of experience in the field of Employee Benefits. He began his career with Aetna Life and Casualty as a group insurance underwriter. As Project Team Leader in the Group Actuarial Department he developed procedures for the coordination of operations among departments within the Group Insurance Division.

He then spent 15 years with MetLife in the sale and servicing of large group accounts, support for regional sales staff, and budget administration.

Most recently, he was responsible for integration of capitated services with fee-for-service contracts, and the installation of risk pool arrangements for MetLife networks. He also was responsible for interfacing with corporate MIS.

Mr. Kent holds a BA from Harvard University.

Joyce Sutton, MD, Managing Partner

Dr. Sutton is a specialist in internal medicine with 25 years in practice who has been in leadership positions in managed care organizations since 1983. She has more than eight years experience in two major national insurance companies serving as Regional Medical Director and then as Vice President of Medical Affairs for Prudential in the Brandywine. She later became CEO of MetLife's Pennsylvania HMO. She has established herself as a well respected advisor/consultant within the managed care industry.

Dr. Sutton holds a BA from Wellesley College and a Doctor of Medicine from the University of Pennsylvania School of Medicine.

Charles McAllister, Sales Manager

Mr. McAllister is a sales management professional with a consistently outstanding record of production achievement in employee benefits and managed care sales. He worked first for US Healthcare in their Boston office and was subsequently recruited by John Hancock.

He later joined MetLife Group Benefits in their Tampa regional office and graduated from the MetLife Group Benefits Training Program. With MetLife Health Care, Mr. McAllister led all MetLife sales representatives in 1995 with more than $12 million in managed health care sales.

Mr. McAllister has a current extensive and active client base. He has completed all Health Insurance of America (HIAA) courses with honors. He is a member of the National Association of Health Underwriters, and the Philadelphia Association of Health Underwriters.

Mr. McAllister holds a BA from University of Maine.

6.3—Management Team Gaps

Two current gaps exist within the management team:

1. a Chief Financial Officer

2. a Business Development (Capitalization) Specialist

Both functions will be performed on a consultative basis in the first year of operations (1997). The CFO position can later be filled on a full-time basis, and capitalization will be handled by Investment Banking Relationships.

The interim positions will be staffed by:

John Handy, Interim CFO

Mr. Handy's last position was VP of Finance and Treasurer for Holiday Inn Worldwide headquartered in Philadelphia.

Mr. Handy holds a BA in Finance from The College of Wooster in Ohio and an MBA in Finance from Temple University in Philadelphia.

Mr. Handy is Senior Partner of Swarthmore Capital in suburban Philadelphia.

Timothy Dineen, Interim VP Corporate Development

Mr. Dineen is Principal and Founder of Leprechaun Capital. He is experienced in raising capital for both public and private companies in an advisory capacity.

Mr. Dineen holds a BA from the University of Notre Dame.

6.4—Personnel Plan

The following table illustrates the Personnel Plan for Brandywine Health Plans, Inc. Specific needs, compensation, and timing are indicated for each position. Future branch office staffing needs are lumped together as one line item.

6.5—Other Management Considerations

An advisory board of prominent managed health care professionals is already being assembled. These individuals are available for consultative assignment as well as Strategic Planning for Brandywine Health Plans, Inc. The preliminary advisory board includes:

Dr. Nancy W. Reed, MD, MBA—Dr. Reed is a former CEO of MetLife of Colorado and Utah with responsibility for HMO, POS, and

PERSONNEL PLAN

Personnel	1997	1998	1999
James J. Peters	$60,000	$60,000	$66,000
Joseph Kent	$60,000	$60,000	$66,000
Joyce Sutton	$60,000	$60,000	$66,000
Charles McAllister, Sales Mgr.	$64,992	$66,000	$66,000
Sales Executive	$42,000	$45,000	$48,000
Sales Executive	$42,000	$45,000	$48,000
Sales Executive	$10,500	$45,000	$48,000
Account Service Exec.	$36,000	$38,000	$40,000
Administrative Asst.	$30,000	$30,000	$32,000
Administrative Asst.	$6,000	$24,000	$25,000
VP Corp. Dev.	$18,000	$24,000	$30,000
CFO	$12,000	$60,000	$66,000
Branch Sales	$0	$200,000	$380,000
Other	$0	$0	$0
Other	$0	$0	$0
Total Payroll	$441,492	$757,000	$981,000
Total Headcount	0	0	0
Payroll Burden	$97,128	$166,540	$215,820
Total Payroll Expenditures	$538,620	$923,540	$1,196,820

PPO products. Her areas of expertise include outcomes management, reference standard benefits, and doctor/plan relationships.

Dr. Leslie Johnson, MD—Dr. Johnson is a psychiatrist who was formerly the National Director of Mental Health and Chemical Dependency Services at MetLife Health Care Management Corporation. Her special interest is in the integration of mental health and chemical dependency programs into health plans as a whole.

Dr. James Grant, MD—Dr. Grant has been Medical Director for a national managed care company with more than 200,000 HMO members and 1,250,000 PPO members. He has been a partner and director in a medical software and hardware company. He also advises Fortune 500 clients on issues pertaining to managed care, particularly preventative care and quality improvement.

7.0—Financial Plan

The financial plan for rapid, but controlled growth for Brandywine Health Plans, Inc. is presented in detail in the following sections.

Initial capitalization (after $300 thousand founder's seed funding) is pegged at $1 million (with cash streaming in from April through September). This capitalization is intended to grow a company with retained equity in excess of $3.35 million in year five.

The company will be debt free at that point (barring any interim management decisions to accelerate growth further). The company will also have significant IPO potential in the future and/or be an acquisition candidate in an industry that traditionally undergoes consolidation.

7.1—Important Assumptions

The financial assumptions upon which this plan is based are outlined in the following table:

GENERAL ASSUMPTIONS

	1997	1998	1999
Short-term Interest Rate %	8.00%	8.00%	8.00%
Long-term Interest Rate %	8.00%	8.00%	8.00%
Payment Days Estimator	**30**	**30**	**30**
Tax Rate %	33.00%	33.00%	33.00%
Expenses in Cash %	100.00%	100.00%	100.00%
Personnel Burden %	22.00%	22.00%	22.00%

7.2—Key Financial Indicators

Key financial indicators are increasing sales volume coupled with maintenance and improvement of margins. On-going cost control is paramount to success.

Benchmark Comparison

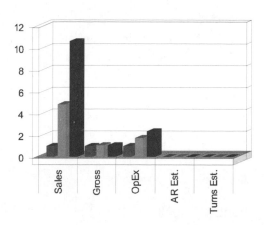

7.3—Break-Even Analysis

Break-even, based upon fixed initial market over-
heads, will be attained prior to the end of year two.

Cost control and market maturation will then
accelerate profitability which increases dispropor-
tionately as market development costs are offset
with a critical mass of baseline business in each new
market.

Break-Even Analysis	
Monthly Units Break-Even	73,259
Monthly Sales Break-Even	$73,259

Assumptions	
Average Per-Unit Revenue	$1.00
Average Per-Unit Variable Cost	$0.20
Estimated Monthly Fixed Cost	$58,608

Breakeven Analysis

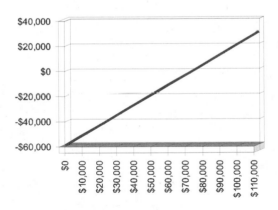

7.4—Projected Profit and Loss

Brandywine Health Plans, Inc. projects over-all profitability in year three. Profits after tax will exceed
$560K in year three and $1.6 million in year five
(shown in long-term plan in the appendix).

PROFIT AND LOSS (INCOME STATEMENT)

	1997	1998	1999
Sales	$288,599	$1,399,223	$3,067,966
Direct Cost of Sales	$57,000	$201,000	$427,500
Other	$0	$0	$0
	————	————	————
Total Cost of Sales	$57,000	$201,000	$427,500
Gross Margin	$231,599	$1,198,223	$2,640,466
Gross Margin %	80.25%	85.63%	86.07%
Operating expenses			
Advertising/Promotion	$90,000	$180,000	$300,000
Travel	$24,000	$48,000	$66,000
Miscellaneous	$30,000	$60,000	$90,000
Other	$0	$0	$0
Payroll Expense	$441,492	$757,000	$981,000
Payroll Burden	$97,128	$166,540	$215,820
Depreciation	$0	$0	$0
Leased Equipment	$0	$0	$0
Telephone/Utilities	$12,000	$24,000	$30,000
Insurance	$0	$0	$0
Rent	$30,000	$90,000	$120,000
Other	$0	$0	$0
Other	$0	$0	$0
Contract/Consultants	$36,000	$0	$0
	————	————	————
Total Operating Expenses	$760,620	$1,325,540	$1,802,820
Profit Before Interest and Taxes	($529,021)	($127,317)	$837,646
Interest Expense Short-term	$0	$0	$0
Interest Expense Long-term	$0	$0	$0
Taxes Incurred	($174,577)	($42,015)	$276,423
Net Profit	($354,444)	($85,302)	$561,223
Net Profit/Sales	-122.82%	-6.10%	18.29%

7.5—Projected Cash Flow

Cash flow is the most critical indicator of business success.

At no point does our business model run out of cash. Significant margin for error is included. Initial and second round investment is procured prior to need and allowing for potential time lag to close.

All future growth is based upon a debt-free internally funded model. Attainment of targeted sales revenues will ensure the accumulation of required cash to execute expansion plans as presented.

Plans can always be curtailed or postponed in the event of future sales shortfalls.

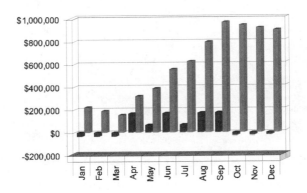

Cash Analysis

Cash Flow
Cash Balance

PRO-FORMA CASH FLOW

	1997	1998	1999
Net Profit	($354,444)	($85,302)	$561,223
Plus:			
Depreciation	$0	$0	$0
Change in Accounts Payable	$0	$0	$0
Current Borrowing (repayment)	$0	$0	$0
Increase (decrease) Other Liabilities	$0	$0	$0
Long-term Borrowing (repayment)	$0	$0	$0
Capital Input	$1,000,000	$0	$0
Subtotal	$645,556	($85,302)	$561,223
Less:	**1997**	**1998**	**1999**
Change in Other ST Assets	$0	$0	$0
Capital Expenditure	$0	$0	$0
Dividends	$0	$0	$0
Subtotal	$0	$0	$0
Net Cash Flow	$645,556	($85,302)	$561,223
Cash Balance	$901,556	$816,253	$1,377,476

7.6—Projected Balance Sheet

Projected Balance Sheets follow:

PRO-FORMA BALANCE SHEET

Assets

Short-term Assets	Starting Balances	1997	1998	1999
Cash	$256,000	$901,556	$816,253	$1,377,476
Other Short-term Assets	$0	$0	$0	$0
Total Short-term Assets	$256,000	$901,556	$816,253	$1,377,476

Long-term Assets

Capital Assets	$0	$0	$0	$0
Accumulated Depreciation	$0	$0	$0	$0
Total Long-term Assets	$0	$0	$0	$0
Total Assets	$256,000	$901,556	$816,253	$1,377,476

Liabilities and Capital

		1997	1998	1999
Accounts Payable	$0	$0	$0	$0
Short-term Notes	$0	$0	$0	$0
Other Short-term Liabilities	$0	$0	$0	$0
Subtotal Short-term Liabilities	$0	$0	$0	$0

Liabilities

Long-term Liabilities	$0	$0	$0	$0
Total Liabilities	$0	$0	$0	$0

Paid in Capital	$300,000	$1,300,000	$1,300,000	$1,300,000
Retained Earnings	($44,000)	($44,000)	($398,444)	($483,747)
Earnings		$0	($354,444)	($85,302)	$561,223
Total Capital	$256,000	$901,556	$816,253	$1,377,476
Total Liabilities and Capital	$256,000	$901,556	$816,253	$1,377,476
Net Worth	$256,000	$901,556	$816,253	$1,377,476

7.7—Business Ratios

These business ratios are only partially relevant as long as the business is able to remain debt free.

RATIO ANALYSIS

Profitability Ratios:	1997	1998	1999	RMA
Gross Margin	80.25%	85.63%	86.07%	0
Net Profit Margin	−122.82%	−6.10%	18.29%	0
Return on Assets	−39.31%	−10.45%	40.74%	0
Return on Equity	−39.31%	−10.45%	40.74%	0
Activity Ratios	**1997**	**1998**	**1999**	**RMA**
AR Turnover	0.00	0.00	0.00	0
Collection Days	0	0	0	0
Inventory Turnover	0.00	0.00	0.00	0
Accts Payable Turnover	0.00	0.00	0.00	0
Total Asset Turnover	0.32	1.71	2.23	0
Debt Ratios	**1997**	**1998**	**1999**	**RMA**
Debt to Net Worth	0.00	0.00	0.00	0
Short-term Liab. to Liab.	0.00	0.00	0.00	0
Liquidity Ratios	**1997**	**1998**	**1999**	**RMA**
Current Ratio	0.00	0.00	0.00	0
Quick Ratio	0.00	0.00	0.00	0
Net Working Capital	$901,556	$816,253	$1,377,476	0
Interest Coverage	0.00	0.00	0.00	0
Additional Ratios	**1997**	**1998**	**1999**	**RMA**
Assets to Sales	3.12	0.58	0.45	0
Debt/Assets	0%	0%	0%	0
Current Debt/ Total Assets	0%	0%	0%	0
Acid Test	0.00	0.00	0.00	0
Asset Turnover	0.32	1.71	2.23	0
Sales/Net Worth	0.32	1.71	2.23	0

Long-term plan	1997	1998	1999	2000	2001
Sales	$288,599	$1,399,223	$3,067,966	$0	$0
Cost of Sales	$57,000	$201,000	$427,500	$0	$0
Gross Margin	$231,599	$1,198,223	$2,640,466	$0	$0
Gross Margin %	80.25%	85.63%	86.07%	0.00%	0.00%
Operating Expenses	$760,620	$1,325,540	$1,802,820	$0	$0
Operating Income	($529,021)	($127,317)	$837,646	$0	$0
Net Income	($354,444)	($85,302)	$561,223	$0	$0
Short-term Assets	$901,556	$816,253	$1,377,476	$0	$0
Long-term Assets	$0	$0	$0	$0	$0
Short-term Liabilities	$0	$0	$0	$0	$0
Long-term Liabilities	$0	$0	$0	$0	$0
Equity	$901,556	$816,253	$1,377,476	$0	$0

7.8—Long-term Plan

Once again the long-term sales forecast is included here. Also included is the long-term forecast table. This is to illustrate that the company will, in fact, be a marketing company with excellent cash flow and profitability by year five, which will open a myriad of strategic potentials.

Not the least of these potentials is growth via becoming a full-service health plan. Premiums would then flow directly to Brandywine Health Plans, Inc. All that would be necessary is to capitalize government mandated reserve requirements. This could be done partially, if not wholly, with debt, thereby enhancing cash flows, investment incomes, and shareholder value.

The successful establishment of a marketing company creates the platform for all other strategic options.

Trinity Capital
Business plan strategic development by
Timothy J. Dineen
Consultant
Norcross, Pennsylvania
Phone: (770) 935-0480
Fax: (770) 935-1075
E-mail: lepcap@mindspring.com
Copyright Palo Alto Software, Inc. 1998

Sample Marketing Plan Outline

I. Executive Summary
(Write this section last and present a capsule of your findings.)

II. Marketing Objective
(Must be measurable, such as desired market share or percentage growth in sales.)

III. Market Position
A. Do I want to be a market leader, challenger, follower or establish a niche?
B. Who is my competition?
   1. *What are the major strengths/weaknesses of each competitor?*
   2. *What do I know about their product or service lines, location, price structure, advertising, suppliers?*
   3. *Are they planning to expand?*
   4. *What is the market share of each of my competitors?*
C. How many firms have exited this market recently? For what reason?
D. Can I compete with their pricing and make a profit?

IV. Target Market
Carefully define what your customer base will be, considering geographic, psychological, demographic and behavior characteristics.
A. How large is this market?
   1. *What is the geographic area to be served?*
   2. *What is the population?*
   3. *Is the population growing/declining?*
B. What are the demographics of the area?
   1. *Average family size?*
   2. *Age distribution?*
   3. *Per capita income?*
C. What do you know about consumer shopping and spending patterns in this area?

V. Market Strategy
A. Marketing Mix—present specific policies on:
   1. *Product*
   2. *Price*
   3. *Place*
   4. *Promotion*
B. Implementation
   1. *How will your marketing objectives be met?*
   2. *Who is responsible for each segment of the plan?*
C. Contingency Plans—If the marketing mix is not appropriate or effective, what alternatives exist?

VII. Budget

VIII. Review Process

Form W-4 (1999)

Purpose. Complete Form W-4 so your employer can withhold the correct Federal income tax from your pay. Because your tax situation may change, you may want to refigure your withholding each year.

Exemption from withholding. If you are exempt, complete only lines 1, 2, 3, 4, and 7, and sign the form to validate it. Your exemption for 1999 expires February 16, 2000.

Note: *You cannot claim exemption from withholding if (1) your income exceeds $700 and includes more than $250 of unearned income (e.g., interest and dividends) and (2) another person can claim you as a dependent on their tax return.*

Basic instructions. If you are not exempt, complete the Personal Allowances Worksheet. The worksheets on page 2 adjust your withholding allowances based on itemized deductions, adjustments to income, or two-earner/two-job situations. Complete all worksheets that apply. They will help you figure the number of withholding allowances you are entitled to claim. **However, you may claim fewer allowances.**

Child tax and higher education credits. For details on adjusting withholding for these and other credits, see **Pub. 919,** Is My Withholding Correct for 1999?

Head of household. Generally, you may claim head of household filing status on your tax return only if you are unmarried and pay more than 50% of the costs of keeping up a home for yourself and your dependent(s) or other qualifying individuals. See line E below.

Nonwage income. If you have a large amount of nonwage income, such as interest or dividends, you should consider making estimated tax payments using Form 1040-ES. Otherwise, you may owe additional tax.

Two earners/two jobs. If you have a working spouse or more than one job, figure the total number of allowances you are entitled to claim on all jobs using worksheets from only one Form W-4. Your withholding will usually be most accurate when all allowances are claimed on the Form W-4 prepared for the highest paying job and zero allowances are claimed for the others.

Check your withholding. After your Form W-4 takes effect, use Pub. 919 to see how the dollar amount you are having withheld compares to your estimated total annual tax. Get Pub. 919 especially if you used the Two-Earner/Two-Job Worksheet and your earnings exceed $150,000 (Single) or $200,000 (Married).

Recent name change? If your name on line 1 differs from that shown on your social security card, call 1-800-772-1213 for a new social security card.

Personal Allowances Worksheet

A Enter "1" for **yourself** if no one else can claim you as a dependent . . . . **A** _____

B Enter "1" if:
- You are single and have only one job; or
- You are married, have only one job, and your spouse does not work; or
- Your wages from a second job or your spouse's wages (or the total of both) are $1,000 or less.

. . **B** _____

C Enter "1" for your **spouse.** But, you may choose to enter -0- if you are married and have either a working spouse or more than one job. (This may help you avoid having too little tax withheld.) . . . . **C** _____

D Enter number of **dependents** (other than your spouse or yourself) you will claim on your tax return . . . . **D** _____

E Enter "1" if you will file as **head of household** on your tax return (see conditions under **Head of household** above) . **E** _____

F Enter "1" if you have at least $1,500 of **child or dependent care expenses** for which you plan to claim a credit . . **F** _____

G **Child Tax Credit:**
- If your total income will be between $20,000 and $50,000 ($23,000 and $63,000 if married), enter "1" for each eligible child.
- If your total income will be between $50,000 and $80,000 ($63,000 and $115,000 if married), enter "1" if you have two eligible children, enter "2" if you have three or four eligible children, or enter "3" if you have five or more eligible children . . **G** _____

H Add lines A through G and enter total here. **Note:** This amount may be different from the number of exemptions you claim on your return. ▶ **H** _____

For accuracy, complete all worksheets that apply.
- If you plan to **itemize or claim adjustments to income** and want to reduce your withholding, see the Deductions and Adjustments Worksheet on page 2.
- If you are **single**, have **more than one job** and your combined earnings from all jobs exceed $32,000, OR if you are **married** and have a **working spouse or more than one job** and the combined earnings from all jobs exceed $55,000, see the Two-Earner/Two-Job Worksheet on page 2 to avoid having too little tax withheld.
- If **neither** of the above situations applies, **stop here** and enter the number from line H on line 5 of Form W-4 below.

‑ ‑ ‑ ‑ ‑ **Cut here and give the certificate to your employer. Keep the top part for your records.** ‑ ‑ ‑ ‑ ‑

Form **W-4** Department of the Treasury Internal Revenue Service	**Employee's Withholding Allowance Certificate** ▶ **For Privacy Act and Paperwork Reduction Act Notice, see page 2.**	OMB No. 1545-0010 **1999**

1 Type or print your first name and middle initial   Last name | **2** Your social security number

Home address (number and street or rural route)

3 ☐ Single ☐ Married ☐ Married, but withhold at higher Single rate.
Note: *If married, but legally separated, or spouse is a nonresident alien, check the Single box.*

City or town, state, and ZIP code

4 If your last name differs from that on your social security card, check here. **You** must call 1-800-772-1213 for a new card . . . ▶ ☐

5 Total number of allowances you are claiming (from line H above or from the worksheets on page 2 if they apply) . | **5** _____

6 Additional amount, if any, you want withheld from each paycheck . . . . | **6** $ _____

7 I claim exemption from withholding for 1999, and I certify that I meet **BOTH** of the following conditions for exemption:
- Last year I had a right to a refund of **ALL** Federal income tax withheld because I had **NO** tax liability **AND**
- This year I expect a refund of **ALL** Federal income tax withheld because I expect to have **NO** tax liability.
If you meet both conditions, write "EXEMPT" here . . . . ▶ | **7** _____

Under penalties of perjury, I certify that I am entitled to the number of withholding allowances claimed on this certificate, or I am entitled to claim exempt status.
Employee's signature
(Form is not valid unless you sign it) ▶   **Date** ▶

8 Employer's name and address (Employer: Complete 8 and 10 only if sending to the IRS) | **9** Office code (optional) | **10** Employer identification number

Cat. No. 10220Q

Form W-4 (1999)   Page **2**

Deductions and Adjustments Worksheet

Note: *Use this worksheet only if you plan to itemize deductions or claim adjustments to income on your 1999 tax return.*

1   Enter an estimate of your 1999 itemized deductions. These include qualifying home mortgage interest, charitable contributions, state and local taxes (but not sales taxes), medical expenses in excess of 7.5% of your income, and miscellaneous deductions. (For 1999, you may have to reduce your itemized deductions if your income is over $126,600 ($63,300 if married filing separately). Get Pub. 919 for details.)   **1** $ _____

2   Enter: { $7,200 if married filing jointly or qualifying widow(er)
              $6,350 if head of household . . . .   **2** $ _____
              $4,300 if single
              $3,600 if married filing separately }

3   **Subtract** line 2 from line 1. If line 2 is greater than line 1, enter -0- . . . .   **3** $ _____

4   Enter an estimate of your 1999 adjustments to income, including alimony, deductible IRA contributions, and student loan interest . .   **4** $ _____

5   **Add** lines 3 and 4 and enter the total . . . .   **5** $ _____

6   Enter an estimate of your 1999 nonwage income (such as dividends or interest) . . . .   **6** $ _____

7   **Subtract** line 6 from line 5. Enter the result, but not less than -0- . . . .   **7** $ _____

8   **Divide** the amount on line 7 by $3,000 and enter the result here. Drop any fraction . . . . . .   **8**   _____

9   Enter the number from Personal Allowances Worksheet, line H, on page 1 . . . .   **9**   _____

10   **Add** lines 8 and 9 and enter the total here. If you plan to use the Two-Earner/Two-Job Worksheet, also enter this total on line 1 below. Otherwise, **stop here** and enter this total on Form W-4, line 5, on page 1 . . . .   **10**   _____

Two-Earner/Two-Job Worksheet

Note: *Use this worksheet only if the instructions for line H on page 1 direct you here.*

1   Enter the number from line H on page 1 (or from line 10 above if you used the Deductions and Adjustments Worksheet)   **1**   _____

2   Find the number in **Table 1** below that applies to the **LOWEST** paying job and enter it here . . . .   **2**   _____

3   If line 1 is **GREATER THAN OR EQUAL TO** line 2, subtract line 2 from line 1. Enter the result here (if zero, enter -0-) and on Form W-4, line 5, on page 1. **DO NOT** use the rest of this worksheet . . . .   **3**   _____

Note: *If line 1 is **LESS THAN** line 2, enter -0- on Form W-4, line 5, on page 1. Complete lines 4–9 to calculate the additional withholding amount necessary to avoid a year end tax bill.*

4   Enter the number from line 2 of this worksheet . . . .   **4**   _____

5   Enter the number from line 1 of this worksheet . . . .   **5**   _____

6   **Subtract** line 5 from line 4 . . . .   **6**   _____

7   Find the amount in **Table 2** below that applies to the **HIGHEST** paying job and enter it here . . . .   **7** $ _____

8   **Multiply** line 7 by line 6 and enter the result here. This is the additional annual withholding amount needed   **8** $ _____

9   Divide line 8 by the number of pay periods remaining in 1999. (For example, divide by 26 if you are paid every other week and you complete this form in December 1998.) Enter the result here and on Form W-4, line 6, page 1. This is the additional amount to be withheld from each paycheck . . . .   **9** $ _____

Table 1: Two-Earner/Two-Job Worksheet

Married Filing Jointly				All Others			
If wages from **LOWEST** paying job are–	Enter on line 2 above	If wages from **LOWEST** paying job are–	Enter on line 2 above	If wages from **LOWEST** paying job are–	Enter on line 2 above	If wages from **LOWEST** paying job are–	Enter on line 2 above
$0 - $4,000	0	40,001 - 45,000	8	$0 - $5,000	0	65,001 - 80,000	8
4,001 - 7,000	1	45,001 - 54,000	9	5,001 - 11,000	1	80,001 - 100,000	9
7,001 - 12,000	2	54,001 - 62,000	10	11,001 - 16,000	2	100,001 and over	10
12,001 - 18,000	3	62,001 - 70,000	11	16,001 - 21,000	3		
18,001 - 24,000	4	70,001 - 85,000	12	21,001 - 25,000	4		
24,001 - 28,000	5	85,001 - 100,000	13	25,001 - 40,000	5		
28,001 - 35,000	6	100,001 - 110,000	14	40,001 - 50,000	6		
35,001 - 40,000	7	110,001 and over	15	50,001 - 65,000	7		

Table 2: Two-Earner/Two-Job Worksheet

Married Filing Jointly		All Others	
If wages from **HIGHEST** paying job are–	Enter on line 7 above	If wages from **HIGHEST** paying job are–	Enter on line 7 above
$0 - $50,000	$400	$0 - $30,000	$400
50,001 - 100,000	770	30,001 - 60,000	770
100,001 - 130,000	850	60,001 - 120,000	850
130,001 - 240,000	1,000	120,001 - 250,000	1,000
240,001 and over	1,100	250,001 and over	1,100

9595 ☐ VOID ☐ CORRECTED

PAYER'S name, street address, city, state, ZIP code, and telephone no.		1 Rents $	OMB No. 1545-0115	
		2 Royalties $	**1999** Form **1099-MISC**	**Miscellaneous Income**
		3 Other income $		
PAYER'S Federal identification number	RECIPIENT'S identification number	4 Federal income tax withheld $	5 Fishing boat proceeds $	**Copy A**
RECIPIENT'S name		6 Medical and health care payments $	7 Nonemployee compensation $	**For** **Internal Revenue Service Center**
Street address (including apt. no.)		8 Substitute payments in lieu of dividends or interest $	9 Payer made direct sales of $5,000 or more of consumer products to a buyer (recipient) for resale ▶ ☐	**File with Form 1096.** For Privacy Act and Paperwork Reduction Act Notice and
City, state, and ZIP code		10 Crop insurance proceeds $	11 State income tax withheld $	instructions for completing this form, see the
Account number (optional)	2nd TIN Not. ☐	12 State/Payer's state number	13 $	**1999 Instructions for Forms 1099, 1098, 5498, and W-2G.**

Form **1099-MISC**   Cat. No. 14425J   Department of the Treasury - Internal Revenue Service

Sample Loan Application Package

Adapted from an outline in *Small Business Financing*, by the American Bankers Association.

1. **Cover letter describing:**
    - Nature of the business
    - Amount of loan requested
    - Repayment terms
    - Purpose of loan
    - Security or collateral

2. **Personal information:**
    - Credit references
    - Income tax statements
    - Financial statements
    - Educational and work history

3. **Firm information:**
    - Business plan
    - Insurance policies
    - Financial statements
    - Financial projections
    - Federal income tax returns

Sample Application for Employment

An Equal Opportunity Employer

Name: (Last)   (First)   (M.I.)

Position applying for:

Office or Department:

Permanent ❏   Temporary ❏   Part-Time ❏

Local address:

Phone: (Day)   (Evening)

Social Security Number:

Country of citizenship:

Type of visa:

Have you ever been convicted of a misdemeanor or felony?
   ❏ Yes   ❏ No
If yes, please give date, type of offense, place and judgment rendered.

Have you ever served in the U.S. military service?
   ❏ Yes   ❏ No
If yes, complete the following.
Branch of service   Dates of service
Rank   Type of discharge

Are you willing to travel on the job?
   ❏ Yes ❏ No
If yes,
   ❏ Domestically❏ Internationally   # days per month:

Languages:
   ❏ Conversational   ❏ Reading/writing proficiency

Please list additional qualifications, skills, personal interests and publications:

EDUCATION

Name & location of school:

Dates attended: Degree or level completed:

EMPLOYMENT HISTORY

Please list all previous employment including part-time and summer positions (use additional sheets as necessary):

Dates   Company name   Title
Salary: Hours:
Reason for leaving:

Dates   Company Name   Title
Salary: Hours:
Reason for leaving:

REFERENCES

1. Name:
   Address:

   Phone:
   Professional relationship (example: supervisor)

2. Name:
   Address:

   Phone:
   Professional relationship (example: supervisor)

3. Name:
   Address:

   Phone:
   Professional relationship (example: supervisor)

I hereby certify that the information furnished is correct. I understand that any false or incorrect information provided by me will subject me to dismissal.

_____

(signature)   (date)

Guide to the Legality
of Interview Questions

Inquiries Before Hiring	Lawful	Unlawful
1) Name		Inquiry into any title that indicates race, color, religion, sex, national origin, or ancestry
2) Address	Inquiry into place and length of time at previous addresses	Inquiries about financial status such as home or car ownership have been found to result in discrimination against minorities since more non-whites are below the poverty line
3) Age	Request proof of age in form of work permit issued by school authorities	Require birth certificate or baptismal record before hiring inadvisable to ask any question
4) Birthplace or national origin	Ability to read, write or speak English or foreign language if required for specific job	A. Inquiry into place of birth B. Any inquiry into place of birth of parents, grand-parents, or spouse C. Any other inquiry into national origin
5) Race or color		Any inquiry which would indicate race or color
6) Sex		Any inquiry
7) Religion/creed		Inquiry to indicate or identify denomination, religious affiliations, church, pastor, parish or religious holidays observed
8) Citizenship	A. Whether applicant is prevented from lawful employment because of visa or immigration status B. Whether applicant can provide proof of citizenship visa or alien registration # after being hired	A. If native-born or naturalized B. Proof of citizenship before hiring C. Whether parents or spouse are native-born or naturalized
9) Handicap	Whether applicant has a specific mental or physical handicap that relates to fitness to perform the particular job.	General inquiries—e.g., "Do you have any handicaps?" which might reveal handicaps not related to fitness to perform specific job.

Inquiries Before Hiring	Lawful	Unlawful
10) Photographs	May be required after hiring for identification purposes	Request photograph before hiring
11) Education	A. Inquiry into what academic, professional or vocational schools attended B. Inquiry into language skills such as ability to read and write foreign languages	A. Any inquiry asking specifically the racial or religious affiliation of a school B. Inquiry as to what is mother tongue or how foreign language ability was acquired, unless necessary for job
12) Relatives	Inquiry into name, relationship and address of person to be notified in case of emergency. Name of relatives employed by your company	Any inquiry about a relative that is unlawful to ask about the applicant
13) Organization	A. Inquiry into organization memberships, excluding any organization the name or character of which indicates the race, color, religion, sex, national origin or ancestry of its members B. What offices are held, if any	Inquiry into all organizations where membership is held
14) Military Service	A. Inquiry into service in U. S. Armed Services B. Rank attained C. Which branch of service D. Require military discharge certificate after being hired	A. Inquiry into military service in armed service of any country but U.S. B. Request military service records
15) Work Schedule	Inquiry into willingness to work required schedule	Any inquiry into willingness to work any particular religious holiday
16) References	General personal and work references not relating to race, color, sex, national origin	Request references specifically from clergy or any other persons who might reflect race, color, religion, sex, national origin or ancestry of applicant
17) Pregnancy	Inquiries concerning applicant's anticipated duration of stay on job or anticipated absences	Inadvisable to ask any question relating to pregnancy or medical history concerning pregnancy

Sample Job Description

POSITION

1. Title:
2. Rank (if appropriate):
3. Job definition (brief summary of type of job):
4. Location:
5. Office/department:
6. Title of supervisor:
7. Salary range: Overtime rates: Bonus plans:
8. Hours: Overtime:
9. Working conditions (note any specific or unusual conditions, including those which are hazardous):

QUALIFICATIONS REQUIRED

1. Education (school/university, number of years attended, type and year of degree and major, specific courses required for position):
2. Other training:
3. Job experience (minimum length of work experience in what fields):
    Specific job skills necessary: Management experience:
4. Specialized skills or licenses required (Examples: foreign languages, word processing, bookkeeping, computer programming, tractor operator, nursing):

JOB RESPONSIBILITIES

1. Job duties (Describe all job functions and areas of responsibility. Allow room for adding new projects, a change in emphasis, and individual initiative. The phrase: "Other duties as assigned by supervisor" can cover a lot of ground):
2. Use of special equipment, type of machine and nature of operation:
3. Committee membership:

WORKING RELATIONSHIPS

1. Reports to:
2. Supervises:
3. Group leadership:
4. Contact with public:

PROMOTION

1. Possibilities within present job:
2. What positions will job qualify employee for in future:
3. Length of average service at this position:
4. Promotion policy concerning pay increases:

Recommended Reading

Books

Abrahams, Jeffrey. *The Mission Statement Book: 301 Corporate Mission Statements from America's Top Companies.* Ten Speed Press, 1995.

Covello, Joseph, and Brian Hazelgren. *The Complete Book of Business Plans.* Sourcebooks Trade, 1994.

Dyer, W. Gibb. *The Entrepreneurial Experience: Confronting Career Dilemmas of the Start-Up Executive.* Jossey-Bass Publishers, 1992.

Edwards, Paul and Sarah, and Laura Clampitt Douglas. *Getting Business to Come to You.* Putnam Publishing Group, 1998.

Edwards, Paul and Sarah. *The Best Home Businesses for the 90s.* J.P. Tarcher, 1995.

Gerber, Michael. *The E-Myth Revisited.* Harper-Business, 1995.

Goldstein, Arnold, et al. *Starting on a Shoestring: Building a Business Without a Bankroll.* John Wiley & Sons, 1995.

Gray, Douglas. *Start and Run a Profitable Consulting Business: A Step-by-Step Business Plan.* Self-Counsel Press, 1996.

Hicks, Tyler Gregory. *199 Great Home Businesses You Can Start (And Succeed In) for Under $1,000: How to Choose the Best Home Businesses for You based on Your Personality Type.* Prima Publishing, 1992.

Kahrs, Kristin, and Angela Shupe. *Business Plan Handbook.* Gale Research, 1997.

Kamoroff, Bernard. *Small Time Operator.* Bell Springs Publishing, 1999.

Kennedy, Dan. *How to Make Millions with Your Ideas: An Entrepreneur's Guide.* Plume, 1996.

Klein, Ruth. *Manage Your Time/Market Your Business.* Amacom, 1995.

Lonier, Terri. *Working Solo: The Real Guide to Freedom and Financial Success With Your Own Business.* John Wiley & Sons, 1998.

MacKenzie, Alec. *The Time Trap.* Amacom, 1997.

Norman, Jan. *What No One Ever Tells You About Starting Your Own Business: Real Life Start-Up Advice From 101 Successful Entrepreneurs.* Upstate Publishing Company, 1999.

Nulman, Philip. *Start Up Marketing: An Entrepreneur's Guide to Advertising, Marketing and Promoting Your Business.* Career Press, 1996.

Roberts, Edward. *Entrepreneurship in High Technology.* Oxford University Press, 1991.

Schine, Gary. *How to Avoid 101 Small Business Mistakes, Myths and Misconceptions.* Consultant Press, 1992.

Stern, Mitchell. *Buy Your Own Business: The Definitive Guide to Identifying and Purchasing a Business You Can Make a Success.* Macmillan, 1998.

Stolze, William. *START UP: An Entrepreneur's Guide to Launching and Managing a New Business* (4th Ed.). Career Press, 1996.

Zobel, Jan. *Minding Her Own Business: The Self-Employed Woman's Guide to Taxes and Recordkeeping.* Easthill Press, 1998.

Magazines

American Demographics
Black Enterprise
Business @ Home (www.gohome.com)
Business Start-Ups
Business Week Online (www.businessweek.com)
Entrepreneurial Edge Online (www.edgeonline.com)
Entrepreneur Magazine (www.entrepreneurmag.com)
Fast Company (www.fastcompany.com)
Forbes
Fortune
Franchise Times (www.franchisetimes.com)
Home Business Magazine
Home Office Computing (www.smalloffice.com)
Inc. Magazine (www.inc.com)
Journal of Business Strategy
Minority Business Enterprise (www.mbemag.com)
Purchasing Magazine
Sales and Marketing Management
Washington Technology
Women's Web Magazine (womenswebmagazine.com)
Working Woman
Small Business Journal

Newsletters

NMSDC's *Minority Supplier News*

The Guerrilla Marketing Newsletter

Web Promote (www.webpromote.com)

The Bizy Moms Newsletter (www.bizymoms.com)

Small Business Information (Sbinformation.miningco.
com)

Resources

Freebies

Get a free copy of *The Business Incorporating Guide* from The Company Corporation by calling (800) 478-1790 or visiting their Web site at www. incorporate.com.

Blueprint for Success: A Guide for Women Entrepreneurs (1998). Provided by the U.S. Small Business Administration's Office of Women's Business Ownership and Salomon Smith Barney.

Free copy of *How to Really Start Your Own Business*, cosponsored by Visa and SCORE at your local SCORE office or on the SCORE Web site at www.score.org.

Free consumer information guide available by calling (888) 878-3256 or visiting the Web site at www.pueblo.gsa.gov.

Free guides on the following topics at www. bizmove.com/business-plan.htm:

> Financial management
>
> Determining the feasibility of your idea

Developing your business plan

Starting a home business

How to perform low cost market research

How to develop a marketing plan

Developing effective advertising

How to promote your small business

Publicity tips

Pricing in a service firm

Understanding financial statements

Forecasting and obtaining capital

How to reduce costs

How to conduct successful meetings

Free course on using the Internet provided by the Virtual University for Small and Medium Sized Enterprises. Available at www.vusme.org/admin/courses.asp.

Free magazine on sales and marketing available at http://salesdoctors.com.

Free magazine for work-at-home moms at www.wahm.com.

Free software for managing all your Web-related contacts and information. Download at www.liraz.com/cybercontact.

Free business plan writing template at www.scotiabank.com/software.html.

Free business plan template at www.planware.org/busplan.htm?source=goto.

Free template at www.sudburyeast.com/Busplan.htm.

Free interactive business plan package at www.netmiser.com/income/business.html.

Free business plan template at www.bizplanit.com/free.htm.

Free business plan template for starting a manufacturing company at www.bizmove.com/starting/m1f1.htm.

Free business plan template for starting a service firm at www.bizmove.com/starting/m1f2.htm.

Free business plan template for starting a retail store at www.bizmove.com/starting/m1f3.htm.

Free business plan template for starting a home-based business at www.bizmove.com/starting/m1f4.htm.

Free business plan template for starting a construction firm at www.bizmove.com/starting/m1f5.htm.

Free trial of several business magazines at www.free-n-cool.com/wmags.html. Get a free issue of *Black Enterprise, Fast Company, Red Herring,* as well as several others.

Free guide to 206 Marketing Ideas at www.ideasiteforbusiness.com/ideas.htm.

Free and nearly free resources and goodies for the newbie entrepreneur and small business owner at www.businessfreebies.com.

Free Web space available at www.webhell.com/user/atlas/free_bus_r.htm.

A large list of business related freebies at www.freestuffcentral.com/business.shtml.

Free e-mail, free screen savers, free maps, free package tracking at http://usaexports.net/free.shtml.

Free online coupons, freebies and contests available at www.coupondirectory.com. Covers a variety of businesses, services and products.

Directories

American Business Funding Directory (www.businessfinanc.com)

Cahners Business Information (www.cahners.com)

Business Opportunities Handbook
(www.ezines.com)

Encyclopedia of American Industries

Encyclopedia of Associations
(www.galenet.gale.com)

Franchise Annual (www.vaxxine.com/franchise)

Hoover's List of Major U.S. Companies

Million Dollar Directory

Nynex Interactive Yellow Pages

Thomas Register of American Manufacturers

Directory of Franchising Organizations

Trade Show Central (www.tscentral.com)

Small Business Resources Directory
(www.d.umn.edu/~jjacobs1/index.htm)

Organizations

American Association of Franchisees & Dealers
(www.aafd.org)

American Home Business Association (AHBA)
((800) 664-2422 or www.homebusiness.com)

American Payroll Association (www.americanpayroll.
org/new)

American Small Businesses Association
(www.asbaonline.org/)

American Society of Association Executives
(www.asaenet.org/gateway/GatewayHP.html)

Association of Home-based Businesses
(www.AAHBB.org)

Better Business Bureau (www.bbb.org)

The Canadian Home Business Organization
(CHBO) (www.chbo.org/chbo.htm)

Direct Marketing Association (www.the-dma.org)

Home Office Association (www.hoaa.com)

Internal Revenue Service (IRS) ((800) 829-3676)

The International Franchise Association (www.franchise.org)

International Trade Associations (www.webhead.comFITA/home.html)

The Multilevel Marketing International Association (www.mlmia.com)

National Association of Business Leaders (www.nabl.com)

The National Association of Home-Based Businesses (www.usahomebusiness.com)

National Association for the Self-Employed (www.nase.org)

National Business Incubators Association (www.nbia.org)

National Foundation for Women Business Owners (www.nfwbo.org)

National Minority Business Council (www.nmbc.org)

SOHO America (www.soho.org)

The Young Entrepreneurs Organization (YEO) (www.yeo.org)

Agencies

Census Bureau (www.census.gov)

Federal Government (www.business.gov)

Government Contracting (www.govcon.com)

Federal Marketplace (www.fedmarket.com)

Federal Small Business Innovation and Research (www.inknowvation.com)

U.S. Patents and Trademarks Office (www.USPTO.gov)

U.S. Department of Commerce (Washington, DC 20231, (703) 305-8600)

Service Corps of Retired Executives (SCORE) (www.score.org, (800) 634-0245)

Small Business Administration (SBA) (www.sba.gov, [800] U-ASK-SBA)

Web resources

www-sci.lib.uci.edu/HSG/RefCalculators.html—provides calculators for figuring the costs for business startups.

www.hoovers.com—find free brief company profiles for more than 13,500 public and private firms, straight from the popular published guide. For a small fee, you can access more detailed information on those businesses.

www.odci.gov/cia/publications/factbook/index.html—for anyone considering expanding into a new country or importing/exporting, the CIA's World Factbook is a useful place to turn for concise data on more than 250 countries' population, government, economy, and more.

www.entrepreneurialedge.com—an online magazine for entrepreneurs with useful articles, links, and tutorials.

www.edgeonline.com/—Entrepreneurial Edge Online champions the entrepreneurial spirit with searchable full-text databases, monthly features, etc.

www.fedstats.gov—if you're interested in U.S. statistics, this site provides data from 70 agencies, allowing you to search for the consumer price index, crime rates, employment trends, vital statistics, and more.

www.thomasregister.com—this free database of more than 155,000 companies allows you to search by product or service, or company.

www.nua.ia/surveys/index.cgi—virtually every study ever done on Internet-related subjects is available here.

www.smallbiz.suny—State University of New York (SUNY), (800) 732-SBDC. Procurement assistance.

www.wboc.org—The Women Business Owners Corporation Web site provides information and technical assistance about corporate and government purchasing. WBOC also has a national certification program to verify the ownership and control of women-owned firms.

www.nafta.net—NAFTAnet Small Business Information is a resource for Business, Electronic Commerce and Electronic Data Interchange, etc.

www.sohobr.com—SOHO Business Resources. Small and home business development, marketing, advertising, sales and training.

www.tsbr.com—The Small Business Resource.

smallbizhelp.net/—A Small Business Resource and Help Center.

www.microsoft.com/smallbiz/—Microsoft Smallbiz offers suggestions for improving your small business operations.

home-based-business.com/—service dedicated to assisting people who are looking for legitimate home-based business opportunities.

www.cpalink.com/—CPA Link bills itself as the complete online directory of accounting professionals.

www.buysellbiz.com/—BuySellBiz.com is devoted to providing information and services for buying, selling, financing, and valuing small to mid-size businesses.

www.information-sources.com/advice.htm—WorthYourWhile Informations Sources International (WYWISI) Entrepreneur Business Advice and Technology Page.

www.achievenetwork.com/—Achieve! Network offers training, education, opportunities, books, videos, CD-ROMs and more.

www.americanexpress.com/smallbusiness/—American Express provides a wealth of information for small business owners.

ccr.edi.disa.mil/ccr/—Central Contractor Registration (CCR) is worth investigating if you're new to government contracting. It facilitates registering as a trading partner with the Federal government.

www.il.hq.af.mil/aflma/lgc/projects/market/market.html—information-packed government Web site.

www.datamerge—Venture Capital Database.

www.v-capital.com.au—Venture Capital Marketplace.

www.dmsource.com—Direct Marketing Dynamics.

www.nlci.com/response—Direct Marketing Response.

www.tradecompas.com—Export Information.

www.all-biz.com—All Business Network.

www.celcee.edu—Entrepreneurial Education.

www.lowe.org/smbiznet—Small Business Net.

www.smartbiz.com—Smart Biz Supersite.

www.entremkt.com/wfn—Women's Franchise Network.

Business Contacts

Sources cited within book

Chapter 2

Kim Fukui
Infokui
Wilmington, DE
(302) 234-3198
E-mail: fukuik@dca.net

Association Sources
Encyclopedia of Associations

Published by Gale Research. Available at most public libraries.
www.galenet.gale.com

American Society of Association Executives
1575 I Street, NW
Washington, DC 20005-1168
(202) 626-2723
www.asaenet.org/gateway/GatewayHP.html

Article Indexes

Business Periodicals Index

www.hwwilson.com

350 business periodicals indexed. Fee-based.

Business and Industry Database

www.rdsinc.com

For $3.50 per article, this site provides a hefty dose of statistics and trend information.

Electric Library Business Edition

http://Business.elibrary.com

Articles from magazines, books, and other news sources are provided here. Database is free to search but a monthly fee of $14.95 is charged if you want to download articles.

Chapter 3

Hyrum Smith, CEO

Franklin Covey Co.

2200 West Parkway Blvd.

Salt Lake City, UT 84119

(800) 655-1492

www.franklincovey.com

ChannelBind Corp.

275 Gosset Road

Spartanburg, SC 29318

(800) 562-7188

www.channelbind.com

PaperDirect!

1025 East Woodmen Road

Colorado Springs, CO 80920

(800) APAPERS

www.paperdirect.com

Business Planning Help:

Small Business Development Centers

Find a list of SBDC's nationwide at: www6. americanexpress.com/smallbusiness or www.sba.gov

Sample plans

www.bplans.com

www.morebusiness.com

Business Plan Handbook, Kristin Kahrs and Angela Shupe (Gale Research, 1997)

The Complete Book of Business Plans, Joseph Covello and Brian Hazelgren (Sourcebooks Trade, 1994)

START UP: An Entrepreneur's Guide to Launching and Managing a New Business (4th Ed.), William Stolze (Career Press, 1996)

Chapter 4

Richard Glaser
Hudson Ventures
Rochester, N.Y.
(716) 546-7013

Daniel J. Christante
Entity Financial Services
North York, Ontario, Canada
(416) 512-7639

Pratt's Guide to Venture Capital Sources 1999. Stanley Pratt (Ed.) Venture Economics, 1999.

Galante's Complete Venture Capital and Private Equity Directory 1999. Asset Alternatives, Inc., 1999.

Funding Sources

Blue Chip Venture Co.
2000 PNC Center
201 East Fifth Street
Cincinnati, OH 45202
(513) 723-2300

Blue Chip Venture Co. invests in minority- and woman-owned companies in various industries. Funding ranges from $250,000–$1.2 million.

Wells Fargo Bank
420 Montgomery Street
San Francisco, CA 94163
(800) 411-4932
wellsfargo.com/biz

Small Business Administration
409 3rd Street, SW
Washington, DC 20416
(800) U-ASK-SBA
www.sba.gov

Women Incorporated
333 South Grand Avenue, Suite 2450
Los Angeles, CA 90071
(800) 930-3993
www.womeninc.com

Women, Inc. provides seminars, products and services, and micro and small business loans up to $1 million.

Venture Capital
www.moneyhunter.com
www.edgeonline.com/main/resourcepage.venture.shtm
www.businessfinance.com/search.shtml

Chapter 5

The Mission Statement Book: 301 Corporate Mission Statements from America's Top Companies. Jeffrey Abrahams (Ten Speed Press, 1995)

Trademark info:
Patents and Trademarks Office
U.S. Department of Commerce
Washington, DC 20231
(800) 786-9199
www.uspto.gov

U.S. Copyright Office
Library of Congress
101 Independence Avenue, SE
Washington, DC 20559-6000
(202) 707-5000
http://lcweb.loc.gov/copyright

Chapter 6

Matthew Korona
Attorney-at-Law
Olver, Korts, Korona, and Russell
10 Tobey Village Office Park
Pittsford, NY 14534
(716) 387-0500

Home Office Computing Magazine
156 W. 56th Street
New York, NY 10019
(212) 333-7600
www.smalloffice.com

Entrepreneur's Home Office Magazine
Entrepreneur Media, Inc.
2392 Morse Avenue
Irvine, CA 92614
(949) 261-2325
www.homeofficemag.com

Jerry Nietlich
In/House Corporate Real Estate Advisors
Irvine, Calif.
(714) 442-0922
jerryn@inhousecorp.com

Executive Suite Companies
HQ Business Centers
120 Montgomery, Suite 2350
San Francisco, CA 94104
(800) 227-3004
http://hqnet.com

OmniOffices, Inc.
590 Madison Avenue, 21st Floor
New York, NY 10022
(212) 521-4000
www.omnioffices.com

Worldwide Business Centers Network
575 Madison Avenue
New York, NY 10022
(800) 638-6384
www.fbtc.com.hk/buscent.html

Chapter 7
Edith and Roy Quick
Quick Tax & Accounting Service
St. Louis, Mo.

Small Business Tax Review (www.smbiz.com)

Intuit Quickbooks
Intuit Corp.
2535 Garvia Avenue
Mountain View, CA 94043
(800) 446-8848
www.intuit.com

Peachtree Accounting
Peachtree Software
1505 Pavilion Place
Norcross, GA 30093
(800) 247-3224
www.peachtree.com

Minding Her Own Business: The Self-Employed Woman's Guide to Taxes and Recordkeeping, Jan Zobel (Easthill Press, 1998)

National Association of Professional Employer Organizations (NAPEO)
901 N. Pitt Street, Suite 150
Alexandria, VA 22314
(703) 836-0466
www.napeo.org

The Institute of Accreditation for Professional Employer Organizations
Three Financial Centre, Suite 401
900 S. Shackleford Road
Little Rock, AR 72211
(501) 219-2045
www.iapeo.org

What No One Ever Tells You About Starting Your Own Business: Real Life Start-Up Advice From 101 Successful Entrepreneurs, Jan Norman (Upstate Publishing Company, 1999)Cyber Dialogue, 304 Hudson Street, New York, NY 10013, www.cyberdialogue. com

The Canadian Telework Association
52 Stonebriar Drive
Nepean, Ontario
Canada K2G 5X9
(613) 225-5588
www.ivc.ca

The E-Myth Revisited, Michael Gerber (HarperBusiness, 1995)

The Time Trap, Alec MacKenzie (Amacom, 1997)

Tom Hull
Wichita State University
1845 Fairmount
Wichita, Kans. 67260
(316) 978-3045
www.wichita.edu

Chapter 8

Annual Statement Studies 1998-1999, Robert Morris
Associates, 1998

Business StartUps Magazine
Entrepreneur Media, Inc.
2392 Morse Avenue
Irvine, CA 92614
(949) 261-2325
www.bizstartups.com

Chapter 9

American Express Small Business Services
www.americanexpress.com

Business Week
1221 Avenue of the Americas, 39th Floor
New York, NY 10020
(212) 512-2511
www.businessweek.com

International Data Corporation
5 Speen Street
Natick, MA 01701
(508) 872-8200
www.idcresearch.com

PR Newswire
810 Seventh Avenue, 35th Floor
New York, NY 10019
(800) 832-5522
www.prnewswire.com

High Income Consulting, Tom Lambert (Nicholas Brealey, 1997)

Center for Exhibition Industry Research (CEIR)
2301 South Lake Shore Drive, Suite E1002
Chicago, IL 60616
(312) 808-2347
www.ceir.org

Murray Raphel
Raphel Marketing
12 S. Virginia Avenue
Atlantic City, New Jersey 08401
(609) 348-6646
www.raphel.com

Chapter 10

Keith and Wendy Rockcastle
Rockcastle Florist
885 Long Pond Road
Rochester, NY 14626
(716) 225-3640
www.rockcastle.com

Everything I Need to Know About CRM ... I Learned at the Craft Shops, Grace Butland

Customer Relationship Lessons from a Crafts Shop, Grace Butland

Khera Communications
1445 Research Blvd, 5th Floor
Rockville, MD 20850-3125
(301) 545-6999
www.morebusiness.com

Temple, Barker & Sloan, Inc.
375 Park Avenue
New York, NY 10022
(212) 888-4646

Delivering Quality Service: Balancing Customer Perceptions and Expectations, Valarie Zeithaml, A. Parasuvaman, and Leonard Berry (Free Press, 1990)

The Service Edge: 101 Companies that Profit from Customer Care, Ron Zemke, Dick Schaaf (Plume, 1990)

Harvard Business Review
Harvard Business School Publishing
60 Harvard Way
Boston, MA 02163
(617) 495-6700
www.hbsp.harvard.edu

Hey, I'm the Customer/Front Line Tips for Providing Superior Customer Service, Ron Willingham (Prentice Hall Trade, 1992)

Ron Zemke, president
Performance Research Associates
821 Marquette Avenue, #1820
Minneapolis, MN 55402-2920
(612) 338-8523

Delivering Knock Your Socks Off Service, Kristin Anderson and Ron Zemke (AMACOM, 1997)

Chapter 11

Publications to assist you in securing government contracts include:

U.S. Government and Purchasing Directory—This booklet lists products and services purchased by the federal government, broken down by agencies. Available through the SBA at 409 3rd Street, SW, Washington, DC 20416 or by calling 1-202-205-6460.

Doing Business with GSA—This booklet explains the basics of government procurement with the General Services Administration. Available from the

Superintendent of Documents, Government Printing Office, Washington, DC 20402 or at pub.fss.gsa.gov/Sched/do_biz.html.

Small Business Specialists—This booklet lists the names and phone numbers of 600 OSBDU specialists, whose responsibility it is to help small businesses identify potential customers within the Federal government. Publication # DOD 4205-1H. Available from Department of Defense, Office of the Secretary of Defense, Washington, DC 20301.

Selling to the Military—This booklet covers the specifics of doing business with the Department of Defense. Available from the Superintendents of Documents. Publication # DOD 4205.1-M. Available from Department of Defense, Washington, DC 20301.

United States Government Organization Manual—This booklet helps businesses understand all of the government agencies and potential purchasing contacts. Available from the Superintendent of Documents, Government Printing Office, Washington, DC 20402.

Selling to the Federal Government—The SBA offers the publication to business owners who request it. Call the SBA Office of Government Contracting at (202) 205-6460.

Selling to the Giants, Jeffrey Davidson, George-Anne Fay (out-of-print, available at most libraries)

Joset Wright
Ameritech
311 West Washington Street
Chicago, IL 60606
(312) 263-2805

Commerce Business Daily
For subscription to printed newspaper, contact:
Superintendent of Documents
P.O. Box 371954
Pittsburgh, PA 15250-7954
(202) 512-1800

For free online database of procurement opportunities:
cbdnet.gpo.gov

Cheryl Watkins Snead
Banneker Industries, Inc.
678 George Washington Highway
Lincoln, RI 02865
(401) 333-4487

National Minority Supplier Development Council
(NMSDC)
15 W. 39th Street, 9th Floor
New York, NY 10018
(212) 944-2430
www.trainingforum.com/ASN/NMSDC/index.html

Renaldo M. Jensen
Ford Motor Company
16800 Executive Plaza Drive
Dearborn, Mich. 48121
www.ford.com

SBA's PRO-Net
409 3rd Street, SW
Washington, DC 20416
(800) U-ASK-SBA
www.pro-net.sba.gov

Chapter 12
Adams Streetwise Hiring Top Performers, Bob Adams
(Adams Publishing, 1997)

The Small Business Journal
407 Vine Street
Cincinnati, OH 45202
(513) 736-4751
www.tsbj.com

Woods & Poole Economics, Inc.
1794 Columbia Road Northwest #3
Washington, DC 20009
(202) 332-7111

George Silvestri
Bureau of Labor Statistics (BLS)
Office of Employment and Unemployment
Statistics
Occupational Employment Statistics
2 Massachusetts Avenue, NE, Suite 4840
Washington, DC 20212
(202) 606-6569

American Demographics Magazine
P.O. Box 10580
Riverton, NJ 08076-0580
(800) 529-7502
www.demographics.com

America's Job Bank
www.ajb.dni.us

Managing to Have Fun, Matt Weinstein (Fireside,
1997)

Delphi Business Strategies
www0.delphi.com/busstrat

Zweig White & Associates
600 Worcester Road
Natick, Mass. 01760
(508) 651-1559

Firmani & Associates, Inc.
2505 Second Avenue #700
Seattle, WA. 98121
(206) 443-9357

Rick Born
Born Information Services
294 East Grove Lane, Suite 100
Wazyata, MN 55391
(800) 469-BORN
www.born.com

Sharon Anderson Wright
Half Price Books
4234 Oak Lawn Avenue
Dallas, TX 75219
(214) 526-8440
www.halfpricebooks.com

Autumn Harp
61 Pine Street
Bristol, VT 05443
(802) 453-4807

The Bureau of National Affairs
1231 25th Street, NW
Washington, DC 20037
(202) 452-4200
www.bna.com

Chapter 13

The Export Assistance Center
Visit the SBA Web site at www.sbaonline.sba.gov/
OIT/export/useac.html to find the export assis-
tance center in your area

New York State Job Development Authority
One Commerce Plaza
Albany, NY 12210
(518) 474-7580
http://unix2.nysed.gov/ils/executive/jda/jda.htm

Economic Development Department
Look in the blue pages of your local phone book
to find the phone number of your local economic
development department.

Coach University
P.O. Box 881595
Steamboat Springs, CO 80488
(800) 48COACH
www.coachu.com

The Young Entrepreneurs Organization (YEO)
1321 Duke Street, Suite 300
Alexandria, VA 22314
(703) 519-6700
www.yeo.org

Robert E. Spekman
Darden School of Business at the University of
Virginia
P.O. Box 6550
Charlottesville, VA 22906-6500
(804) 973-9549
www.darden.virginia.edu

Think and Grow Rich, Napoleon Hill (Ballantine
Books, 1996)

PricewaterhouseCoopers LLP
1301 Avenue of the Americas
New York, NY 10019
(212) 707-6000
www.pwcglobal.com

Uniformity LLC
531 West Lodi Avenue
Lodi, CA 95240
(209) 369-7343

Richard Hagberg
Hagberg Consulting Group
950 Tower Lane, 7th Floor
Foster City, CA 94404
(650) 377-0232

Chapter 14

The National Association of Home-Based
Businesses
10451 Mill Run Circle, Suite 400
Owings Mills, MD 21117
(410) 581-0071
www.usahomebusiness.com

Entrepreneur Magazine: Starting a Home-Based Business
(John Wiley & Sons, 1999)

Paul and Sarah Edwards
www.paulandsarah.com

Beverley Williams
Association of Home-based Businesses
P.O. Box 10023
Rockville, MD 20849
(800) 447-9710
www.aahbb.org

USATel
Supermarket of LD Services
(800) 390-6891
http://LD.net/?7413

ECHOtel
28001 Dorothy Drive
Agoura Hills, CA 91301
(800) 233-0406
www.echo-inc.com/ECHO/ECHOtellntro.htm

Mothers' Home Business Network
P.O. Box 423
East Meadow, NY 11554
(516) 997-7394
www.homeworkingmom.com/echo

The National Insurance Consumer Helpline
(800) 942-4242

The Insurance Information Institute
Insuring Your Home Business
110 William St.
New York, NY 10038
(212) 669-9200
www.iii.org

Jane Applegate
The Applegate Group
P.O. Box 768
Pelham, NY 10803
(914) 738-6552
www.janeapplegate.com

EKOS Research Associates, Inc.
145 King Street, W
Toronto, Ontario
(416) 214-1424
www.ekos.com

Chapter 15
Forrester Research, Inc.
1033 Massachusetts Avenue
Cambridge, MA 02138
(617) 497-7090
www.forrester.com

Autobytel.com
(323) 960-1360
www.autobytel.com

Rich Scocozza
Bear, Stearns & Co
245 Park Avenue
New York, NY 10167
(888) 473-3819
www.bearstearns.com

Zach Nelson
Network Associates
3965 Freedom Circle
Santa Clara, CA 95054
(408) 988-3832
www.networkassociate.com

Barnes and Noble
33 E. 17th Street
New York, NY 10003
(212) 539-2000
www.barnesandnoble.com

Amazon.com
1516 Second Avenue
Seattle, WA 98101
(206) 622-2335
www.amazon.com

The Expert Marketplace
7395 South Peoria Street
Englewood, CO 80112
(800) 983-9737
http://expert-market.com

Mary Furlong
Third Age Media Inc.
585 Howard Street, First Floor
San Francisco, CA 94105-3001
www.thirdage.com

SmallOffice.com
Home Office Computing Magazine
156 W. 56th Street
New York, NY 10019
(212) 333-7600

U.S. Department of Commerce
(202) 482-4883
www.doc.gov

Council of Better Business Bureaus
BBBOnline
4200 Wilson Blvd., 8th Floor
Arlington, VA 22203
(888) 679-3353
www.bbbonline.org

First Data Corporation
5660 New Northside Drive, Suite 1400
Atlanta, GA 30328
(770) 857-7001
www.firstdatacorp.com

Bank of America Merchant Services
NC1-003-05-08
P.O. Box 1091
Charlotte, NC 28254-3489
(800) 228-5882
www.bankofamerica.com

The Financial Times
FT Publications, Inc.
14 East 60th Street
New York, NY 10022
(212) 752-4500
www.ft.com

CareerPath
523 West 6th Street, Suite 515
Los Angeles, CA 90014
(213) 996-0200
www.careerpath.com

Democrat and Chronicle
55 Exchange Street
Rochester, NY 14604
(716) 232-7100
www.democratandchronicle.com

Digital Impact
177 Bovet Road, Suite 200
San Mateo, CA 94402
(650) 356-3400
www.digital-impact.com

GuestTrack, Inc.
3532 Jasmine Avenue
Los Angeles, CA 90034
(310) 558-3599
www.guesttrack.com

CNET
www.cnet.com

Doing Business on the Internet: How the Electronic Highway is Transforming American Companies, Mary J. Cronin (John Wiley & Sons, 1995)

Our Dumb Century: The Onion Presents 100 Years of Headlines from America's Finest News Source, The Onion (Three Rivers Press, 1999)

Rainbow Play Systems, Inc.
500 Rainbow Parkway
Brookings, SD 57006
(800) RAINBOW
www.rainbowplay.com

Supermarkets Online
(888) SHOP123
www.ValuPage.com

Chapter 16
FranNet
(800) frannet
www.frannet.com Franchise Registry
www.franchiseregistry.com

The Federal Trade Commission (FTC)
CRC-240
Washington, DC 20580
(202) FTC-HELP
www.ftc.gov

Andrew Caffey
Franchise attorney
Chevy Chase, Maryland
Acaffey@compuserve.com

The International Franchise Association
1350 New York Avenue, NW, Suite 900
Washington, DC 20005-4709
(202) 628-8000
www.franchise.org

How to Raise A Family & A Career Under One Roof: A Parent's Guide to Home Business, Lisa Roberts
(Brookhaven Press, 1997)

The Multilevel Marketing International Association
119 Stanford Court
Irvine, CA 92612
(949) 854-0484
www.mlmia.com

Dale Carnegie Program
Visit www.dalecarnegie.com to find a local training center.

Start and Succeed in Multilevel Marketing, Gregory F. Kishel and Patricia Kishel (John Wiley & Sons, 1999)

Chapter 17

How to Avoid 101 Small Business Mistakes, Myths, and Misconceptions, Gary Schine (Consultant Press, 1991)

ASI Solutions, Inc.
780 Third Avenue
New York, NY 10017
(212) 319-8400
www.asisolutions.com

Business Resale Network
Entrepreneur Media, Inc.
2392 Morse Avenue
Irvine, CA 92614
(949) 261-2325
www.br-network.com

Inc. Magazine
38 Commercial Wharf
Boston, MA
www.inc.com

BizQuest
200 N. Mullan Road, Suite 213
Spokane, WA 99206
(509) 928-1757
www.bizquest.com

Business Broker Web
Acquisition and Financial Consulting, Inc.
1120 Wivenhoe Way
Virginia Beach, VA 23454-3046
(804) 496-9349
http://business-broker.com

BizBuySell
120 Flyway Drive
Kiawah Island, SC 29455
(843) 768-9992
www.bizbuysell.com

SmallbizNet
Edward Lowe Foundation
58220 Decatur Road
P.O. Box 8
Cassopolis, MI 49031
(800) 232-LOWE
www.lowe.org/smbiznet/
features/buysell.htm

American Express Small Business Exchange—
www6.americanexpress.com/smallbusiness/

Deloitte & Touche Online
Deloitte & Touche
700 Walnut Street
Cincinnati, OH 45202
(513) 929-3300
www.dtonline.com/Buying/Bycover.htm

The Secrets to Buying and Selling a Business, Ira
Nottonson (Psi Research, 1997)

Chapter 18
Wheel of Life—SBA's Online Women's Business
Center
www.onlinewbc.org/docs/manage/
lifewheel.html

Parenting Magazine Online
www.parenting.com

Marsey Carsey
Carsey-Werner Distribution
4024 Radford Avenue
Los Angeles, CA 91604
(818) 655-5598

201 Great Ideas For Your Small Business, Jane
Applegate (Bloomberg Press, 1998)

Simplify Your Life, Elaine St. James (Hyperion, 1994)

Jennifer White
JWC Group
2640 Sheridan Drive
Cincinnati, Ohio 45212
(513) 351-1289
www.successu.com

Work Less, Make More, Jennifer White
(Kendall/Hunt Publishing, 1998)

Families and Work Institute
330 Seventh Avenue, 14th Floor
New York, N.Y. 10001
(212) 465-2044
www.familiesand workinst.org

Women's Wire Web site
Women.com Networks
1820 Gateway Drive, Suite 100
San Mateo, CA 94404
(650) 378-4952
www.womenswire.com

A

The *Unofficial Guide*™ Reader Questionnaire

If you would like to express your opinion about starting a small business or this guide, please complete this questionnaire and mail it to:

The Unofficial Guide™ Reader Questionnaire
Lifestyle Guides
Hungry Minds, Inc.
909 Third Ave.
New York, NY 10022

Gender: ___ M ___ F

Age: ___ Under 30 ___ 31–40
___ 41–50 ___ Over 50

Education: ___ High school ___ College
___ Graduate/Professional

What is your occupation?
_____

How did you hear about this guide?
___ Friend or relative
___ Newspaper, magazine, or Internet
___ Radio or TV
___ Recommended at bookstore
___ Recommended by librarian
___ Picked it up on my own
___ Familiar with the *Unofficial Guide*™ travel series

Did you go to the bookstore specifically for a book on starting a small business? Yes ___ No ___

Have you used any other *Unofficial Guides*™?
Yes ___ No ___

If "Yes," which ones?
_____
_____
_____

What other book(s) on starting a small business have you purchased?

_____

_____

_____

Was this book:
____ more helpful than other(s)
____ less helpful than other(s)

Do you think this book was worth its price?
Yes ____   No ____

Did this book cover all topics related to starting a small business adequately?   Yes ____   No ____

Please explain your answer:

_____

_____

_____

Were there any specific sections in this book that were of particular help to you?   Yes ____   No ____

Please explain your answer:

_____

_____

_____

On a scale of 1 to 10, with 10 being the best rating, how would you rate this guide? ____

What other titles would you like to see published in the _Unofficial Guide_™ series?

_____

_____

_____

Are _Unofficial Guides_™ readily available in your area?
Yes ____   No ____

Other comments:

_____

_____

_____

Get the inside scoop...
with the *Unofficial Guides*™!

Health and Fitness

The Unofficial Guide to Alternative Medicine
ISBN: 0-02-862526-9

The Unofficial Guide to Coping with Menopause
ISBN: 0-02-862694-X

The Unofficial Guide to Dieting Safely
ISBN: 0-02-862521-8

The Unofficial Guide to Having a Baby
ISBN: 0-02-862695-8

The Unofficial Guide to Living with Diabetes
ISBN: 0-02-862919-1

The Unofficial Guide to Smart Nutrition
ISBN: 0-02-863589-2

The Unofficial Guide to Surviving Breast Cancer
ISBN: 0-02-863491-8

Career Planning

The Unofficial Guide to Acing the Interview
ISBN: 0-02-862924-8

The Unofficial Guide to Earning What You Deserve
ISBN: 0-02-862716-4

The Unofficial Guide to Hiring and Firing People
ISBN: 0-02-862523-4

Business and Personal Finance

The Unofficial Guide to Beating Debt
ISBN: 0-02-863337-7

The Unofficial Guide to Investing
ISBN: 0-02-862458-0

The Unofficial Guide to Investing in Mutual Funds
ISBN: 0-02-862920-5

The Unofficial Guide to Managing Your Personal Finances
ISBN: 0-02-862921-3

All books in the *Unofficial Guide*™ series are available at your local bookseller.

About the Author

Marcia Layton Turner started her first business at the ripe old age of eight, selling vegetables from her family's garden curbside in their neighborhood. The venture was extremely profitable, due in good measure to Mom and Dad having funded the raw material and production costs.

In the ensuing years, Marcia honed her business skills through MBA training, consulting assignments, and corporate experience at the Eastman Kodak Company, which brought her full circle to starting her own marketing consulting firm, Layton & Co., in the early 1990s.

Marcia has been profiled or quoted as a start-up expert in *Money Magazine, Entrepreneur, USA Weekend,* and several other national publications. Her entrepreneurial know-how was also noted by iVillage and Macmillan, which hired her to serve as their small business guru during the start-up phases of their Web communities.

In addition to offering business guidance online, Marcia has also written several books. She co-authored with Ed Paulson *The Complete Idiot's Guide to Starting a Business,* as well as penning *The Complete Idiot's Guide to Terrific Business Writing* and *Successful Fine Art Marketing* on her own.

This book for the Unofficial Guides has given Marcia the chance to pass along much of her hard-won wisdom about starting a business with the hopes that it will directly contribute to the success of its readers' new business ventures.